Backyard Birds of North America

Fred J. Alsop III

CRANE HILL
PUBLISHERS

To the two women in my life—

Cathi Jo,

my wife,
for all the birding trips we've taken together,
for running the wildbird feeding store,
and for loving a birder;

and in memory of

Billie Johnston Alsop,

my mother,
who loved her yard, her flowers,
and feeding the birds.

Copyright © 2003 by Fred J. Alsop III
Illustrations by Ray Harm
All rights reserved
Printed in China
Published by Crane Hill Publishers
www.cranehill.com

Library of Congress Cataloging-in-Publication Data

Alsop, Fred.
  Backyard birds of North America / Fred J. Alsop III ; illustrations by
Ray Harm.
       p. cm.
Includes bibliographical references and index.
  ISBN 1-57587-209-9
  1. Birds--North America--Identification. I. Title.
  QL681.A6215 2003
  598'.097--dc21
                                        2003005398

10 9 8 7 6 5 4 3 2 1

Table of Contents

Preface

The first time I remember seeing anyone feed birds was one winter morning at my grandfather's house in Kentucky when I was four or five years old. When I walked into the kitchen, I saw my grandfather standing at one of the windows looking outside at the snow-covered lawn. He was watching birds eating the cracked corn he had placed on a patch of grass he had swept clean of snow. He pointed out "red birds" (Northern Cardinals), "snowbirds" (Dark-eyed Juncos), doves, jays, and sparrows (he did not distinguish between species of sparrows; any small brown bird not a wren was a sparrow). Fascinated, I stood and watched with him for many minutes that morning. I had never really noticed birds much before, and it had never occurred to me that anyone would feed them. And, though we lived on a small farm with cows, pigs, mules, chickens, dogs, and cats, I had never seen my grandfather feed a wild animal before or take pleasure in watching them.

Although I hunted, fished, and spent countless hours roaming outdoors during my boyhood days, I was not particularly interested in birds. It was not until my junior year in college that they became important to me, and ever since then the study, identification, and pleasure of watching them has been both my vocation as an ornithologist and my avocation as a birder. My interest in birds has benefited me beyond measure. It has carried me to many extraordinary places in the world, where I have seen thousands of species of birds and countless other wonders I never dreamed of in my ol' Kentucky home.

For many years I have fed birds in my backyard. I have enjoyed trying various types of seed, making suet cakes, feeding hummingbirds, building feeders and nesting boxes, trying to outwit squirrels, and planting trees, shrubs, and flowers—in short, becoming involved in all the things you do when you begin to feed birds. I have studied birds, identified birds, photographed birds, and written about them. I remain as fascinated with these colorful, delightful creatures as I was that morning fifty-five years ago when I took my first innocent look out my grandfather's kitchen window.

I hope that some of the experience I have gained will help you attract birds to your backyard. It doesn't matter if you plan to put out a single feeder to watch for minutes a day or you are planning a multi-year project to turn your backyard into a world-class naturescape. We already share a common bond—our love of nature.

May all the woodland creatures you desire to attract become your daily companions in your backyard. Enjoy!

Fred J. Alsop III, Ph.D.
Johnson City, Tennessee

Geographical Area Covered In This Book

This book focuses on birds that can be readily seen in backyards in North America. The birds described in this book are correlated to the six regions illustrated on the map below.

Northeast = ■
Southeast = ■
South Florida = ■
Western Grasslands = ■
Deserts and Western Mountains = ■
Pacific Coast = ■

Attracting Birds to Your Backyard

Many people attract birds to their backyard as a way of getting back in touch with nature, getting back to a time when people lived as an integral part of the natural world. Other people attract birds to help reverse the current decrease in songbird populations, especially the neotropical migratory species that breed in North America but winter south of the United States in the New World tropics (neotropics). Urbanization continues to destroy natural wildlife habitats, and even the relatively small efforts we make to provide foraging areas and breeding sites in our backyards can make a tremendous difference in the survival of these birds. Also singing birds make most people feel better than traffic, sirens, machinery, and other man-made background sounds.

Still other people attract birds to upgrade their property. National Wildlife Federation studies show that landscaping increases property values as much as twenty percent and that landscaping to attract wildlife adds as much value as commercial landscaping plus the bonus of letting you watch birds and other animals in your backyard. Plantings that provide protective shading, wind screening, and humidity also reduce your home heating and cooling bills, make your home blend in better with its natural surroundings, and give you and your wildlife guests a greater degree of privacy. Providing for and watching birds and other wildlife will give you a tremendous amount of aesthetic pleasure, a quality hands-on natural history and ecology experience, and a way of relieving the stress of modern life.

Attracting birds to your backyard will let you enjoy their speedy action, great feather colors, interesting songs, and fascinating habits up close and personal. You will be able to observe the rushed stopovers of spring and fall migrant birds, the more leisurely stays of breeding birds and their fledglings, and the seasonal visits of wintering birds. You will have a front-row seat to nonstop action: the fierce diving dogfights of hummers (hummingbirds) around your nectar feeders between visits to the flowers in your yard. The constant comings and goings of chickadees and titmice as they pick out one sunflower seed at a time and fly off to a perch to peck away the seed coat. Courting male doves inflating their chests and necks and aggressively pursuing the look-alike females on the ground beneath your feeders. White-breasted Nuthatches spreading their wings and tails while pivoting in short semicircles over your suet feeder to stand off

Ron Austing

woodpeckers. The constant fluttering of activity as birds jockey for position at your feeder as well as long periods when no bird moves, as they freeze in place like feathered statues and rivet their eyes on an encroaching hawk. The shrill alarm note of a Blue Jay that sends the entire company madly dashing for the nearest cover before a predator gets close enough to launch its attack. Adults and fledglings drinking and splashing in your birdbath.

The term "backyard" does not limit you to the backyard of your house by any means. Make plans to attract birds to your backyard, side yards, and front yard as well as the land around your property. If you can talk your neighbors into sharing your interest in attracting birds, you will be able to offer a wider variety of planned habitats and thereby increase the number and variety of birds you attract. If you live in a subdivision or discrete residential area, you might see if you can organize the entire neighborhood into "wildlifescaping." You may even want to hang a feeder or mount a nesting box or ledge at your workplace (see Feeders, page 9, and Nesting Sites, page 27).

If you provide suitable food, shelter, and water, birds will come to your backyard—and if you offer a wide variety of these basic necessities, you will attract a wide variety of birds. You can provide food and shelter by planting and maintaining trees, shrubs, flowers, and other vegetation (see Plantings, page 38, and Just for Hummingbirds, page 54). You can supplement the fruit, seeds, nectar, sap, and insects provided by the plants by offering feeders filled with seeds, suet, or nectar (see Feeders, page 9; Foods, page 17; and Just for Hummingbirds, page 54). You can supplement the available natural shelter by providing nesting boxes (see Nesting Sites, page 27) and making brush piles and other suitable "covers" (see Brush Piles, Stumps, and Snags, page 47). Nearby streams, pools, ponds, and lakes, as well as birdbaths and other sources of water (see Water Sources, page 50) will attract some species that, because of their insect or fruit diets, may not be tempted to visit your feeders. For instance, robins, bluebirds, waxwings, and a host of warblers and vireos frequent good water holes but rarely come to feeders.

Place your feeders, nesting boxes, and birdbaths where the birds will feel safe from people as well as squirrels, cats, and other animals (see Other Backyard Wildlife, page 60)—and where you can readily see the birds as you go about your daily routine. You may want to place at least one feeder a few inches from your favorite viewing window. You can buy feeders that have a one-way mirror at the back and either attach directly to the window or fit into the window like an air-conditioning unit; the birds feed in a box almost inside your home! You may find yourself spending big chunks of your day learning about the birds you see right outside your windowpane.

You are probably already interested in birds and feeding them—or you wouldn't be reading this book. If you are one of the more than sixty million Americans already hooked on making your backyard better for both you and birds, the information in the pages that follow should help you improve on the good thing you already have going.

If you haven't fed your first bird yet, just get a package of black oil sunflower seeds at your supermarket, garden center, or backyard bird feeding store, and scatter the seeds on the ground. It's that easy—you've taken your first step in attracting birds to your backyard. You can stop here or you can naturescape your entire property to attract birds and other wildlife by adding appropriate plantings (including brush piles, stumps, and snags), birdbaths and cascading waterfalls, feeders of all varieties, and hundreds of nesting boxes and shelves. You might even mount outdoor microphones connected to indoor speakers to bring the sounds of your backyard birds right inside your house.

Whether you stick with throwing seed on the ground or go on to create the ultimate backyard for birdwatching, perhaps the best reward of all is watching a wild creature accept your offering of food, shelter, or water. So use the following suggestions for adding feeders, food, nesting sites, plantings, dust baths, and water sources to attract birds—then pick up your binoculars and enjoy watching.

Ron Austing

Creating the Ultimate Backyard for Birdwatching

Turning your backyard into a sanctuary for birds and other wildlife will be one of the most rewarding experiences of your life. You can make this project as simple or involved as you want, and you can do a little bit at a time or undertake major ecological "grassroots" changes all at once. Whatever changes you make will bring you hours of pleasure as you watch birds and other wild creatures come and go on a daily basis and learn firsthand about their interesting behaviors.

Getting started is as easy as hanging your first feeder, setting up a birdbath, or mounting a nesting box. You can readily buy these items, but you may want to spend an afternoon or evening building them yourself.

You may find that taking this first step and continuing to provide food, water, and shelter satisfies your desire to attract and watch birds in your backyard. Or this may be just the beginning of a project that will continue for years and include finding out about different kinds of plants and planting the trees, shrubs, and flowers that will attract the widest variety of birds to your backyard. Don't be impatient—taking your time in creating your ultimate backyard will alert you to new possibilities and also spread out the pleasure of learning more about the natural world around you.

After you have placed a feeder, birdbath, or nesting box close enough to a window so you can watch the birds up close on a daily basis, take an inventory of the elements in your backyard that already attract birds. Make a list of the established plants and what "food" they provide (nuts, berries, nectar, seeds, and fruit). Also list the kinds of insects you see in your backyard (grasshoppers, earthworms, moths, caterpillars, and others). Note natural places in your backyard that provide shelter for birds (dense shrubs, hedges, conifers, brush piles, hollow trees, rock walls, and others). Also note all the seasonal or permanent sources of water (a birdbath that can be heated in winter, and nearby springs, ponds, and streams).

Next make a sketch of your existing backyard and the surrounding natural and man-made areas, including buildings, walkways and driveways, fences, water sources, trees, gardens, and other plantings. Notice what kinds of birds frequent the natural areas outside your backyard and think about ways you can "connect" these areas to your property by planting trees and shrubs to form sheltered "traveling" corridors and safety "islands." Your goal is to provide natural dense covering, both at ground level and above, so birds and other animals can easily and safely reach your backyard sanctuary.

After you have completed your sketch, think about what ecological changes you want to make to attract the widest variety of birds to your backyard. Keep in mind both what the birds need (food, water, and shelter) and what you and the other people living in the area need (formal or informal walkways to reach different parts of the yard, etc.). Unless you are starting from scratch with only a house on a flat lawn, you already have some of the habitat diversity needed to attract a small parade of birds. Before you clear out underbrush or fencerows, burn brush piles, or cut down hollow trees, decide from the birds' point of view whether or not these natural areas meet any of their basic needs.

Before you carry out your plans, you should decide the primary purpose of your sanctuary. Do you want to attract mostly birds, and if so do you want to create a haven for them year-round or just during the winter season? Or do you want to create the ultimate backyard for all kinds of wildlife—birds, squirrels, chipmunks, bats, insects, lizards, butterflies, rabbits, frogs and toads, raccoons, and more? Knowing your primary purpose will help you make the best choices in creating your ultimate backyard.

Ron Austing

The following pages will give you detailed information about feeders, food, nesting sites, plantings, dust baths, and water sources. You can find additional ideas in bird and wildlife magazines and other bird books, as well as from your county extension agent's office, your state wildlife resources agency, and the National Wildlife Federation (for more information, write to the National Wildlife Federation, Backyard Wildlife Habitat Program, 1400 Sixteenth Street Northwest, Washington, D.C. 20036-2266).

Feeders

The greater the variety of feeders and food you provide, the greater the variety of birds that will come to your backyard. Perhaps the ultimate feeding station would have at least one of every kind of feeder available and would offer a wide variety of seeds, suet and suet mixes, and nectars.

Some feeders, such as thistle (niger) feeders for goldfinches and siskins and nectar feeders for hummingbirds, are specifically designed to attract only one or two species of birds. Others, such as platform feeders, are more generic and attract a wide range of species.

You can easily build some types of feeders using scrap wood and other materials you already have or can buy very inexpensively. If you decide to build your own feeder, check your local library for books with plans for building feeders and nesting boxes. You can also find lots of helpful information on feeders and bird-related topics on the internet.

Retailers and mail-order companies offer a wide selection of well-made, long-lasting feeders made from wood, metals, plastics, ceramics, and other materials ranging from rustic to space-age design. All of the major variety stores now have a bird-feeding section, as do building supply stores, nurseries, feed stores, farmers' co-ops, and even supermarkets. A number of national franchises specialize in backyard bird-feeding supplies. The salespeople can often tell you what food works best for each kind of feeder and the species it attracts.

The descriptions below will help you choose the feeders you need for the feeding stations in your ultimate backyard.

Platform Feeders

Platform feeders, the simplest of all feeders, take you one step up from placing the food directly on the ground. You can make a platform feeder simply by mounting a piece of plywood on a pole. If you attach a baffle between the platform and the ground, it will make it harder for climbing animals to reach the food.

Because platform feeders offer open landing areas, they attract both small and large birds, ranging from chickadees and finches to cardinals, jays, doves, rock doves (pigeons), and even woodpeckers. You can fill your platform feeders with any kind of food, and one bird or another will eagerly take almost everything you offer.

Platform feeders have several advantages. They give an open view of the birds that come to feed on it, and they are extremely easy to clean. Their big drawback is that the food is exposed to the elements. You can add a roof to help keep the food drier and free from snow, but it will cut down on your viewing area, cast a shadow that will make it harder to clearly see and photograph the birds, and perhaps discourage larger birds from trying to land on the limited exposed area.

To attract the widest variety of birds, use at least two platform feeders, one standing about a foot off the ground and the other about window height. The lower platform feeder will attract ground-feeding species, including towhees, juncos, sparrows, doves, and Northern Bobwhites, that are not comfortable at higher feeders. Almost all the other birds will come to the higher feeder, and they'll come often, making it the most popular feeder in your backyard.

Ron Austing

Hopper Feeders

Hopper feeders also attract a great variety of birds and have the added advantage of protecting the food from the weather. You can fill them with all kinds of food: small and large seeds, shelled seeds, nuts, and cracked corn. The only seed not recommended for hopper feeders is thistle—these extremely small seeds tend to attract moisture and will form lumps in feeders not especially designed for them (see Tube Feeders, page 11).

Hopper feeders provide ample landing perches for most birds, and their roofs sometimes help keep feeding birds dry.

The sides of these feeders are often made of glass or clear plastic, which lets you track the amount of food inside. A hinged or lift-up roof or a trapdoor in the roof allows quick, easy refilling.

You can easily build a hopper feeder. Traditionally they are made of wood, and some look quite rustic. They vary in size from small to gigantic. I built one for my backyard that holds more than 200 pounds of seed—plenty to feed the birds for several weeks in the winter if my wife and I leave town on an extended birding trip. To discourage squirrels from chewing on my hopper feeder and enlarging the feeding holes, I treated them with Ro-pel, a nontoxic foul-tasting chemical that penetrates wood without staining it. You can buy Ro-pel at most garden supply shops; you can also use it to stop woodpeckers from pecking at the wood part of your house and other buildings.

Tube Feeders

Tube feeders attract chickadees, titmice, finches, nuthatches, and small woodpeckers, especially Downy Woodpeckers. Tube feeders are usually made of clear plastic, which lets you easily track the amount of food inside. The best tube feeders are made of Lexan and have metal rims around the feeding holes, which makes them squirrel resistant—squirrels may still be able to reach the feeder depending on how it is mounted, but the metal generally will prevent them from enlarging the feeding holes and damaging the feeder.

Most tube feeders have short perches below the feeding holes, but some are designed for exclusive use by goldfinches and siskins and have the perch above the holes, which requires the birds to hang upside down to feed. Some of them have an attached feed tray or the option of adding an inexpensive food tray at the bottom. The small size of the perches discourages jays, doves, cardinals, and other larger birds from coming to tube feeders. If you want to attract larger birds, build or buy feeders that have a food tray, or attach one.

Tube feeders come in two distinct types: basic large-hole feeders that can dispense a variety of foods and small-hole feeders that dispense only thistle (niger) seed. Thistle feeders are designed especially for finches and will attract American Goldfinches and Pine Siskins, close "northerly" relatives of the goldfinches that occasionally invade the South for the winter. The thistle seeds that are sold commercially for these feeders do not come from the purple-flowered, sticker-laden thistle plants you see growing along roadsides—commercial thistle seeds come from a yellow, daisylike-flowered plant (niger) that grows in India and northeast Africa. Many people are reluctant to fill feeders with thistle seeds because they are afraid that dropped seeds will germinate and the aggressive plants will establish themselves. Fear not—because niger is a non-native plant, the seeds are rendered inactive by heating and they will not germinate. The very small holes in thistle feeders keep the tiny black seeds from falling out and from getting wet and sticking together. You may think it would take the birds a long time to empty a feeder one tiny seed at a time, but you will be surprised at how skillfully the goldfinches manipulate these little seeds and how quickly the seed level drops. You will find yourself glued to your windowpane watching these agile birds twist themselves upside down on the perches and gobble up the seeds.

You can also attract goldfinches and siskins with inexpensive "thistle socks," open-mesh nylon bags. The birds will land on the socks and pull out the seeds from the small openings in the mesh.

You can fill large-hole tube feeders with sunflower seeds, cracked nuts, mixed seeds, or cracked corn. Since most seed mixes contain millet and other small grains preferred by ground-feeding species, I fill my tube feeders with sunflower seeds and cracked nuts, and I use the seed mixes in my platform and hopper feeders.

Many people begin with one small tube feeder filled with black oil sunflower seeds. This setup meets the basics of "feeding the birds" and provides quite a bit of enjoyment—and it makes a great gift for that difficult-to-shop-for person of any age. I suggest using a number of tube feeders and filling them with a wide variety of foods to attract the most species to your backyard.

Ball Feeders

Ball feeders are round, bowl, or satellite-shaped containers with no attached perches—only round openings at the base. They usually have an attached squirrel guard at the top.

Their design excludes all birds except those that have strong feet and are used to clinging. Chickadees, titmice, nuthatches, and woodpeckers use ball feeders with ease, and you will enjoy watching the skilled aerial acrobatics these birds perform as they perch and feed.

I suggest using only black oil sunflower seeds in ball feeders.

Ron Austing

Window Feeders

Window feeders let you bring birds right up to your house—
sometimes right into your house—so you can see them
close-up without using binoculars, which allows children
and housebound adults to easily enjoy these colorful, active
creatures. Window feeders work well if you live in an
apartment building or a house with limited yard space. You
may also want to mount a window feeder at your workplace
(see Workplace Feeders, page 17).

Some window feeders attach directly to the window frame
or sill, while others hang from the eaves or guttering. Some

of my favorite window feeders are small, clear-plastic tubes with suction cups that attach to the windowpane. I fill one of these feeders with sunflower chips and enjoy watching the chickadees, titmice, and several finch species that regularly visit. In the summer I add a suction-cup-equipped hummingbird feeder. Ruby-throated Hummingbirds come and feed so close that I can see their long tongues taking up the sugar-water nectar.

Several companies make feeders that are designed to fit into a window. All you have to do is place one of these three-sided box-style feeders into an open window with the outside of the feeder flush with the outside of your house (you fill the open space between the sides of the feeder and window frame with insulating material). The sides of the feeder, which jut into the room, are one-way mirrors that let you closely observe the birds while they feed but doesn't let them see you—or your house cat. You don't have to go outside to fill these window feeders—you add food through a port in the top from inside your room.

Nectar Feeders

Most nectar feeders are designed to attract hummingbirds and have very small feeding holes and perches. Other birds are also fond of nectar, so don't be surprised if you see orioles, mockingbirds, tanagers, chickadees, House Finches, and woodpeckers attempting to drink from your hummingbird feeder.

You can choose from a wide selection of commercial feeders ranging from small feeders that have to be filled daily to ones that hold a quart or more of nectar. Or you can make a nectar feeder from bent glass tubing, a rubber stopper, and a test-tube. You may want to add one of the new nectar feeders with larger perches and fill it with a citrus-flavored nectar mix to attract orioles or fill inexpensive poultry chick water dispensers with sugar-water nectar for larger birds.

Ants, bees, and other insects also feed on nectar. You can attach an ant moat above the feeder, fill it with water, and effectively block ants from reaching the feeder. Most nectar feeders have bee guards, barriers that prevent insects from getting close enough to suck up the nectar.

I suggest placing several nectar feeders in your backyard, spacing them apart and mounting them on or near viewing windows. You can fill the feeders with commercial ready-to-use or ready-to-mix nectar, or you can make your own nectar (see Nectar, page 24).

Hot summer sun has a greenhouse heating effect and ferments nectar in a feeder within a few days, making it unusable to the birds. Every three to four days, rinse out your feeders and add fresh nectar. (For more about hummingbirds and nectar feeders, see Nectar, page 24, and Just for Hummingbirds, page 54.)

Fred J. Alsop III

Suet Feeders

Suet feeders are among the most interesting, effective, and inexpensive feeders. They attract woodpeckers, chickadees, titmice, nuthatches, woodpeckers, Carolina Wrens, Brown Creepers, and often wintering warblers and kinglets.

You can offer suet or suet mixes in a variety of ways, but I recommend using one of the plastic-coated wire baskets designed for them. Anchor the wire cage securely to a tree, post, or other solid object to prevent raccoons and opossums from carrying it away. (For information about commercial and homemade suet foods, see Suet and Suet Mixes, page 22.)

I keep my suet feeders filled year-round, and I especially enjoy watching adult woodpeckers bring their fledglings just out of the nest to feed. Starlings sometimes visit suet feeders, but if you want to discourage them, buy a wire basket that has a peaked roof over it so the suet can only be reached by clinging to the underside of the feeder—something starlings are loathe to do.

Fred J. Alsop III

Bluebird Feeders

Several hopper-type feeders on the market are designed to dispense currents, raisins, cornbread, fruit, berries, or commercial "bluebird mix." They lack the usual feeding holes, and birds enter the feeders from the ends through bluebird-size holes. Tufted Titmice also quickly learn to use bluebird feeders.

Personally I have had poor results attracting bluebirds to these feeders, but other people I know have been more successful. One person in my area attracts bluebirds to a platform feeder in her backyard. She feeds them a steady diet of cornbread that she makes "with as much corn oil as it will hold." I have seen as many as six Eastern Bluebirds at a time eagerly downing her crumbled cornbread in winter.

Woodpecker Feeders

Perches on tube feeders tend to exclude woodpeckers, and they have a hard time trying to find a place on hopper and platform feeders to brace their stiff tails so they can feed in an upright position. Feeders designed for woodpeckers have a support they can use to brace their tails. These feeders also have ¾-inch-thick walls that prevent almost all birds except woodpeckers from feeding on the nuts, corn kernels, sunflower seeds, or peanuts inside. Only woodpeckers and White-breasted Nuthatches have bills long enough to reach the food.

If you're looking for a feeder that your neighbors probably don't own, or for a feeder for a backyard birder who has everything, get a woodpecker feeder.

Workplace Feeders

You don't have to limit your enjoyment of feeding birds or watching wildlife to the time you spend at home. Even if your work keeps you indoors for most of the day, you may be able to find a spot outside the building to mount one or more feeders that you and your coworkers can enjoy. My dentist keeps several bird feeders positioned outside the large windows of his office, and I always enjoy (as I am sure his other patients do) the diversion of watching birds coming to and going from these feeders when I sit in his dentist's chair.

If you have a window in the area where you work you may be able to put up a small window ledge feeder or a nectar feeder (see Window Feeders, page 13, and Nectar Feeders, page 14). Window feeders are easy to maintain, and they attract a lot of birds. Being able to look up from your work occasionally and watch a colorful bird at your feeder is both satisfying and relaxing.

Foods

To attract the widest variety of birds to your feeding stations, offer as many foods in as many different kinds of feeders as you can. Use the information on the following pages to help you choose foods to attract the birds you especially want to watch in your ultimate backyard.

Seeds

Americans spend more than $2 billion on birdseed each year. Seeds are easy to store and dispense, they're relatively inexpensive, and birds eat them year-round. Sunflower seeds and "wild bird mixes" have been widely available for many years, and other seeds can now be found at local stores and through mail-order sources.

Striped Sunflower Seeds

Striped sunflower seeds are larger (they can be up to $1/2$ inch long) than black oil sunflower seeds (see below) and have longitudinal dark and light stripes on the seed coat. Since the hulls are too thick for most small birds to break open, striped sunflower seeds tend to pile up quickly under feeders.

Birds that like sunflower seeds: cardinals, jays, grosbeaks, chickadees, titmice, nuthatches, and woodpeckers.

Black Oil Sunflower Seeds

Black oil sunflower seeds are the generic seeds of birdfeeding—if you want to put only one kind of seed in your feeders, this is it! More bird species will eat these small, oil-rich (calorie-rich) seeds than any other kind. Be sure to offer black oil sunflower seeds in at least one of your feeders.

Black oil sunflower seeds are easily distinguished by their small size (they are about $1/4$ inch long) and dark, almost black seed coat. Their small size makes them easy for birds to carry off, and their thinner hull makes them easier than striped sunflower seeds to break open. Their smaller seed coats also mean that less waste will pile up under your feeders.

Ron Austing

Birds that like black oil sunflower seeds: all seed-eating birds, including woodpeckers.

Hulled Sunflower Seeds (Chips/Hearts)

Choose hulled sunflower seeds (also called sunflower chips or hearts) if you want to feed the birds without having to periodically rake up the seed coats that accumulate beneath your feeders. I almost always use hulled sunflower seeds in window feeders that are over patios, walks, porches, or driveways. Hulled sunflower seeds cost more per pound, but remember that you are not paying for the weight of the seed coats as you do for unhulled seeds.

Birds that like hulled sunflower seeds: all seed-eating birds, especially goldfinches, siskins, House Finches, and chickadees.

Safflower Seeds

If you have not offered safflower seeds before, you may have to introduce these white seeds to your birds by mixing them with sunflower seeds and gradually working to straight safflower seeds. If you want to discourage squirrels and blackbirds from using your feeders, fill them with safflower seeds—neither species likes them.

Birds that like safflower seeds: doves, cardinals, House Finches, sparrows, and titmice.

White Proso Millet Seeds

These small, round, bone-colored seeds are often found in wild bird seed mixes. Ground-feeding birds relish white proso millet, and it works well in mixes used for hopper and platform feeders.

Birds that like white proso millet seeds: doves, cardinals, towhees, juncos, and all species of sparrows.

Red Millet Seeds

These small, round reddish seeds (not to be confused with the larger BB-size milo seeds) are often found in seed mixes. Birds don't like it as much as white millet.

Birds that like red millet seeds: doves and most sparrows.

Milo Seeds

Milo is one of the sorghum grains, and BB-size reddish-brown milo seeds are often found in wild bird mixes. Seeds from mature milo grain have very hard seed coats and taste somewhat bitter. Birds that eat milo seeds tend to swallow them whole. While birds in the Midwest and southwestern United States eat great quantities of milo seeds, most Southern birds rake them out of feeders, leaving them to germinate in your backyard. I suggest buying mixes that contain little or no milo seeds.

Birds that like milo seeds: Northern Bobwhites, quails, Wild Turkeys, doves, and ducks.

Thistle (Niger) Seeds

These tiny black seeds do not come from the wild thistle plants you see growing in fields and along roadsides; they come from the niger plant (a yellow-flowering, daisylike plant that doesn't have stickers on leaves and stems) that grows in India and northeast Africa. These imported seeds are heat-treated to prevent them from germinating. Thistle seeds should be used in feeders especially designed to dispense them (for more about thistle feeders, see Tube Feeders, page 11).

Perhaps the only drawback to using thistle seeds is their price—these tiny, oil-rich seeds generally cost more per pound than other seeds. But when you consider the slow rate at which they disappear based on the huge number of them it takes to fill a feeder (there are more than 150,000 thistle seeds in a pound), you get a lot of viewing pleasure and birdfeeding for your dollar. I heartily suggest trying a thistle feeder in your backyard.

Birds that like thistle (niger) seeds: goldfinches, Pine Siskins, Purple Finches, House Finches, chickadees, and titmice.

Corn

Whole kernels and shelled corn, which are available in bulk from most feed stores and farmers' co-ops, work well for platform feeders. Placing some ears of corn on the cob on the ground will help keep squirrels and raccoons away from the more expensive foods in your feeders and from interfering with feeding birds.

Birds that like corn: Northern Bobwhites, quails, Wild Turkeys, doves, pigeons, jays, grackles, blackbirds, and crows.

Cracked Corn

Birds can carry off and eat cracked corn easier than whole corn. It works well in mixes for hopper and platform feeders.

Ron Austing

I don't recommend using cracked corn in feeders in urban areas unless you want to attract lots of House Sparrows and Rock Doves (pigeons).

Birds that like cracked corn: doves, sparrows, Northern Bobwhites, quails, Wild Turkeys, ducks, blackbirds, and starlings.

Nuts

Peanuts

A great variety of birds will eagerly feed on peanuts and a commercial mix called "peanut pickouts." Placed in hopper, platform, and even tube feeders, either alone or in a mix, peanuts will disappear quickly. To thwart the squirrels from eating up all the peanuts, place them in a feeder made from 1/4-inch mesh hardware cloth.

Birds that like peanuts: chickadees, titmice, goldfinches, Pine Siskins, sparrows, jays, crows, and kinglets.

Unsalted Peanuts in the Shell

Bags of these unsalted peanuts in the shell can be used as a substitute for suet in the summer. You can either place the peanuts on platform feeders or just throw them on the ground.

Birds that like unsalted peanuts in the shell: titmice, jays, and woodpeckers.

Ron Austing

Nut Meats (Walnuts, Almonds, Pecans, and Others)

While nut meats may be expensive fare compared with other foods for birds, they are sometimes available at co-ops and farmers' markets in bulk. Whenever you offer them, the birds will surely enjoy them.

Birds that like nut meats: chickadees, titmice, nuthatches, jays, and woodpeckers.

Suet and Suet Mixes

Pure suet is nothing more than beef fat and is available at your supermarket meat counter or meat market. Raw suet attracts many birds, including woodpeckers, but it goes rancid quickly in hot summer days. I suggest using raw suet only during cooler weather.

If you want to make suet cakes, cut raw suet into $1/2$-inch chunks and cook it over low heat until the oil is rendered out. Then mix in as much cornmeal (the cheapest brand you can buy) as it will hold, along with peanut butter, raisins, and mixed seeds. Pack the suet mixture into a wax-paper milk carton or Tupperware® container, and refrigerate it overnight. Cut off pieces of the "set" mixture to fit your wire baskets. The rendered fat will not spoil, even in the summer heat.

You can also buy suet cakes. You will find a bewildering array of suet mixtures at stores that sell birdseed. The cheapest high-energy cakes are as good as any other kinds, and the birds will love them all. In hot weather months, look for no-melt suet "dough" cakes—they won't melt and run out of the holder like regular suet cakes do.

Birds that like suet and suet mixes: woodpeckers, chickadees, titmice, wrens, nuthatches, warblers, European Starlings, and some thrushes.

Fruit

You may not have considered fruit as a part of the larder you can offer to birds, but some birds prefer fruit and berries. Bluebirds, tanagers, and orioles will never frequent your seed feeders no matter how many different varieties of seeds or how many different kinds of feeders you place in your backyard. But apples will lure colorful bluebirds to a feeder, and citrus fruit may entice richly plumaged orange-and-black orioles to be regular visitors.

Apples

Slice apples in half and offer them cut side out on a nail driven into a post, feeder, or tree. Or dice apples and place them in a food dish attached to a feeder to attract bluebirds and American Robins.

Birds that like apples: jays, orioles, robins, bluebirds, mockingbirds, grosbeaks, and woodpeckers.

Bananas

Lots of tropical birds eat bananas and many of our summering songbirds spend their winters in the tropics, but we don't often think of or see bananas offered to birds at feeders because they spoil so quickly. You can make bananas last longer by leaving on the peel and slicing them into inch-long sections and placing them on the feeder or by removing only one longitudinal section of peel. (Also see Ripe Bananas, page 24.)

Birds that like bananas: Northern Mockingbirds, tanagers, American Robins, orioles, and warblers.

Grapes, Raisins, and Soaked Raisins

Grapes are readily taken by a number of species of birds and will go further if you slice them before placing them in your feeders. Many birds eat raisins as they are, but for variety try soaking them in water and offer the "instant" grapes at your feeders—you'll cause quite a commotion!

Birds that like grapes, raisins, and soaked raisins: bluebirds, American Robins, Cedar Waxwings, Northern Mockingbirds, Gray Catbirds, thrashers, woodpeckers, grosbeaks, European Starlings, and wrens.

Oranges

Slice oranges in half and offer them cut side out on a nail driven into a post, feeder, or tree (loose sliced and sectioned oranges are quickly carried away). You can also fasten orange halves to a platform feeder, a plank placed on the ground, or a tree branch close to the ground.

Birds that like oranges: orioles, tanagers, mockingbirds, thrashers, and woodpeckers.

Ripe Bananas

You can hang ripe bananas near your bird feeders to attract fruit-eating birds as well as insects, including fruit flies—which in turn will attract small insectivorous birds that will enjoy the concentration of live, fast food. (Also see Bananas, page 23.)

Birds that like ripe bananas: hummingbirds (they will feed on the fruit flies), warblers, and gnatcatchers.

Nectar

For most of us, attracting hummingbirds by filling feeders with sugar-water nectar is a summertime ritual, and if you live in the Deep South, you may have also used sugar-water feeders to attract wintering hummingbirds as well. In recent winters hummingbirds have been seen in almost all of the Southeastern states, and some people provide nectar year-round to attract these seasonal visitors from the West—as well as a number of other species.

Commercial ready-to-use and ready-to-mix nectars are available, but most contain red dyes that may be harmful to birds' kidneys. (Red flowers are known to attract hummingbirds, and most hummingbird feeder manufacturers add sufficient red areas to their feeders so that no red is needed in the nectar itself.)

You can easily make sugar-water nectar by adding one part sugar to four parts boiling water. Do not add red dye or honey to your homemade nectar; neither ingredient is needed to attract birds. Let the nectar cool before filling your feeders,

Ron Austing

and refrigerate any leftovers. (For more about nectar, see Nectar Feeders, page 14).

Birds that like nectar: hummingbirds, orioles, woodpeckers, and some finches.

Extras on the Menu

Here are some suggested foods that have been featured in magazines for birders or passed around in bird-feeding circles.

Peanut Butter

This high-energy food that lots of birds like is inexpensive (the cheapest brand suits the birds just fine), readily available, and easy to use. If you are concerned about it being too sticky for the birds to eat, mix the peanut butter with cornmeal (which the birds also like). You can experiment by adding suet, cracked corn, seeds, and raisins, and then cooking the mixture to blend the ingredients.

Spread peanut butter or your peanut butter mixture into the crevices of pine cones, cracks in a log or tree trunk, or 1/2-inch holes drilled in a limb or piece of 4 x 4 (suspend the 4 x 4 from a limb or other hanger)—and enjoy watching the birds flock to it. Peanut butter will also attract ants—which the birds may eat as well, but if you don't want to be overrun with ants, you may want to save this treat for colder weather.

Birds that like peanut butter: wrens, warblers, finches, jays, woodpeckers, thrashers, bluebirds, chickadees, titmice, and nuthatches.

Grape Jelly

You can attract orioles by placing some inexpensive generic-brand grape jelly in small, shallow ($1/2$ to 1-inch deep, 3 to 4-inch wide) trays fastened to your bird feeders. Try this in the summer when the orioles are around—it may be just the ticket to get them down out of the treetops on a daily basis.

Birds that like grape jelly: Baltimore Orioles, Bullock's Orioles, Orchard Orioles, Gray Catbirds, and American Robins.

Crushed Eggshells

Birds, particularly adult females, especially like crushed eggshells in the spring and summer when they are nesting. Female birds produce the shells for the eggs they lay from calcium they obtain from the foods they eat and from their own skeletal system.

Birds that like crushed eggshells: almost all birds.

Grit

"Rare as hen's teeth" is an old cliche that points out the fact that no modern bird has teeth. Many birds, especially seed-eating species, use powerful muscles in their gizzards to help grind up their food. The gizzard, a muscular stomach-like organ, holds grit in the form of sand and small stones swallowed by birds to help in the grinding process. Grit is readily available most of the year except in those states where winter snows cover the ground for lengthy periods. Birds will appreciate having a scoop of sand on a platform feeder or in a shallow container near a feeder.

Birds that like grit: almost all seed-eating birds.

Live Food

For a special treat that many birds will relish, place a scoop of live insects on your feeding platforms or trays. Many species that won't visit your feeders for any other reason will come again and again if you offer live insects.

Offering live insects is not as difficult or expensive as you may think. You can find inexpensive mealworms at many pet shops, pet sections in some of the larger variety stores, and sometimes at bait supply stores. Or you can raise mealworms. A starter set of 1,000 mealworms costs less than $5. Place the mealworms in a plastic container with cornmeal, oatmeal, or bran flakes topped with shredded newspaper and a slice of apple or potato. Cover the container with screen wire to keep in the insects and add a fresh slice of apple or potato once a week. Place some of the mealworms in a dish each day on the feeder, and watch how quickly they are snapped up by the birds.

If you have a bug-zapper, you have another easy source of live insects. Try suspending a steep-sided plastic tray beneath the bug-zapper to catch insects that would normally fall to the porch floor or ground. Many of the insects are not killed but will be trapped in your tray. Leave enough space between the tray and the bug-zapper for birds to fly in and retrieve the bugs. If you don't have a bug-zapper, just put an ultraviolet lightbulb in your porch light fixture and hang your collecting tray under the light.

Birds that like live insects: vireos, warblers, woodpeckers, sparrows, finches, chickadees, titmice, gnatcatchers, bluebirds, American Robins, wrens, nuthatches, kinglets, jays, and mimic thrushes.

Ron Austing

Nesting Sites

Providing suitable nesting habitats will attract both permanent residents and migratory breeding birds. Once again, creating this part of your ultimate backyard can be as simple or involved as you want to make it.

Much of the naturescaping you have done or plan to do will provide the necessary shelter for many bird species (see Plantings, page 38). You can also buy or build nesting boxes and platforms to meet the specific needs of birds you particularly want to watch.

Ron Austing

Woodpeckers and other primary-cavity nesters excavate their own cavities, while secondary-cavity nesters either find suitable natural cavities or abandoned woodpecker holes. The cavity nests birds make in trees or wooden posts are naturally rustic—so even if your carpentry skills are rudimentary, you will probably be able to build a nesting box that at least one homeless secondary-cavity nester would welcome.

Suitable nesting cavities are often at a premium and in such demand that birds compete fiercely for them. Scientific studies have shown that the lack of nesting cavities limits the number of some bird species. When researchers supplied artificial nesting boxes over several consecutive breeding seasons, some bird populations increased significantly. Some birds have become so adapted to nesting in manmade nesting cavities that they are rarely seen in natural settings. When was the last time you saw a Purple Martin or a Chimney Swift nesting in something other than a manmade nesting box, a hollowed-out gourd, or a chimney (for swifts)?

Birds other than cavity nesters also sometimes have trouble finding suitable nesting sites and will accept help from people. Dr. Jerry Nagel, a colleague and friend of mind, became interested in the nesting success of Eastern Phoebes several summers ago. He checked under ten concrete high-way culverts in Upper East Tennessee and found three nesting pairs of Eastern Phoebes. That fall, after the phoebes had stopped all their breeding activities and the year's fledglings had left the nests, Jerry glued small wooden nesting ledges inside each of the culverts. When we checked the culverts the next year, all ten of them had nesting phoebes—and every phoebe nest was built squarely on one of Jerry's wooden ledges.

Years ago two other friends, Ron Austing and Jack Holt, built artificial nests from old automobile tires, hardware cloth, straw, and sticks and placed them forty feet or higher in trees in scattered woodlots in the rolling hill country of southwestern Ohio. More than seventy percent of the artificial nests were used by Great Horned Owls that evidently had been unable to locate natural suitable nesting sites in the region's cut-over forests.

American Robins, Eastern Phoebes, and Barn Swallows will nest on simple wooden shelves attached to buildings or under bridges and culverts, particularly if the shelves are placed under the shelter of an overhanging eave, porch, awning, or other protective covering. If you live by a large pond, lake, river, or other body of water, you may want to build nesting platforms for area waterbirds. A 20- to 30-foot pole set in open water with a 45-inch-square platform on top will attract ospreys. Place some sticks on the platforms to get them started on building their nests, and enjoy watching these fish-eating birds of prey raise their young.

Great Blue Herons prefer platforms raised about 30 feet above the water either near or on the shore. To protect young herons from ground predators, add a metal guard around the pole about 5 feet above the water or shore. For the nesting platform, use wooden slats to build an open 30-inch-long triangular structure. Make one side of the triangle 84 inches long—the extra 4 feet will serve as a perch; rounding the slats of the perch will make it easier for the birds to stand on it.

Canada Geese prefer "island" nesting sites. You can create artificial islands by placing 48-inch-square platforms on log or rigid-foam rafts. Attach either a metal washtub or an old tire to the top of the wooden platforms, and then anchor the rafts well out in the water to protect the nesting adults, eggs, and fledglings from ground predators.

If you are not handy with tools or don't have the time, materials, or equipment to build nesting boxes or platforms, you can find a wide variety of ready-made and precut nesting materials at hardware, variety, and bird-feeding stores.

Use the information on the following pages to help you provide a variety of nesting sites at both your house and workplace. Being a landlord for the birds doesn't take much time or effort, and the excitement of watching birds court their mates and raise their families will provide hours of pleasure.

Building Nesting Boxes, Platforms, and Ledges

The Tennessee Wildlife Resources Agency offers a free forty-page booklet called *Woodworking for Wildlife in Tennessee.* This booklet gives drawings and instructions for building a variety of nesting boxes and platforms that can be made by anyone who has basic carpentry skills. The nesting structures shown can be used in backyards across the country. To get your free copy, write to Tennessee Wildlife Resources Agency, Ellington Agricultural Center, P.O. Box 40407, Nashville, TN 37204. Many state wildlife agencies, or your local library, will also have plans and instructions.

To make sure that the nesting sites you build have the best chance of attracting birds and providing safe shelter for them for at least ten years, keep the following tips in mind.

- Build each box or platform for a specific kind of bird rather than just building for the "birds." Different species have different house-size and entrance-hole requirements, and birds will be attracted to nesting sites that are just right for them (see Providing Nesting Sites for the Birds You Want to Attract, page 36).

- Nesting boxes must have a hinged side, front, or roof so they can be easily checked and cleaned out after each brood of fledglings has left and at the end of the breeding season. Be sure to use rust-proof hinges when you make nesting boxes.

- Use locking clips (like those on dog leashes) instead of hooks and eyes to secure the hinged opening on Wood Duck and owl boxes to prevent raccoons from opening them. If you can't find locking clips, add a row of large-head roofing nails on the side of the roof and a matching row on the upper edge of the box sides; run wire around the "pairs" of nails to hold the hinged opening tightly shut.

- Extend the roof of the nesting box at least two inches beyond the front to help prevent water from getting inside during heavy rainstorms. (Mounting nesting boxes with the entrance holes facing away from prevailing winds will also help keep out rainwater.) Drill at least one ($1/4$-inch) drain hole in each corner of the floor. Drill several ($1/4$-inch) holes or cut several slots near the top of the box to allow warm air to escape on hot summer days.

- Almost every carpenter thinks that a "proper" birdhouse has to have a perch below the entrance hole, but avoid the temptation. North American cavity-nesting birds have

Ron Austing

strong grasping feet and don't need perches. House Sparrows and European Starlings don't need perches, but perches make it easier for them to successfully prevent other birds from using the nesting boxes. Bluebirds, Tree Swallows, and other native species can often displace House Sparrows and European Starlings when these non-native "undesirables" don't have the advantage of a perch. So if you buy or already have nesting boxes that have perches, take them off. The only time you might want to attach a "perch" is when you build a Wood Duck nesting box. Fastening a slab of wood, with the bark still on it, horizontally under the entrance hole of Wood Duck nesting boxes makes it easier for these birds to land at the opening, although they, too, will do fine without a perch.

Ron Austing

- Use ³/₄-inch-thick wood when you make nesting boxes to insulate the interior from the cold snaps of late spring and the heat of summer. Pine works well for smaller boxes, but use cedar, redwood, or cypress for most larger ones. You can use pine or plywood for Wood Duck, owl, flicker, and martin nesting boxes if you treat the outside surfaces of the boxes with earthtone paints, stains, or preservatives (you can use white paint for martins only).
  If you plan to mount a nesting box on a post or tree, put several coats of paint, stain, or preservative on the back side to help keep it from rotting. Do not paint or otherwise treat the inside of nesting boxes.
  Do not use wood treated with green copper-based preservative because it can produce poisonous vapors when it is exposed to water, and do not paint, stain or treat a wooden nesting box with creosote.

- *Do not* make nesting boxes from tin cans or other metal materials, or from milk cartons. Metals heat up like ovens in direct sun and the heat will "cook" the eggs and nestlings. Milk cartons provide little insulation and temperatures inside range widely, often lethally.
  Commercial Purple Martin houses made from lightweight, airplane-grade aluminum and artificial gourd houses for martins, wrens, and other birds have been well field-tested for keeping inside temperatures in a healthy

range. Commercial plastic Wood Duck houses have also been tested and approved, but be sure to place them in shady locations.

- Use galvanized nails or screws because they don't rust. Screws work better than nails because they accommodate the expansion, contraction, and warping of wood as it heats, cools, and weathers. Use concrete-coated or ring shank nails to prevent the sides, roof, and floorboards from loosening.

- Nail the sides of the nesting box to the edges (rather than the top) of the floorboard to keep rainwater from seeping into the crack between the sides and the floor and then up into the nest. Recess the floorboard about 1/4 inch up from the bottom of the sides to help prevent moisture from seeping across the underside of the floor and up the sides.

- You can suspend small nesting boxes for wrens under the eaves of your house or from a tree limb, but all other nesting boxes should be firmly attached to a post, tree, or building. Use lag screws and washers when you attach nesting boxes to living trees so you can gradually unscrew them to allow for the tree's growth—otherwise the tree will slowly pull the screws through the wood and damage the house.

- Mount bluebird nesting boxes on posts out in the open. Do not mount bluebird boxes on trees because bluebirds don't like overhanging branches and the many birds that do prefer houses on trees will compete strongly for them.

- Space nesting boxes far apart to reduce competition and territorial conflicts. A good rule-of-thumb is to allow about an acre of habitat for birds of the same species, but there are some exceptions. Bluebird boxes should be placed at least 100 yards apart, but you can mount two of them back-to-back and often have the second box occupied by the pair that just finished their first nesting of the season in the first box. Since Purple Martins and Wood Ducks tolerate other birds from their species, place martin boxes in "apartment style" colonies and place gourds in clusters. You can group Wood Duck boxes in clusters of two, three, or four.

- Small animals may take up residence in your bird nesting boxes—after all they don't know the boxes were intended for other tenants. If you don't want resident mice, squirrels, flying squirrels, opossums, and raccoons or visiting snakes (usually just looking for dinner), you will have to evict them. On the other hand, if you are creating an ultimate backyard for the benefit of all wildlife, you may decide just to provide enough boxes to accommodate the birds as well as unexpected creatures.

● In early spring check your nesting boxes for mice nests, and evict the mice before the birds start looking for nesting sites. Some people advise just leaving the "door" of the nesting box open during the winter to discourage mice, but many birds, including bluebirds, use the boxes as nightly roosts, especially during cold winter weather when a whole family of birds may snuggle inside for protection and shared body heat.

● To evict wasps and bees, spray the insects and their nests with insecticide and remove the nests after the adults are dead. Then spray the interior of the box with Lysol® or another disinfectant.

● To evict ants, spray the colony with Terro® or another commercial ant killer or spray some of the ant killer into a bottle cap and place it under the nesting box.

● Blowfly eggs and larvae will sometimes become established in a bluebird nest, and the larvae will suck blood from the young birds, weakening them and sometimes causing death. If you see blowflies, gently lift up the bluebird nest and lightly tap it with your fingers. The larvae will fall through the nesting material to the floorboard, and then you can brush them out of the box.

● House Sparrows and European Starlings are non-native bird species brought to the United States from Europe, and they are not protected by our state or federal laws. So if you really don't want them in your nesting boxes, you can legally remove them—nests, eggs, and fledglings. These birds are often persistent, and you may have to evict them five or six times before they give up and abandon your nesting box. You can trap adult birds on their nests at night by placing a plastic bag over the entrance hole and opening the box or tapping on it sharply to drive them into the bag. Double check the descriptions for House Sparrows (see page 198) and European Starlings (see page 159) to positively identify the birds occupying your nesting box so you don't toss out or discourage "desirable" species that are protected by law.

    I don't advocate killing any animal though, and personally I find House Sparrows and European Starlings

Ron Austing

just as fascinating as our native birds. Instead of killing these birds, I suggest discouraging them from nesting by providing nesting boxes designed specifically for other species (see Providing Nesting Sites for the Birds You Want to Attract, page 36).

- Any nesting box with an entrance hole at least 1³/₈ inches or larger will admit House Sparrows, and an entrance hole 1¹/₂ inches or larger will admit European Starlings. To prevent these "undesirable" species, don't make entrance holes any larger than needed to fit the species you want to attract.

- Place wood chips rather then sawdust in your nesting boxes for birds that prefer woody materials as a base for their nests and for birds that don't deposit their eggs directly on the floorboard. Sawdust is small with lots of surface area, and it tends to pack down and hold moisture when it gets wet. Wood chips retain less water and provide better drainage for the nest.

  Owls, American Kestrels, Wood Ducks, and Hooded Mergansers like to have a layer of wood chips on the floor of their nesting boxes. Woodpeckers and nuthatches prefer that you overfill their nesting boxes with wood chips so they can toss out a lot of them and at least partially satisfy their instinct to "dig" a cavity.

- You do not need to equip your nesting boxes with "escape ladders" for most bird species, with the possible exception of Tree Swallows. Adults caught by early spring cold snaps often take refuge in nesting boxes, and sometimes an escape ladder—a piece of hardware cloth fastened inside the box from just beneath the entrance hole to the floorboard—may make the difference of whether or not a weakened adult can get back up to the hole and leave the box when the weather improves.

● Always mount a metal cone as a predator guard on any wooden post or tree used to hold a nesting box or platform.

Providing Nesting Sites for the Birds You Want to Attract

The table on the next page lists the nesting box require-ments of some of the species you may want to attract to nesting boxes in your backyard. I did not include House Sparrows or European Starlings because they will come whether or not you build specifically for them. Most woodpeckers prefer to excavate their own nesting cavities, and I listed only those species that will accept a nesting box on a somewhat regular basis.

In general, drill the entrance hole one or two inches from the top on the front side of each nesting box. For Purple Martins, drill the entrance hole one inch from the floor.

Woodworking for Wildlife in Tennessee, the free booklet offered by the Tennessee Wildlife Resources Agency (see page 30), includes building plans for all of the nesting boxes listed on page 37.

Ron Austing

Nesting Boxes

Species	Size of Box Height (in.)	Floor (in.)	Entrance Hole Diameter (in.)	Height above Ground (ft.)	Remarks
American Kestrel	14-16	9 x 9	3	12-30	on tree/post in open country
Screech-Owls (all species)	15-18	8 x 8	3	10-30	on tree/post/building in wooded area
Northern Flicker	16-18	7 x 7	2½	8-20	on tree in wooded area
Red-headed Woodpecker	12-16	6 x 6	2	12-20	on tree in wooded area
Red-bellied Woodpecker	12-16	6 x 6	2½	12-20	on tree in wooded area
Great Crested Flycatcher	10-12	6 x 6	2	8-20	on tree/post in wooded area
Purple Martin	6	6 x 6	2¼	8-20	on post in open area; best near water
Tree Swallow	6-8	5 x 5	1½	5-15	on post in open area; best near water
Titmice (all species)	8-10	4 x 4	1⅛	5-15	on tree/post in wooded area
Chickadees (all species)	8-10	4 x 4	1⅛	5-15	on tree/post in wooded area
Nuthatches (all species)	8-10	4 x 4	1¼	10-20	on tree in wooded area
Carolina & Bewick's Wrens	6-8	4 x 4	1½	5-10	on tree/post/building in wooded area
House Wren	6-8	4 x 4	1⅛	5-10	on tree/post/building near people
Bluebirds (all species)	8	5 x 5	1½	5-10	on post in open area/meadow
House Finch (occasional user)	6	6 x 6	1½	6-12	on tree/post/building near people

Plantings

Think of planting trees, shrubs, and other vegetation as an investment. They add to the resale value of your property, make your home more energy-efficient, improve the appearance of your property, cut down on the amount of grass you have to mow—and they also provide food and cover for birds and other wildlife. When you consider all the benefits, you can readily justify the cost of naturescaping.

When you are planning your ultimate backyard, include a diversity of plants that will attract a variety of birds. Decide what species you especially want to see, and then use the information in this book (see descriptions of birds commonly seen in backyards, starting on page 91) and other books (see Helpful Resource Materials, page 199) to determine what plants meet the food and shelter needs of those species.

As you decide what existing plants to keep on your property and what new ones to add, remember that your backyard must meet your needs as well as the birds. Also keep in mind that the larger the area you naturescape, the greater the diversity and number of birds you can attract.

You may want to invite your neighbors to join you in creating wildlife corridors and continuous strips of natural areas that cross property lines. Working together to naturescape an entire neighborhood will not only provide a wider diversity of natural food and shelter, but it will also increase the value of everyone's property. Whether or not your neighbors take an active role in your naturescaping project, be sure the changes you make to your property don't adversely affect their property.

Evaluating Your Existing Naturescape

The first step in naturescaping is to evaluate what you already have on your property.

STEP 1: Draw a "map" that shows your property lines, existing buildings, fences, walkways, driveways, areas of trees/shrubbery/lawn, and streams/ponds/other natural sources of water. Also sketch in above and below-ground wiring, water pipes, septic tanks and drain fields, sewer lines, gas lines, and any other features you know about.

Being aware of what's already on your property will help you plan where to fit in "new" plantings so roots don't grow into drain tiles and trees don't reach up into wiring. It will also let you know areas to avoid so you don't inadvertently cut into underground wiring with a shovel or break a water pipe with a backhoe.

STEP 2: Notice what areas of your property get sun at different times of the day and during different seasons. Indicate these areas on a piece of clear plastic that you can place over your property "map." Also indicate on the plastic overlay any low-lying areas that tend to stay moist.

Examine the soil in various areas on your property and note on the plastic overlay where you have top soil, clay, sand, sandy loam, fill dirt, or some combination. Buy a soil test kit at a garden supply or variety store and check the soil pH of the different areas.

The amount of sunlight and moisture, the type of soil, and the pH of the soil will determine what plants will grow best in each area of your property.

STEP 3: Make a list of the trees, shrubs, vines, and other plants already growing on your property. Note their size, age, health, whether they are native to your state, their energy conservation value (do they lower cooling/heating costs by shading your home in summer or acting as windbreaks in the winter?), and their maintenance requirements (do they require extra watering, fertilizing, or pruning?).

Also note if the plants you already have provide food or shelter for birds and other wildlife. Birds native to your area have adapted to the available native plants, so having a wide variety of native plants will encourage a wide variety of native birds to live in your backyard year-round. In general, native plants grow better and produce more food and shelter than non-native ones. Also, non-native plants sometimes become out-of-control pests because there are few natural controls to restrict their growth and propagation.

Notice if existing plantings on your property give adequate cover and safe travel corridors for birds and small animals. Look for areas you can naturescape to provide natural shelter.

STEP 4: Consider your space requirements for work, entertainment, security, and comfort. Realistically decide how much and what type of space you need for each activity, and sketch these areas onto another piece of clear plastic that you can place over your property map.

STEP 5: List the wildlife that now visits your yard. If you have dogs or cats that live outside, you will probably attract fewer birds and other wildlife animals to your backyard.

Improving Your Naturescape

Use your property map, plastic overlays, and lists as the starting point for developing your naturescaping master plan. Ask the staff of local nurseries and garden shops to tell you about native and non-native plants that thrive in your area.

You can use the listings on pages 42–45 to get started. There is also information available from your county cooperative extension service and your state Wildlife, Game, and Fisheries Agency (many of these agencies have developed detailed "backyard wildlife habitat improvement" kits). Or you can write to The National Wildlife Federation (1400 Sixteenth Street Northwest, Washington, D.C. 20036-2266) and ask about their Backyard Wildlife Habitat Program.

Once you have gathered information about what plants will do well in your backyard, decide what existing plantings you want to keep and what plants you want to add. Keep in mind that you can make your naturescaping project as simple or extensive as you want—and you don't have to do it all at once. For most of us with somewhat limited time and means, naturescaping will be an ongoing project that will continue for years—and perhaps never be completely finished! Remember too that no matter how big your green thumb is or how much water and fertilizer you use, it just takes time for trees and plants to grow.

The information on the following pages will help you get started on your master naturescaping plan, whether you are starting from scratch, making major changes, or just modifying your existing plantings.

Starting from Scratch or Making Major Changes

STEP 1: Begin by planting a variety of native evergreen and deciduous trees along the edges of your property. These will simulate a forest canopy and provide food, shelter, and nesting sites for birds and other wildlife. They will also screen your property from streets and neighboring properties.

Plant deciduous trees on the south side of your house for summer shade and combine deciduous trees with evergreens on the west side to give winter windbreaks. These should be native overstory trees that will reach fifty feet or taller.

Surround solitary trees with small shrubs (see Step 3 below) to provide ground cover and traveling corridors for birds and other wildlife. Allow enough room for tree growth when planting near buildings and overhead wires to avoid having to severely prune or move a tree that gets too big for its space.

See page 42 for suggested deciduous and evergreen trees.

STEP 2: Provide an understory layer by planting smaller flowering trees in clusters, not in rows, near the taller trees along the edges of your property. Irregular borders attract birds and other wildlife because they provide more "edge," more cover, and sometimes more food than rows of plants. Understory trees will reach from 20 to 50 feet. Mix several species of varying height, shape, and density, and select trees that bear fruit at different times of the year to provide year-round feeding opportunities for birds and other wildlife. Plant fruit trees that thrive without the use of toxic sprays.

See page 43 for suggested understory trees.

STEP 3: Plant shrubs and ground covers around the smaller trees to provide both shelter and food for ground-feeding birds and other wildlife. Select shrubs and woody plants that have multiple stems and reach no more than twenty feet. Buy plants that have several years' growth so they will mature quickly, and plant them in the fall to allow them several months of dormancy to acclimate to local conditions. Remember not to mount your feeders too close to shrubs because they make excellent ambush areas for cats.

See page 44 for suggested woody plants and ground covers.

STEP 4: Although you may want to have some lawn for recreational use, large sprawling lawns are labor and energy intensive, and monocultured, manicured lawns do not provide much food or shelter for birds or other wildlife. Consider replacing some lawn area with flower beds, gardens, shrubbery, and natural landscaping. You may want to develop unneeded lawn area into wildflower meadows. Your local county cooperative extension service or state wildlife resources agency can help you choose warm-season grasses and native wildflowers that will make selected sections of your lawn wilder, more interesting and beautiful, and more attractive to birds and other wildlife.

Modifying Your Existing Plantings

STEP 1: Add enough new plantings to give you a wide variety of evergreen and deciduous trees, understory trees, shrubs, and ground covers (see Starting from Scratch or Making Major Changes, Steps 1, 2, and 3, page 40).

STEP 2: Add mulch around your trees and shrubs to keep soil moisture from evaporating quickly and to inhibit weeds. The mulch you add will eventually break down and begin forming nutrient-rich soil. Spread mulch two to threee inches deep between and around trees and plants, but not directly against their trunks.

Suggested mulch: dried leaves, conifer needles, bark chips, and lawn clippings.

STEP 3: Replace non-native plants with native ones. Native plants are adapted to your area's soil and climatic conditions, often are more disease resistant, and are generally preferred by native birds and other wildlife.

Plant List by Regions

Use the lists on the following pages to plan your new naturescape, or make changes to your existing environment. The plants are keyed by the regions that appear on the map on page VI.

Northeast = ■
Southeast = ■
South Florida = ■
Western Grasslands = ■
Deserts and Western Mountains = ■
Pacific Coast = ■

Trees:

Common Name	Scientific Name	Regions
White Pine	*Pinus strobes*	■
Pitch Pine	*Pinus rigida*	■
Red Pine	*Pinus resinosa*	■
Slash Pine	*Pinus elliottii*	■
Longleaf Pine	*Pinus palustris*	■
Shortleaf Pine	*Pinus echinata*	■
Virginia (Scrub) Pine	*Pinus virginiana*	■
Loblolly Pine	*Pinus taeda*	■
Ponderosa Pine	*Pinus ponderosa*	■
Jeffrey Pine	*Pinus jeffreyi*	■
Sugar Pine	*Pinus lambertiana*	■
Lodgepole Pine	*Pinus murrayana*	■
Pinyon Pine	*Pinus monophylla*	■
Eastern Hemlock	*Tsuga canadensis*	■ ■
Western Hemlock	*Tsuga heterophylla*	■
Colorado Blue Spruce	*Picea pungens*	■
White Spruce	*Picea glauca*	■
Englemann Spruce	*Picea engelmannii*	■
Red Fir	*Abies magnifica*	■
White Fir	*Abies concolor*	■
Eastern Red Cedar	*Juniperus virginiana*	■ ■ ■
American Beech	*Fagus grandifloia*	■
American Elm	*Ulmus americana*	■
Black Cherry	*Prunus serotina*	■ ■
Persimmon	*Diospyros virginiana*	■ ■ ■
White Oak	*Quercus alba*	■
Live Oak	*Quercus virginiana*	■
Chapman Oak	*Quercus chapmanii*	■
Southern Red Oak	*Quercus falcate*	■
Laurel Oak	*Quercus laurifolia*	■
Turkey Oak	*Quercus laevis*	■
Bur Oak	*Quercus macrocarpa*	■

Chinkapin Oak	*Quercus muehlenbergii*	
Post Oak	*Quercus stellata*	
Coast Live Oak	*Quercus agrifolia*	
Canyon Live Oak	*Quercus chrysolepis*	
Interior Live Oak	*Quercus wislizeni*	
Sugar Maple	*Acer saccharum*	
Red Maple	*Acer rubrum*	
Box Elder	*Acer negundo*	
Hickories	*Carya* sp.	
Pecan	*Carya illinoensis*	
California Sycamore	*Platanus racemosa*	
Sycamore	*Platanus occidentalis*	
Arizona Ash	*Fraxinus velutina*	
Green Ash	*Fraxinus pennsylvanica*	
Mountain Ash	*Sorbus scopulina*	
Black Walnut	*Juglans nigra*	
Red Mulberry	*Morus ruba*	
American Basswood	*Tilia americana*	
Blackgum	*Nyssa sylvatica*	
Southern Magnolia	*Magnolia grandiflora*	
Sweetbay Magnolia	*Magnolia virginiana*	
Sassafras	*Sassafras albidum*	
Sweetgum	*Liquidambar styraciflua*	
Western Cottonwood	*Populus fremontii*	
Serviceberry (shadbush)	*Amelanchier canadensis*	
Pacific Madrone	*Arbutus menziesii*	
Netted Hackberry	*Celtis reticulata*	
Common Hackberry	*Celtis occidentalis*	
Yellow Buckeye	*Aesculus octandra*	
Sourwood	*Oxydendrum arboreum*	
Paurotis Palm	*Acoelorraphe wrightii*	
Gumbo Limbo	*Bursera simaruba*	
Cabbage Palm	*Sabal palmetto*	
Shortleaf Fig	*Ficus citrifolia*	

Understory trees:

Southern Red Cedar	*Juniperus silicicola*	
Western Juniper	*Juniperus occidentalis*	
Western Redcedar	*Thuja plicata*	
Mountain Ash	*Sorbus americana*	
River Birch	*Betula nigra*	
Sweet Back Birch	*Betula lenta*	
American Holly	*Ilex opaca*	
Flowering Dogwood	*Cornus florida*	
Alternate-leaved Dogwood	*Cornus alternifolia*	
Mountain Dogwood	*Cornus nuttallii*	
Rough-leaved Dogwood	*Cornus drummondii*	
Downy Serviceberry	*Amelanchier arborea*	

Common Name	Scientific Name	
Saskatoon Serviceberry	*Amelanchier alnifolia*	▫
Western Serviceberry	*Amelanchier alnifolia*	■
Western Hawthorn	*Crataegus douglasii*	■
Pigeon Plum	*Coccoloba diversifolia*	■
Sea Grape	*Coccoloba uvifera*	■
Fringetree	*Chionanthus virginicus*	■
Hercules Club	*Aralia spinosa*	■
Wild Crabapple	*Malus angustifolia*	■
White Alder	*Alnus rhombifolia*	▫
Mountain Alder	*Alnus incana*	▫
Horsebean Palo Verde	*Parkinsonia aculeate*	▫

Woody plants:

Common Name	Scientific Name	
Staghorn Sumac	*Rhus typhina*	■ ■
Smooth Sumac	*Rhus glabra*	■ ■ ▫
Winged Sumac	*Rhus copallina*	■ ■
Witch Hazel	*Hamamelis virginiana*	■
Northern Arrowwood	*Viburnum recognitum*	■
Southern Arrowwood	*Viburnum dentatum*	■
Rusty Haw	*Viburnum rufidulum*	▫
Nannyberry	*Viburnum lentago*	▫
Wild Hydrangea	*Hydrangea arborescens*	■
Gray Dogwood	*Cornus racemosa*	■
Common Spicebush	*Lindera benzoin*	■ ■
Sweet Gallberry	*Ilex coriacea*	■
Dahoon Holly	*Ilex cassine*	■
Yaupon Holly	*Ilex vomitoria*	■
Deciduous Holly	*Ilex decidua*	▫
Winterberry	*Ilex verticillata*	■
California Holly	*Heteromeles arbutifolia*	▫
American Elderberry	*Sambucus canadensis*	■ ■ ▫
Red Elderberry	*Sambucus pubens*	■ ■
Blue Elderberry	*Sambucus caerulea*	▫
Mexican Elderberry	*Sambucus mexicana*	■
Bayberrys	*Myrica* spp.	■
Blackberry	*Rubus* sp.	■ ■ ▫
Raspberry	*Rubus* sp.	■ ▫
Blueberry	*Vaccinium* sp.	■
Highbush Blueberry	*Vaccinium corymbosum*	■
Lowbush Blueberry	*Vaccinium angustifolium*	■
Deerberry	*Vaccinium stamineum*	■
Huckleberries	*Vaccinium* spp.	▫
Coralberry	*Symphoricarpos orbiculatus*	■
Beautyberry	*Callicarpa americana*	■
Wax Myrtle	*Myrica cerifera*	■
Chickasaw Plum	*Prunus angustifolia*	■
Common Chokecherry	*Prunus virginiana*	▫
Hollyleaf Cherry	*Prunus ilicifolia*	▫

Redbud	*Cercis canadensis*	■
Dog-hobble	*Leucothoe fontanesiana*	■
Carolina Buckthorn	*Rhamnus caroliniana*	■
Rhododendrons	*Rhododendron* spp.	■
Chokeberrys	*Pyrus* spp.	■
Lignum Vitae	*Guaiacum sanctum*	■
Coral Bean	*Erythrina herbacea*	■
Joewood	*Jacquinia keyensis*	■
Christmas Berry	*Lycium carolinianum*	■
Cocoplum	*Chrysobalanus icaco*	■
Wild Coffee	*Psychotria nervosa*	■
Fire Bush	*Hamelia patens*	■
Florida Privet	*Forestiera segregata*	■
Sea Lavender	*Argusia gnaphaoldes*	■
Ink Berry	*Scaevola plumieri*	■
Pigeon Berry	*Bourreria succulenta*	■
Bay Cedar	*Suriana maritime*	■
Hazelnut	*Corylus americana*	▨
Buffalo Berry	*Shepherdia argentea*	▨
Missouri Gooseberry	*Ribes missouriense*	▨
Texas Mandrone	*Arbutus texana*	▨
Western Snowberry	*Symphoricarpos occidentalis*	▨
Western Soapberry	*Sapindus drumondii*	▨
Brittlebush	*Encelia farinose*	▢
Creosote Bush	*Larrea tridentate*	▢
Manzanita	*Arctostaphylos pungens*	▨ ■
Quailbush	*Atriplex lentiformis*	▢
Desert Willow	*Chilopsis linearis*	▢
Mesquite	*Prosopis velutina*	▢
Flowering Currant	*Ribes sanguineum*	▢
Golden Current	*Ribes aureum*	■
Mexican Bush Sage	*Salvia leucantha*	■
Pacific Wax Myrtle	*Myrica californica*	▨
Black Huckleberry	*Gaylussacia baccata*	■

Ground covers:

American Bittersweet	*Celastrus scandens*	■ ■
Trumpet Creeper	*Campsis radicans*	■ ▨
Coral Honeysuckle	*Lonicera sempervirens*	■
Twinberry	*Lonicera involucrate*	■
Crossvine	*Bignonia capreolata*	■
Wild Grapes	*Vitis* spp.	▨ ■
Canyon Grape	*Vitis arizonica*	▢
Prickly Pear/Cholla Cacti	*Opuntia* spp.	▢
Ocotillo	*Fouquieria splendens*	▢
Native Sunflowers	*Helianthus* spp.	▨

Maintaining Your Naturescape

Lawn Areas: You can convert some of your lawn into a mini-meadow by mowing it just twice in the summer to control tree and weed invasion. Or you can mow the grass once every two to three weeks and set the blade at the highest cutting position. (If you live within city or township limits, check mowing ordinances before you create a mini-meadow or let your grass grow too high.)

Paths: Maintain mulched, stone, or concrete paths as walkways through your backyard when the vegetation is wet. Plant ground covers and shrubs along these paths to provide natural shelter for birds and other wildlife.

Pruning: Check with garden shop or nursery personnel to find out when and how to prune the plantings in your yard. Proper pruning prevents overcrowding, promotes denser growth, and produces more lateral branches, more flowering, and more fruit—all things that will benefit the birds and other wildlife. Be careful not to prune during the nesting season. Add your pruning debris to your brush piles to provide additional cover for birds (see Brush Piles, Stumps, and Snags, below).

Hedges: Create hedges from both evergreen shrubs (their dense needles and stickery branches make ideal cover and nesting areas) and thorny shrubs (they provide great escapes from predators and also discourage human interference). When pruning your hedges, vary the heights to provide a variety of shelter. Keep in mind that birds prefer somewhat unkempt, informal hedges.

Small Trees: Don't prune all the dead limbs—leave some for woodpeckers and other insectivorous birds to feed on. And don't take all the fruit from fruit trees for yourself—leave some for the birds.

Large Trees: Once a year mow under large trees to control unwanted seedlings. Also, maintain dead trees and limbs that are not hazardous—you may even "plant" some dead snags in your yard (see Brush Piles, Stumps, and Snags, below). Dead trees and limbs provide nesting and roosting cavities as well as woodboring insects for food.

Dead Wood "Plantings"

Not everything you add to attract birds has to be new. Try adding some old dead wood. Start thinking of brush piles, stumps, snags, fallen limbs, and leaf litter in a "new" way—with an eye toward providing shelter and food for wildlife.

Brush Piles, Stumps, and Snags

A brush pile is one of the easiest wildlife features you can add to your naturescape. For years I have piled fallen branches and cut Christmas trees along the fencerow in my backyard. They now make an impressive brush pile that is used daily by many ground-dwelling birds, including Eastern Towhees, Song and White-throated sparrows, Mourning Doves, Dark-eyed Juncos, Northern Cardinals, and wrens. The brush pile serves as a refuge from predators and is one of the first places birds on my nearby feeders dash to when an alarm note is sounded. It also provides a welcome winter haven, and birds gather there regularly between foraging bouts at my feeders. The brush pile provides sanctuary for other wildlife as well, including reptiles, chipmunks, rabbits, an occasional skunk, and other small mammals.

Build your brush pile about ten feet away from food sources and from other cover to help prevent cats from hiding in the brush pile and ambushing birds and small animals. Crisscross some big logs, stumps, and snags on the ground, leaving 8 to 12 inches between each piece. Add larger brush next and then smaller limbs, until you have a mound about 3 to 6 feet wide and 3 to 6 feet tall. Continue to add downed and pruned limbs and branches to your brush pile throughout the year. If your property is large enough, make several smaller brush piles instead of one large pile.

Stumps and snags provide excellent shelter for nesting, roosting, foraging, storing food, and hibernating. Decaying wood hosts a succession of invading fungi and insects that make stumps and snags much more suitable for birds that excavate nesting cavities, and the woodboring and wood-dwelling insects provide a convenient source of food. Open-armed snags also provide lookout perches for hawks and owls as well as for birds that hawk insects in flight, such as Red-headed Woodpeckers, phoebes, Eastern Wood-pewees, and Great Crested Flycatchers.

Unless a large dead tree or its overhanging branches pose a danger to people, buildings, power lines, or other property, leave it and watch the parade of animals, including birds, that make it their home. If the dead tree is too tall to leave standing safely, you can cut down part of it, leaving as much of the stump as you can, and use some of the limbs to create a snag.

Woodpeckers (with the exception of the Red-cockaded Woodpecker, a federally endangered species that excavates its nesting and roosting cavities in living pine trees) excavate roosting and nesting cavities in dead wood. If the dead wood is soft enough, chickadees, titmice, and nuthatches also can dig out their cavities. Once a cavity has been excavated, skinks and other small reptiles may lay their eggs in it.

Snags with cavities provide nesting sites for secondary-cavity nesting species, birds that depend on other species or nature to create cavities because they aren't strong enough to do the excavating. Chickadees, titmice, nuthatches, bluebirds, Great Crested Flycatchers, Tree Swallows, Prothonotary Warblers, starlings, and wrens frequent snags.
If the cavity is large enough, American Kestrels, screech-owls, and Wood Ducks may nest in them; screech-owls may also use it as a daytime roost. Squirrels, flying squirrels, and raccoons may also call snag cavities home.

The lack of suitable cavities has been cited in countless scientific studies as an important factor in restricting the size of cavity-nesting bird populations. You can promote nesting and help increase bird population by providing dead snags on your property.

If you're sold on the need for a dead tree or two in your backyard but you don't have one, don't kill a live tree—unless it's an old deformed one that you were planning to cut down anyway. If that's the case, cut away the bark in a 1 to 2-foot-wide circle around the trunk, and watch the birds and other wildlife attracted to the dying tree.

A more practical option is to "plant" dead snags and stumps by inserting a large section of a dead tree or branch into a hole dug into the ground. This way you can pick the size snags you want and place them where you want (in a location good for viewing and photographing birds but where they won't damage anything if they fall).

When my friend Johnny Lynch created several shallow ponds for nesting ducks and geese on his eighty-acre farm, he cut down dead Eastern Red Cedars (junipers) on his woodlot and "planted" the 8 to 15-foot skeletal trees in the water along one part of the shoreline of each pond. The dense wood of Red Cedar weathers well and takes a long time to decay, and these dead "plantings" have taken on new life as active perches for Tree Swallows that nest in boxes on shore and hunt for insects over the water. Red-winged Blackbirds use the dead trees as song perches from which
to advertise and defend their territories, Belted Kingfishers use them as hunting perches when they scan the pond for minnows just below the surface, and American Robins, American Goldfinches, Cedar Waxwings, and other birds come to preen and rest in the open arms of the trees.

Keep your eyes peeled for dead trees in your neighborhood. Most folks will part with a dead tree or two just for the asking—and perhaps for an explanation of why you want them.

Ron Austing

Fallen Limbs

Don't drag all your fallen limbs to your brush pile—place one or two in a convenient place in your backyard as a ready food source for woodpeckers and other birds that eat woodboring insects. Large fallen limbs also provide shelter and food-storage areas for squirrels and deer mice.

As they decay, fallen limbs absorb and retain water, creating a moist habitat that will attract salamanders and lizards. If you want to watch salamanders, place fallen limbs on north-facing slopes of a forested hill; if you want to watch lizards, place fallen limbs on south-facing slopes, which tend to be sunnier and thus warmer and drier than north-facing slopes.

Leaf Litter

Leaf litter releases nutrients back to the soil and offers a number of wildlife creatures shelter and food. Leaving leaf litter under your trees and shrubs will slow down the evaporation of moisture and attract insects eaten by wrens, towhees, sparrows, thrushes, and other ground-feeding birds. Leaf litter also attracts lizards, salamanders, and frogs. Gray and Cope's Gray Treefrogs hibernate in deep leaf litter.

So don't rush to rake all the fallen leaves from your yard. Leave some for the birds and other wildlife to enjoy.

Dust Baths

Dust baths help absorb excess oils on birds' feathers and discourage mites and other feather parasites. Sparrows, jays, robins, titmice, cardinals, and wrens regularly take dust baths.

Wet dust bath areas provide mud for Barn Swallows, Purple Martins, American Robins, Eastern Phoebes and other birds to use for their nests. Butterflies also frequent wet dust bath areas to "puddle."

You can create "natural" dust bath areas by scraping the vegetation away from a three-foot-square sunny area. Till the top layer of soil to a fine consistency, and keep the area vegetation free.

You can build a dust bath by constructing a two-foot-square wooden tray with two or three-inch sides. Fill the tray with fine loose soil and some ashes, and place it on the ground in an open area.

Fred J. Alsop III

Water Sources

Birds need water as much as they need food. Although the food they eat provides some water, they depend primarily on clean freshwater sources in their environment. If you include just one source of water in your ultimate backyard, you will attract the greatest number of different species. Birds of all kinds will flock to it to drink, bathe, cool off, and sometimes make mud for building their nests.

Offering water can be as simple as filling a shallow container and placing it in an accessible place, or it can involve digging a pond or constructing a living stream with a triple waterfall and lost lagoon. The most important thing is to have fun—don't make providing water so complicated that you don't enjoy doing it.

The best water containers are shallow (one–three inches deep); if the container is deeper than three inches, provide rocks or perches so birds can rest and preen their feathers. Containers with shallow, gradually sloping bottoms are ideal.

Since birds don't have nonskid feet, make sure the containers have rough-textured bottoms. You can roughen up the texture by adding nonskid stick-on strips, or you can paint the bottoms with adhesive and pat on sand for traction.

Your first water container can be an upside-down garbage can lid, a shallow plastic bowl, or an inexpensive birdbath. Once the birds spot your water container, they will continue to visit the container if you keep it clean and filled. Change the water daily, and scrub out the container with a brush and high-pressure hose to remove droppings, algae, and debris. Don't use swimming pool or other chemicals to kill algae in a container used by the birds—the chemicals will harm them. If you use soap to clean the container, rinse it thoroughly.

Place water containers in open areas that have at least partial shade—shaded areas not only keep the water cooler, but the absence of sunlight slows the growth of algae. Place the containers away from feeders so that seed hulls and bird droppings from these high traffic areas don't foul the water. Although the containers should be in open areas, make sure they are within ten feet of protective shrubbery and low trees to protect birds from cats, hawks, and other predators.

If you live in an area where the winters are cold enough to freeze water, place a forty-watt lightbulb under the container or use one of the commercially available birdbath heaters. Don't use an aquarium heater because they are built for indoor use. Be sure to use grounded outdoor wiring to connect your heater to your household electrical power supply.

The heater does not create a hot tub or sauna for the birds amid the ice and snow—it just keeps the water from freezing so thirsty birds can get the water they need. Do not put antifreeze (glycerin), alcohol, or other chemicals in the water in an attempt to keep it from icing over—these chemicals are toxic.

Birdbaths

There are many styles of birdbaths available at nature supply stores, stores specializing in backyard bird feeding, hardware stores, larger variety stores, and garden centers. Traditional birdbaths have a shallow bowl placed on a hollow pedestal. Shallow dishes that hang from slender chains or rope have the advantage of being mobile and can be moved over and over until you find that perfect spot. Place hanging baths high enough off the ground to protect birds from ground predators, and tuck them under a limb that provides convenient perches.

You can make your own birdbath by tying a brick to the handle of a garbage can lid and placing the lid upside down on an upright cylinder of plastic or ceramic drain tile. The weight of the brick hanging in the cylinder makes the birdbath so secure that it will not easily tip over, even when a squirrel hops aboard.

Ground-level birdbaths appeal not only to birds that spend most of their time on the ground but also to those that live in understory trees and shrubs. You can purchase sunken or ground-level pools, or you can simply dig a shallow hole or series of holes and line them with concrete, tough plastic pool liner, or wooden or plastic barrels cut in half (cut off more of the barrels if the sides are too high).

Freeze-proof plastic water birdbaths made from poly-propylene are extremely durable and can be used year-round without breaking in freezing weather. Birdbaths and pools made of concrete or ceramic often crack in freezing weather and do not hold up well over the years.

Child-size wading pools, which are often available at discount bargain prices at the end of summer, make great pools for birds. Just add rocks to make part of the pool shallow enough for birds, and use deeper parts of the pool for aquatic plants to make the pool a natural part of the landscape.

Pools and Ponds

Look at garden or nursery shops for booklets with ideas and designs for pools, ponds, recirculating streams, and other water-related features. Your library will also have books with plans, suggestions, and how-to-do-it directions, and you can find even more information on the World Wide Web.

If you have natural seep or wet areas in low places on your property, you might consider turning them into pools instead of fighting nature and trying to make the "swamp" into dry land. Using a little aquatic engineering, you may be able to turn these areas into natural "wet" lands, with shallow pools for birds and other wildlife at the higher end, with the water trickling down to the deeper end.

Creating larger pools or ponds may require some profes-sional assistance. Before starting on an extensive project, check on your neighborhood and local ordinances for restrictions on waterscaping. Also check with your insurance company for liabilities related to having a pool or pond on your property.

If you decide to add a pool, use a length of rope to outline the shape and size in the location where you want it. When you get it positioned and shaped to your satisfaction, mark the outline with a lime "chalk line" or small wooden stakes, and start digging. Slope the sides of your pool so birds can enter the deeper water gradually.

Running or Dripping Water

Many birds come to water when they hear running streams or dripping water. Using drippers, misters, waterfalls or cascades, or recirculating pumps will add the magical sound of water, giving you great opportunities to see species that might not come to your feeders. Many of the outstanding photographs in magazines of warblers, tanagers, orioles, vireos, and other treetop birds were taken when birds were initially attracted to the sound of water.

Drippers are easy to install, and their real value is in the noise they make. You can simply hang a garden hose over your birdbath or pool and adjust the tap so that a few drops per minute create a steady drip into the water below. You can also make a pinhole in one bottom corner of a plastic milk container, fill the container, screw on the lid, and suspend the container above your birdbath or pool; regulate the rate of the drip by loosening or tightening the lid. Saline-solution IV bottles used by medical-care facilities also make superb drippers. If you want to buy a dripper, look for them in stores that sell birdbaths.

You may also want to add misters to your waterscape. They have recirculating pumps and can be placed in birdbaths to produce a cascading fountain effect. They can also be placed on a tree branch or shrub above birdbaths and pools. Many birds like the mister's simulation of a light shower and will perch under its spray or, in the case of hummingbirds, fly back and forth through it.

You can use a submergible or recirculating pump to create a small stream with waterfalls and rills that invite birds down for a drink or cool, lingering bath. The decor can have a natural look or be as fancy as you can imagine.

Just for Hummingbirds

What beautiful and fascinating creatures hummingbirds are! These tiniest of birds (a nonmigrating Ruby-throated Hummingbird weighs only about 3.5 grams and measures about 2 3/4 inches) dazzle us with their iridescent plumage and aerial acrobatics. Hummingbirds, which feed primarily on the high-energy nectar of flowers, serve as the principal pollinators of many flower species. As hummingbirds and flowers continue to co-evolve, hummingbirds are increasingly found almost everywhere in the Western Hemisphere that flowers grow—including our backyards.

Once only people living in the Southwest, along the Gulf Coast or in Florida could feed hummingbirds year-round, but now it seems everyone in the Southeast has a chance of seeing wintering visitors from the western U.S. visit feeders from October to well into January. Although only Ruby-throated Hummingbirds regularly breed in the Southeast, Bob and Martha Sargent of Trussville, Alabama, have banded eleven species of wintering hummingbirds. In the past fifteen years birders in my "northerly" state of Tennessee have recorded seeing six species—Ruby-throated Hummingbirds and five wintering western species: Black-chinned, Anna's, Allen's, Rufous, and Calliope Hummingbirds.

You can attract hummingbirds (often called "hummers" for the humming sound made by their rapidly beating wings) by providing flowering plants and nectar feeders. The plants they feed on are often too fragile to support even their lightweight bodies, so they feed by hovering in front of the flowers, which requires a high level of energy. It takes a lot of flower nectar (sucrose usually combined with glucose or fructose) or sugar-water nectar to keep a hummingbird going. Researchers have found that hummingbirds normally consume several times their body weight in nectar and small insects daily, and if the nectar is calorie-poor, they may consume up to fourteen times their body weight daily. When high-calorie nectar is available, the birds may have to eat only four or five times an hour, but when the nectar is low in calories, they may have to feed every four or five minutes. Most of the sugar hummers consume goes directly from their digestive tracts to their muscles, although some of it is stored as fat for an energy reserve to get the bird through a short summer night or long migration flight.

Planting a Hummingbird Garden

Hummingbirds find their food primarily by sight, and they seem to prefer tubular blossoms that are red, orange, or yellow—but they also visit flowers of other colors and shapes. Plant lots of flowering plants, both perennials and annuals, as well as woody vines, shrubs, and trees to attract hummers.

Your hummingbird garden will also provide food and shelter for the small insects hummers eat for protein and other nutrients. And hummers use the silk from spiders' webs to fasten lichens and other plant materials to their nests.

The following list, keyed to the map on page VI, will give you an idea of plants to include in your ultimate backyard to attract hummingbirds. Use as many native plants as you can because they are already acclimated and will grow and propagate better and also produce more nutritious nectars.

Native perennials:

Beardtongue, smooth	*Penstemon digitalis*	■
Beardtongue, hairy	*Penstemon hirstus*	■
Beardtongue, common	*Penstemon barbatus*	■
Bee-balm	*Monarda didyma*	■
Bergamots	*Monarda* spp.	■ ▨
Blazing Stars	*Liatris* spp.	■
Bouvardia	*Bouvardia ternifolia*	▨
Cardinal Flower	*Lobelia cardinalis*	■ ▨ ■
Columbine	*Aquilegia pubescens*	▨
Columbine, wild	*Aquilegia canadensis*	■
Evening Primrose	*Oenothera biennis*	■
Fire Pink	*Silene virginica*	■ ▨ ▨
Fireweed	*Epilobium angustifolium*	▨
Indian Paintbrush	*Castillija lineariaefolia*	■ ▨ ▨
Lupines	*Lupinus* spp.	▨ ■
Lupine, sky	*Lupinus nanus*	■
Mexican Honeysuckle	*Justicia spicigera*	■ ▨
Obedient Plant	*Physostegia virginiana*	■
Phlox, annual	*Phlox drummondii*	■
Phlox, tall	*Phlox paniculata*	■
Phlox, wild blue	*Phlox divericata*	■
Rose Mallow	*Hisbiscus moscheustos*	■
Royal Catchfly	*Silene regia*	■
Sage, blue	*Salvia azurea*	■
Sage, scarlet	*Salvia coccinea*	■
Sage, Mexican bush	*Salvia leucantha*	■
Sage, pineapple	*Salvia elegans*	■
Scarlet Creeper	*Ipomoea coccinea*	▨
Touch-me-nots (Jewelweed)	*Impatiens* spp.	■ ▨
Yellow Monkey Flower	*Mimulus guttatus*	■

Annuals and non-native perennials:

Canna	*Canna* spp.	■
Coralbell	*Heuchera* spp.	■
Dahlia	*Dahlia* spp.	■
Flowering Tobacco	*Nicotania* spp.	■
Fuschia	*Fuschia* spp.	■
Larkspur	*Delphinium* spp.	■
Nasturtium	*Nasturtium* spp.	■
Petunia	*Petunia* spp.	■
Scarlet Sage	*Salvia coccinea*	■
Salvias	*Salvia* spp.	■ ■ ■ ■

Native trees, shrubs, and vines:

Agaves	*Agave* spp.	■
Azalea	*Rhododendron* spp.	■ ■
Beauty Bush	*Callipara americana*	■
Butterfly Bush	*Buddleia davidii*	■ ■
Coral Bean	*Erythrina herbacea*	■ ■
Coral-berry	*Symphoricarpos orbiculatus*	■ ■
Coral Honeysuckle	*Lonicera sempervirens*	■
Cross-vine	*Bignonia capreolata*	■ ■
Desert Honeysuckle	*Anisacanthus thurberi*	■
Desert Willow	*Chilopsis linearis*	■
Flowering Currant	*Ribes sanguineum*	■
Fuchsia-flowering Gooseberry	*Ribes speciosum*	■
Hawthorn	*Crataegus crusgalli*	■ ■
Honeysuckle	*Lonicera maackii*	■ ■
Hummingbird Trumpet	*Epiobium canum*	■ ■
Lilac	*Syringia* spp.	■ ■
Mesquite	*Prosopis velutina*	■
Mimosa (non-native)	*Albissa julibrissin*	■ ■
New Mexico Locust	*Robinia neomexicana*	■ ■
Ocotillo	*Fouquieria splendens*	■
Prickly Pear Cacti	*Opuntia* spp.	■
Red Buckeye	*Aesculus pavia*	■ ■
Rhododendron	*Rhododendron* spp.	■ ■
Trumpet Creeper	*Campsis radicans*	■ ■
Tuliptree (Tulip Poplar)	*Liriodendron tulipifera*	■ ■
Weigelia	*Weigelia* spp.	■

Note: Many non-native trees, such as mimosa (sensitive tree), and shrubs that grow well in the Southeastern United States also attract hummingbirds. Watch all the flowering plants in your area during your local hummingbird season and note which ones the birds feed on.

Ron Austing

Hummingbird Feeders and Nectar

Hummingbirds seem to like red, and almost all hummingbird feeders have enough red on them to attract the birds like a magnet. If you feel you need even more red to help hummers find your feeders the first time, hang some red ribbons from the feeder or nearby twigs, or place the feeder near red flowers. Once hummers discover your feeder, they will be steady customers.

Clean feeders are a must, so choose ones that have openings large enough to insert a bottlebrush or toothbrush to scrub the inside. Plastic feeders are generally easier to maintain than glass, and they don't shatter if they fall. Buy several small feeders rather than one large one—it takes a lot of hummingbirds making lots of trips to empty a quart-size feeder before the nectar sours and ferments. And since hummers tend to be aggressively territorial, you will probably attract more of them if you provide a number of feeders and space them in open areas throughout your backyard.

Insects often compete with hummingbirds at nectar feeders. Ants love the nectar, as do several species of bees and wasps. Ants can be stopped in their tracks with a simple device called an ant moat, a small plastic "cup" with eye loops at the top and bottom that fits between the feeder and the hanger. Fill the cup with water or salad oil to prevent the ants from crawling out of it and reaching the feeder. Bees, wasps, and other flying insects can often be discouraged by using feeders with bee guards, small plastic baskets that attach to the feeding holes. Bee guards allow hummers to reach the nectar with their long tongues, but they prevent insects from reaching it with their feeding mouthparts.

Except for people who live in southern states that are warm enough to have hummingbirds year-round, most birdwatchers don't maintain hummingbird feeders after the birds migrate south in the fall. But having feeders up and waiting when the first males arrive in the spring can be the key to having them stay around your yard for the summer. Check with the staff of bird specialty stores or other birdwatchers to find out when the first birds will arrive in your area. Watching hummingbirds has become so popular that many newspapers run articles about their arrival and when to set out feeders. For those of you who live in my area (near Johnson City in Upper East Tennessee), the first male Ruby-throated Hummingbirds of the season arrive around April 6.

Sometimes after the first few weeks of the spring migration, the number of birds visiting your feeders drops off and you may think the hummers have deserted your backyard. Keep your feeders filled though because when the new food sources they have been exploiting begin to fade, they may come back with an appetite. And when the young birds come out of their nests in June, they will visit your feeders regularly.

Lots of people here in Upper East Tennessee think all the hummingbirds have flown south by Labor Day, but that is way ahead of their migration schedule. Many Ruby-throated Hummingbirds are still passing through as late as the third week of October, and they need as much food as they can get as fuel for their migrating flights. The farther south you live, the longer you can expect hummers to come to your feeder. Perhaps a good rule of thumb is to take down your feeders two weeks after you have seen the last hummingbird—but remember, leaving feeders up through October often attracts a visiting western hummingbird species long after the Ruby-throated Hummingbirds have left. And there's no danger of leaving a feeder up "too long" and enticing hummingbirds to overwinter where it is too cold for them to survive—the instinct to migrate is stronger than any nectar you can offer at your feeder.

Most commercial hummingbird nectar and nectar mixes contain red dyes that have been reported to be harmful to the birds' kidneys. Look for commercial nectar and mixes without the red dye. Or make your own sugar-water nectar by adding one part sugar (sucrose) to four parts boiling water—don't add red food coloring, honey (honey often contains a fungus that can kill the birds), or artificial sweeteners (they have no food value). Let the sugar water cool before you fill your feeders, and refrigerate leftover nectar.

You can safely vary the amount of sugar in your nectar and offer "stronger" nectar (one part sugar to two parts water) when the birds need more calories, such as just after they arrive in spring, when they are building up fat deposits before their fall migration, and after several days of unseasonably damp, cool weather. Don't worry—the birds will not "overdose" on the sugar; they just won't have to feed as often.

Replace the nectar in your feeders every three or four days, especially in summer. The hot sun has a greenhouse effect that quickly sours and ferments the nectar, making it unusable to the birds. Every time you replace the nectar, scrub out the inside of the feeder using a bottlebrush or old toothbrush and mild soapy water—but do not use strong household cleaners. Rinse the feeder thoroughly to remove all traces of the soap before you refill it. (For more about hummingbird feeders and nectar, see Nectar Feeders, page 14, and Nectar, page 24.)

Water Sources for Hummingbirds

Like all other birds, hummers look for a dependable supply of daily water, and they seem to especially relish taking baths. One December day in Oaxaca, Mexico, I watched a hummingbird hover over a dew-covered leaf for at least ten minutes while it brushed its breast and belly over and over against the wet surface and then preened its wet feathers. I have also seen several species stand in shallow pools and splash water over their bodies with their whirling wings.

I had read about hummingbirds visiting birdbaths, but I didn't see it for myself until I saw them enjoying a mister at a birdbath. The mister seemed to have a magnetic effect on the birds—they kept flying through it and perching under it, all the while working water into their feathers. Some birders have reported seeing hummers flying back and forth through lawn sprinklers.

You might want to include a mister in your ultimate backyard to attract not only hummers but other birds as well. Misters are inexpensive. Some attach to garden hoses and others attach to pumps immersed in a birdbath or shallow pool.

Other Backyard Wildlife

The naturescaping you do to attract birds will attract other wildlife as well, including squirrels, chipmunks, opossums, rabbits, skunks, bats, raccoons, snakes, lizards, box turtles, salamanders, frogs, and toads. Your life will be easier and your enjoyment greater if you welcome all of these creatures instead of trying to exclude predators or other "undesirables."

Some people have birds they just don't like come to their feeders. Starlings, jays, hawks, House Sparrows, and other birds you may not especially want to watch will come whether you want them to or not. You will probably react very negatively if you see a hawk preying on the birds at your feeders, but this doesn't happen very often, and it is part of the necessary balance of nature. You can "protect" the birds from hawks by placing your feeders within 10 feet of shrubs (be careful not to inadvertently provide ambush cover for cats on the hunt, though) or trees where they can take quick refuge.

Hawks and other birds of prey usually need an open area to successfully stalk their prey. Birds have keen vision and are very aware of movement, and it's very difficult for birds of prey to get close to a group of birds at a feeder without being spotted while they're still too far away to be more than a passing threat. When a bird sounds the "alarm" that a hawk is nearby, every bird at your feeders will sit dead still. Not until the hawk flies off and the "all clear" call is sounded will the birds begin to move again. Hawks are not as common as the bird species they may prey on, and you are most fortunate to have the opportunity to see one on your property.

If you don't want to feed jays, grackles, Mourning Doves, Rock Doves (Pigeons), and crows, surround your feeders with wire mesh that has holes small enough to keep out the "undesirables" but large to let smaller birds reach the food. Unfortunately the wire mesh won't keep out "undesirable" smaller birds such as European Starlings, House Sparrows, and Brown-headed Cowbirds.

Another way of attracting specific birds and discouraging others is to offer foods preferred by the "desirable" species. (See Foods, page 17.)

Keep in mind that there are no "good" or "bad" birds or other creatures—each one is instinctively playing the role its species has evolved to play in the natural world. As birds and other wildlife accept your offerings of food, shelter, and water, you will be able to watch closeup how the various species interact. You'll be fascinated—guaranteed!

Squirrels

You will probably see squirrels as often as you see birds in your backyard. Squirrels have always been common woodland species, and they have become concentrated in the wooded sections of our urban areas as more and more forests have been cleared for houses.

Squirrels are accomplished climbers and agile leapers, and they are smart. They have time to figure out how to get to the food in your bird feeders. Squirrels do not think that food in their territory is "for the birds only." In fact, the food offered in bird feeders has given squirrel populations a boost! Squirrels live at least five or six years in the wild (well-fed backyard squirrels probably live much longer), and they raise two litters a year, with two to five young in each litter—so there may be several of them living on your property.

You have three options when it comes to squirrels in your backyard: You can try to eliminate them altogether, you can battle them in an ongoing squirrel war, or you can learn to live with them. Trying to eliminate them almost never works. In most states squirrels are protected by law as a game species, and even during legal hunting season, most municipalities bar the discharge of firearms.

You can trap the squirrels in your backyard and relocate them (they probably won't survive in their new territory, especially if you relocate them during winter months). But the vacuum created by the removal of one squirrel seems to fill almost immediately with one or two newcomers. Besides, trapping can be difficult, and you put yourself at risk by handling a trap holding an angry live squirrel armed with teeth that can crack nuts. And there may be legal restrictions on trapping and transporting protected wildlife.

Also, once you've trapped the squirrels, where do you release them? Several years ago two men were excitedly telling me their latest squirrel-elimination stories when all three of us suddenly realized that one of the men was releasing his trapped squirrels at a "perfect wooded spot" on the other man's property!

Poisons aren't a good way to eliminate squirrels either. Most poisons are broad spectrum and will kill any animal that ingests them, birds included.

The bottom line is that there is no way to effectively eliminate all the squirrels from a wooded lot. To help you put your ongoing squirrel war in perspective, I heartily suggest you read *Outwitting Squirrels: 101 Cunning Stratagems to Reduce Dramatically the Egregious Misappropriation of Seed from Your Birdfeeder by Squirrels,* by Bill Adler Jr.

Ron Austing

You can attempt to separate squirrels from the food in your feeders, but it's not easy and you will probably lose in the end. There will always be one squirrel that will figure out even the most ingenious barrier and get to the food sooner or later—and time is always on the squirrels' side. You can buy squirrel-resistant feeders that are encased in plastic-coated wire mesh or have metal perches and rims around the feeding holes (don't worry—the birds' feet won't stick to the metal in cold weather). These feeders don't prevent squirrels from physically reaching the food, but they do prevent them from chewing on the feeders and destroying them.

Some squirrel-proof feeders prevent squirrels from staying on the feeders if they reach them; the Mandarin Sky Cafe model, made of Lexan plastic—the stuff bulletproof glass is made of, is the best one of this type on the market. Other feeders prevent squirrels from reaching the food inside the feeders by having a counter-weighted bar that shuts the feeding holes when a creature heavier than a bird lands on the feeder, or a wire mesh cage that has holes large enough to let in small-to-medium-size birds, but is too small for squirrels. If you buy a wire-mesh cage model, make sure the cage will keep the squirrels far enough away to stop them from stretching their "arms" inside and reaching the feeding holes.

Unless you use the Mandarin Sky Cafe model, it's almost impossible to squirrel-proof a hanging feeder. You can discourage—or at least slow down—squirrels and other climbing animals by hanging large baffles over them or using feeders that have domed tops, such as Droll Yankee's Big Top model. You can buy plastic and metal baffles, both cone and disk shaped, at bird feeding supply stores or by mail order through birding magazines. You can easily make a baffle using a cylinder of galvanized stovepipe, but it's worth the investment to buy one that is the right size and readily attaches to the pole.

Here are other strategies for your ongoing squirrel war:

- Choose a spot on a limb at least ten feet out from the trunk and five feet off the ground so very athletic squirrels can't jump out or up and reach it.

- Hang the feeder with thin wire. Do not use monofilament fishing line, string, or rope—all a squirrel would have to do is take one quick bite with its sharp chisel-shaped incisors to bring down the feeder.

- Alway put a baffle between the hanger and the feeder because squirrels can slide down even the thinest of wire with the skill of seasoned circus performers.

- I mount my feeders on poles and place a baffle right beneath each feeder. If you hang the feeder from a shepherd's-crook pole, you will still need to put a baffle on the pole to keep the squirrels from climbing it. Squirrels can shin up the skinniest of poles.

- Some people grease the poles with petroleum jelly, but I don't recommend it because it is potentially harmful to the squirrels as well as birds and other wildlife. Petroleum jelly can harm the animals eyes and mat their fur or feathers, reducing their insulating value.

- Fill your feeders with safflower instead of sunflower seeds. Safflower seeds have a somewhat bitter taste that the birds don't seem to mind once they get used to it (use a mixture of safflower and sunflower seeds for a few weeks before you switch to all safflower seeds). Squirrels—and black-birds, starlings, and Rock Doves—don't seem to like it (caution—the squirrels in your backyard may not know they're not supposed to like it and may eat it passionately!).

- Or fill your feeders with the "hot" new bird food—prepackaged sunflower (and other seed) laced with a film of hot red-pepper powder. You can also buy the pepper powder and sprinkle it on other bird food. The theory is that squirrels' keen sense of smell and taste will make them avoid your spicy offering, but most "desirable" birds will readily accept the pepper taste (many species feed on hot peppers in the wild). From my own personal experience and the experiences of others, I know birds will eat pepper-coated seeds but squirrels have mixed reactions. Some squirrels take one taste and immediately leave the feeders, and some squirrels relish the peppered mix as if it were just what they were looking for to spice up the bland seeds. You might want do your own taste experiment and see which side of the table your backyard squirrels choose.

Once you have accepted the fact that you will never get rid of the squirrels on your property and that you are spending a lot of time and energy battling them, you might decide to just accept them as part of your backyard wildlife. You can still use squirrel-resistant or squirrel-proof feeders equipped with baffles and stocked with food squirrels don't particularly like.

You may even decide to feed the squirrels so you can watch them—after all, they are agile, clever, and cute. Mix corn with more costly seed on platform feeders or set up a "squirrel-feeding" station away from your bird feeders and stock it with dried corn on the cob. Squirrel feeding is fast becoming a popular activity, and you can find feeders designed to offer corn on the cob—from little wooden table and chair sets, where squirrels can sit quietly and eat, to whirls, twirls, and wheels you attach to an ear of corn so the squirrels turn end to end as they eat. Or you can easily make a feeder by attaching a large eyescrew to one end of a 24 to 30-inch length of light chain and a snap clip to the opposite end. Insert the screw into the large end of a corn cob and clip the chain around a tree or limb. The squirrels won't be able to drag away the corn, so you'll be able to watch them.

Raccoons

Raccoons are very intelligent mammals that are attracted to feeders, and they are not as easy to discourage as squirrels because they are larger, stronger, and perhaps have more manual dexterity. Raccoons can reach around most baffles and through wire-mesh cages to scoop food out of feeders.

You can make life harder for raccoons by placing large stovepipe baffles above or below your feeders. You can also limit the amount of food they get by filling your feeders with only enough seed to satisfy the birds, leaving little, if any, at the end of the day. Some people even resort to taking their feeders inside every night.

Raccoons are not as plentiful as squirrels, and you might be able to remove them from your backyard by trapping

(Havahart® type traps work well) and relocating them. Before you buy or set any traps though, check with local wildlife agencies to find out if any laws protect raccoons in your area and if you need permits to trap, transport, and relocate them.

You may decide after all that life is simpler if you just try to accept raccoons as part of your backyard wildlife and allow them a nightly share of the spoils. You will probably enjoy watching these bright, clever creatures perform their nightly antics right outside your windows.

As tame as they may seem once they have lost their fear of man, it's not a good idea to try to handfeed raccoons. They sometimes carry rabies, and their strong teeth and claws can cause serious wounds.

Mice, Rats, and Other Small Rodents

House mice, deer mice, rats, and other small rodents will feed at platform and sometimes hanging feeders and also on seed that invariably falls on the ground under your feeders. You will rarely see these nocturnal creatures unless you catch them off guard when you turn on the outside lights or walk through your backyard at night.

In the East, Flying Squirrels may regularly come to your platform and hopper feeders after dark, especially for corn and sunflower and other large seeds. If you want to get a close-up look at these tiny creatures that have big, dark eyes, try standing close to your feeders in the dark. They will glide noiselessly past you, land on the feeder, and immediately run to the opposite side before getting close enough to the food to eat. They are often very tame and may let you get close to them. They may even adjust to having outside lights on, which would allow you to watch them more easily.

Eliminating mice, rats, and other rodents can be a problem. Don't use poisons because they will kill all creatures that eat them, including birds. You can try trapping and relocating them, but beware of the risk you take in handling frightened, angry, sharp-toothed animals. If you rake or sweep away most of the spilled seed that falls from your feeders, you will reduce the food supply and reduce the rodent populations.

Attracting screech-owls to your backyard will also help reduce rodent populations. I have several screech-owl nesting boxes in my backyard, and I have often seen the owls sitting in the entrance holes at dusk while keeping a sharp eye out for mice. I prefer using this natural food chain of events to trapping or killing the rodents myself.

Predators

Predators, including native wildlife like hawks, foxes, and snakes as well as domestic pets, will prey on the birds you attract to your property. There is nothing wrong with predation—it is a natural way of life for species that do not eat seeds, fruit, or plants. Predators are not "wrong" or "bad"—they are simply playing out the ecological role their species has evolved to play in the natural world.

Even so, having a hawk show up in your backyard, finding the contents of a nest hanging out of one of your nesting boxes, or seeing a cat catch a bird at your feeder can be disheartening. Just remember that the predators (the wild ones, at least) are only providing food for themselves and their young—and the animals they prey on generally reproduce at a rate high enough to sustain losses and still maintain a healthy population. In fact, predators may even help strengthen the species they prey on. As biologists' studies have shown, predators often catch older, weaker animals and young, inexperienced ones, which reduces the number of birds competing for the food, shelter, and water.

Aside from hawks and owls, only a few other birds prey on the eggs or young of other birds. House Wrens sometimes peck open eggs of other species, and crows and jays occasionally feed on eggs and young birds.

House Sparrows and European Starlings, non-native species that were first introduced in the northeastern United States, don't eat other birds, but they are predators in the sense that they actively compete—usually successfully—with titmice, nuthatches, chickadees, bluebirds, and many species of woodpeckers for available nesting sites. House Sparrows and European Starlings are so aggressive that they sometimes build their own nests over the active nests of other species, break their eggs, and kill their young. You can thwart these "predators" by building nesting boxes to meet the specific needs of other species (see Providing Nesting Sites for the Birds You Want to Attract, page 36) and by providing nesting boxes without perches (perches make it easier for House Sparrows and European Starlings to defend their sites).

Male House Wrens can also be considered predators because they arrive in their breeding territories early and fill most of the available nesting boxes with "dummy" nests made of sticks. When the females arrive, each one will choose only one of the nesting sites, but in the meantime the males have driven off other species that will not attempt to nest in a box already filled with sticks.

Cowbirds act as predators in a different way. Each morning during the breeding season, each female lays eggs (sometimes more than thirty each season) in open-cup nests of other species. The unsuspecting "foster" parents often raise the cowbird young at the expense of their own young.

Snakes, raccoons, chipmunks, and squirrels all eat birds, adult as well as eggs and young, as part of their normal diet. Cats, both domestic and feral (the offspring of domestic cats that have been turned loose in the wild), kill many millions of songbirds each year. Estimates suggest that more than 30 million feral cats roam the United States, and if each killed only five birds (a very conservative guess) a year, we would be 150 million birds poorer. Add to this the number of birds killed each year by house cats, and the number is almost unbelievable.

You can give the birds you attract to your backyard an advantage over cats and other predators by doing the following:

● Place your feeders, birdbaths and other water sources as well as dust baths in the open, at least 10 or 12 feet from the nearest low brushy or shrubby cover so birds have a chance of seeing an approaching cat or other ground-traveling predator.

● If you have a house cat that goes outside, put at least two small bells on its collar to warn birds. (One bell is not enough because sometimes the sound is muffled—or the cat learns to move in such a way to minimize its ringing; but two bells will always sound a warning). Try to get your neighbors who have cats to do the same.

● If you have feral cats frequenting your backyard, try to get some help from your local authorities in trapping and relocating them.

● Keeping a dog on your property may help keep cats away, but dogs sometimes attack birds, especially young, sick, or injured ones that are more easily caught.

● Naturescape your yard so it has safe "traveling" corridors and patches of dense cover between the corridors that will help protect birds from predators (see Plantings, page 38).

● Place baffles around trees or poles supporting nesting boxes and feeders to thwart most climbing mammals from reaching the birds.

Photographing Birds

If you decide to try your hand at photographing birds, you probably want your pictures to look like the ones you see in wildlife magazines or the videos you see on PBS or the Discovery Channel. If you haven't already guessed, photographing wildlife in the field is difficult, so before you rush out and buy sophisticated equipment and plan trips to exotic places, start with a basic camera setup and practice photographing the birds in your backyard. Many professional photographers supplement their portfolios by photographing the wildlife that inhabit their own backyards because these birds and other animals are somewhat accustomed to seeing people in their "natural" environment, and their backyard feeders, water sources, dustbaths, plantings, and nesting sites provide camera-ready props and sets.

The information below about cameras, lenses, and related photographic items will help you get started on capturing birds on film. I suggest practicing with relatively inexpensive equipment and adding more expensive pieces as your interest and skill increase.

Cameras

Start with a 35mm camera with a single-lens reflex body that allows you to interchange lenses. Most 35mm cameras come with a 50mm lens, which is a good general-purpose lens but doesn't work well for photographing small subjects—you will need a longer, faster lens (see Lenses, page 70). The popular one-piece 35mm Instamatic cameras do not work for photographing birds because of their built-in small lens.

If you already have a good basic 35mm camera body, all you have to do is add an appropriate lens. If you need to purchase a camera body, you will have to choose from a multitude of available options. For a beginning photographer, simple is best. You can always add autofocus and the other "bells and whistles" later if you decide you need them.

I highly recommend using a camera with a TTL (through the lens) metering system. A good spot metering system pays dividends in nature photography where the proper exposure of the subject—not the background—is of prime importance.

If you want to capture the action and sounds of birds, you will need a video camera. The zoom lens format of available video cameras will give you a wide selection of focal lengths. Adding an inexpensive 2X teleconverter will give you even larger images and let you shoot from greater distances.

Lenses

With lenses, you get what you pay for, and the rule of thumb is buy the best you can afford. To capture the images of 5 to 9-inch songbirds, which nearly "fill the frame" of even 400mm telephoto lenses, you have to get within twenty feet. So in general, the longer and faster (smaller f-stop) the lens, the better.

Longer lenses, 300mm and larger, let you photograph from farther away because they decrease the apparent distance to the subject optically—they give you bigger images. A 300mm lens on a 35mm camera magnifies the subject six times; a 400mm magnifies eight times. Faster lenses (which have smaller f-stop numbers) allow more light to enter the camera, letting you photograph at faster shutter speeds—which is very important in catching the action of fast-moving birds. But longer and faster lenses (with f-stops of 4.5 and 2.8) come with higher price tags. Somewhere you will strike a balance between what lens you need to get the quality you want and what you can comfortably afford.

For most bird photography you need a telephoto lens in the 300mm to 500mm range to increase the size of the image, let you photograph the subject at a greater distance (perhaps as close as the animal will tolerate), and narrow the viewing angle to mask distracting background objects. A 400mm lens is perhaps the "standard" focal length.

I don't recommend buying less-expensive mirror lenses with fixed apertures. Although they are shorter, lighter, and somewhat easier to use, they have a fixed f-stop, so the only control you have over exposure is adjusting your camera's shutter speed. They also record any bright objects in the field of view, but these objects will appear as out of focus star-bursts on your final picture.

Zoom lenses let you choose focal lengths within the range of the lens. A zoom lens in the range of 100mm to 300mm will provide good backup for your longer fixed-focal length lens. To stop the action and get sharp pictures, shoot with the lens opened all the way (set at the smallest f-stop). This gives you the shortest depth of field, which puts your subject in sharp focus and the background out of focus.

No telephoto lens, no matter how long, can reach out and bring your subject in to the desired image size under all lighting and background conditions, and someday you will need a bigger lens—but the cost may prevent you from buying one. A relatively inexpensive option is to buy a teleconverter, a lens that attaches between your camera body and telephoto lens (either fixed or zoom). Teleconverters come in a variety of magnifications and magnify the image size of the lens you

Ron Austing

are using. For example, a 300mm lens coupled with a 2X teleconverter becomes a 600mm telephoto lens. Most teleconverters don't change the clarity of the image, and your camera will meter the light coming through the lens combination correctly. The price you pay for the increased magnification is losing some light from the film plane—a 2X teleconverter loses about 2 f-stops, but under most lighting conditions you can compensate for this by adjusting the shutter speed or aperture opening.

Another inexpensive accessory you will find very useful is a set of extension tubes, hollow rings of various lengths that mount between the camera body and the lens to allow the lens to focus closer than it normally would. Extension tubes offer the perfect solution when your long lens doesn't focus as close as you need because of your distance from the subject. Extension tubes won't let you focus on "infinity," but they will let you work in the 5 to 12-foot range where most of your pictures will be taken. Only the longest extension tubes reduce the amount of light falling on your film, so you meter light as you normally do.

Flash Photography

You may want to use electronic flash or strobe lighting later, but at first concentrate on working with natural light. This approach has the advantage of simplicity and gives you more flexibility in tracking and shooting your wildlife subjects. With flash photography you have to maneuver your subject into the narrow field where your flash is focused, and in

Ron Austing

daylight situations the artificial lighting can override the natural light, blacking out the background and making the subject appear to have been photographed at midnight.

So focus on using natural light now, and as your skill increases, experiment with flash photography.

Film Choices

Print films give you a little more latitude with proper light exposure than do slide films, and you can use film speeds ranging from 50 to 400 ISO (ASA) with good results. The faster films (higher ISO numbers) require less exposure time, which translates into faster shutter speeds and sharper images of active subjects.

I shoot mostly color slide (transparency) films for my teaching, lecture, and publishing work, and I get good results with 50, 64, 100 and 200 ISO films. The slower speed films show almost no grain and are adequate in good light with a fast lens. Images made on 200 or higher ISO films show some grain, and the higher the ISO, the more granular the results. If you want high resolution and little or no grain, use films with a low ISO number. If grain doesn't matter, use films in the 400 to 1600 ISO range.

Don't forget about experimenting with black-and-white films. Although your photographs will lack the pizzazz and punch of color, you can create interesting black-and-white prints by shooting strong subjects in carefully composed settings that include a range of textures. And you can develop and print your pictures yourself if you invest a little in making a dark room, which can be as simple as a large closet in your home.

Whatever film you use, be sure to take a light reading every time with either the light meter built into the camera or a handheld meter. Avoid bright sunlight in the middle of the day when light on subjects is harsh and there are few shadows. Natural light is usually best early in the morning and late in the afternoon. Try shooting on overcast days—you may find that the color saturation of the natural light is surprisingly good.

One recommended accessory that costs pennies and is worth its weight in gold is a "gray card," a medium-gray stock card available at camera stores. Meter off your "gray card" to get average lighting conditions so your light meter will indicate the exact exposure you need to use.

Tripods

When shooting with a telephoto lens, you need to use a tripod. If you want a sharp image, the camera must be on a stable mount, and the bigger the lens you are using, the heavier the tripod must be.

Most good tripods come without a head to hold the camera/lens, and you must choose one to fit your particular needs. Be sure to buy a ball head, which has one lever that lets you move and pan your camera, rather than the standard tilt-type, which has three levers.

Blinds

Blinds (or "hides," as the English call them) are anything that can conceal you from your wildlife subjects. Using a blind you can make a "too-short" telephoto lens just the right length by getting both you and the camera closer to your subjects.

Even if you choose to shoot the birds coming into your backyard feeders from an open kitchen window, you still need to cover the window area so the birds will not see you and be frightened away by your movements. You can't get clear photographs by shooting through the glass in the window, so first raise the window and then hang paper or cloth over the entire area, leaving a port for the camera lens to poke through and a small opening for you to observe the comings and goings of your subjects.

Camera stores and photography magazines offer many types of portable blinds, but you can easily build one. Since the birds in your backyard are already accustomed to manmade objects, your blind doesn't have to blend into the background. I have seen great photos taken from inside cardboard boxes, tents, from under blankets, inside vehicles (they make great blinds as long as you stay inside them), umbrellas with "skirts" added, projector stands with adjustable telescoping legs with a tailored cloth over them, and many other simple blinds.

The basic requirements for a blind are:

—It should be large enough for you and your gear to fit comfortably inside, either seated or standing.

—It should be made of materials the birds cannot see through.

—It should have no pieces loose enough to blow or flap in the wind.

Birds accept blinds as part of the landscape in a surprisingly short time and quickly resume their normal behavior and activities. You can make them settle down even quicker by having someone walk with you to your blind and then leave after you are settled. Numbers don't mean much to most birds (crows and their kin are the exception—they can "count" up to 5), so the birds "lose count" when the other person leaves and behave as if both of you have left.

Props and Backgrounds

Birds are small, fast, and active, and you will be more successful in your efforts to capture them on film if you take some time to learn their habits and plan some backyard "studio" areas. Many birds take the same routes to and from nesting/roosting sites, feeders, foraging areas, dust baths, and water sources—just watch them for several days, and you will see some good photo spots. Searching for nests during breeding season will also give you clues for good photo opportunities.

If you have placed your feeders and water sources where they can be easily viewed from inside your home, you can set up your camera equipment, including a blind (see Blinds, page 73), and be ready to shoot whenever your subjects appear. Feel free to move or add more feeders or bird baths to get better camera angles—the birds will quickly adjust.

Before you start shooting, take a close look at the background in your viewing area. It should be simple, so it

Ron Austing

doesn't compete with the subjects in your photographs, and it should be well behind the subjects, so it will be out of focus and create a soft image that contrasts with the sharper image of your subjects. Shooting with the lens open wide will create a shorter depth of field and "soften" backgrounds, which will be out of focus.

Also make sure the background is natural, not something manmade. Manmade objects tend to have a repeated, geometric design that will pull the viewer's attention away from the subjects of your photographs. Strive for camera angles that show sky, grass, flowers, shrubs, and trees rather than a fence or side of a building.

You will want most of your subjects to be at about the same level as your camera lens. If you are seated in a blind, this will probably be 3 1/2 to 4 feet above the ground, and somewhat higher if you are standing, so place some of your feeders, nesting boxes, and water sources about this height for photo opportunities.

Also provide some natural props in areas with good lighting and suitable backgrounds that your wildlife subjects can perch on to "pose" for photographs. Small sticks, limbs, and branches with blossoms or fruit placed near feeders, water sources, and nesting boxes will often become temporary perches that will provide interesting settings for good photos. These temporary props can be attached to posts driven into the ground, to the top of a spare tripod, or to the feeder or

Ron Austing

birdbath itself with wire, tape, string, or C-clamps. Change your props often to avoid a series of pictures of different birds all posed on the same branch or twig.

To encourage woodpeckers, nuthatches, chickadees, and other birds to "pose" on trees, press some suet or peanut butter mix into crevices or drilled holes on the backside of the tree. Then get into your blind and wait. Before long birds will be climbing and feeding in perfect camera view.

Identifying Birds

Placing feeders and a birdbath in your backyard will give you a good chance to observe birds close-up every day. And mounting birdhouses on poles and in trees will encourage birds to nest on your property, letting you see both young and adult birds.

Once you start watching the birds regularly, you will begin to readily identify cardinals, jays, wrens, woodpeckers, starlings, and other common species. But sooner or later, you'll notice an unfamiliar bird and want to know what it is. Here are some tips to help you identity that "mystery" bird.

Field Marks

Birders and biologists use **field marks** to compare one species to another and help identify an unknown bird. Each species has its own distinctive combination of field marks, which include behavior, relative size and shape, patches of contrasting plumage, bill size and shape, wing length and shape, tail length and shape, and sounds. When you see a new bird, take a close look at the entire bird and make notes about the bird's field marks (see What to Look for on a Bird, page 78, and Which Is It? page 80) Then look at the photographs and read the descriptions (starting on page 91) in this book for species with similar field marks.

Usually only one or two species will have a combination of field marks that are very similar. The more details you notice about your "mystery" bird's field marks, the easier it will be for you to decide which particular species it is.

What to Look for on a Bird

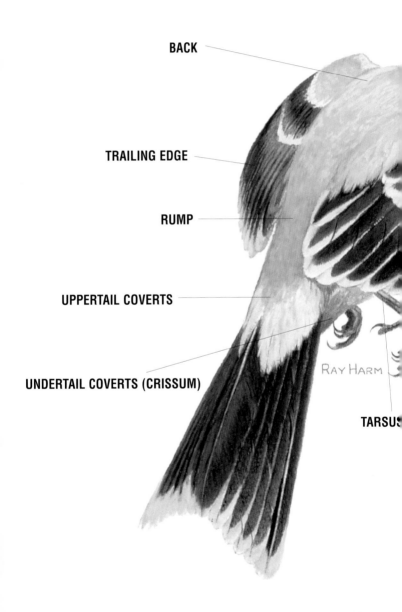

BACK

TRAILING EDGE

RUMP

UPPERTAIL COVERTS

UNDERTAIL COVERTS (CRISSUM)

RAY HARM

TARSUS

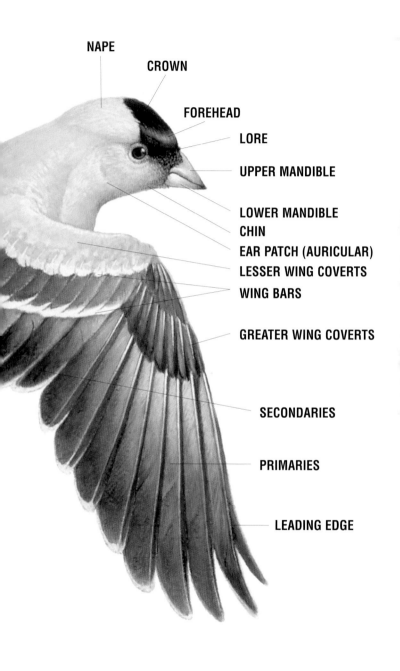

NAPE

CROWN

FOREHEAD

LORE

UPPER MANDIBLE

LOWER MANDIBLE
CHIN
EAR PATCH (AURICULAR)
LESSER WING COVERTS
WING BARS

GREATER WING COVERTS

SECONDARIES

PRIMARIES

LEADING EDGE

Which Is It?

This **WHICH IS IT?** checklist will help you identify birds.

Where and When
Habitat
Impression
Comparison
Habits

Identification Flashes
Sounds

Important Details
Tail and Wings

Where and When

Where refers to geographic region. Birds are among the most mobile and far-ranging species on earth, but almost all birds spend most of their lives within rather strict geographic ranges. So one important clue to a "mystery" bird's identity is where you see it. (For more about geographic regions, consult a bird-watching field guide; see Helpful Resource Materials, page 199.)

Occasionally an individual or small group of birds turns up in an unexpected location—much to the delight of ardent birders—but this is uncommon. If you are having trouble identifying a new bird and think it might be a "rare and accidental" visitor to your geographic region, invite an experienced birder to check out the stranger. In the excitement of seeing an unfamiliar bird, beginning birdwatchers often misidentify an expected local species.

When refers to the season of the year, another important clue in identifying a "mystery" bird. "When" will be different for many species depending on what part of the U.S. or Canada you live in. The examples below refer to birds that range in the Southeast where I live. Consult a field guide's range maps to learn "when" for birds occurring where you live.

Permanent residents live in the same geographic region all year long. Blue Jays, Northern Mockingbirds, Eastern Bluebirds, and European Starlings are permanent residents in the Southeastern United States.

Summer residents breed and raise their young in one region and then leave to winter in warmer regions. Ruby-throated Hummingbirds, Purple Martins, Wood Thrushes, and Red-eyed Vireos are summer residents in the Southeast.

Winter visitors come to a geographic region only during winter months, after their breeding season. Purple Finches, Evening Grosbeaks, White-throated Sparrows, Ruby-crowned Kinglets, Yellow-rumped Warblers, and Hermit Thrushes are winter visitors in the Southeast. If you feed birds only during the colder months of the year, you will see mostly permanent residents and winter visitors.

Transients pass through a geographic region only once or twice a year during their spring and/or fall migrations. Southeastern transients winter in Central America, South America, or the Caribbean and breed in geographic regions in the northern U. S. and in Canada, and we may see them in our yards for only a few days or weeks each year. Rose-breasted Grosbeaks; Bay-breasted, Blackpoll, Tennessee, and Magnolia Warblers are transients in the Southeast.

Accidentals are birds that are not expected in a particular geographic region any time of year. Most new birdwatchers "see" many accidental species, but as they gain experience they realize they may have made erroneous or hasty calls. But look carefully—an accidental bird may just choose your backyard as the place to give the birding world a thrill! For example, one October a Green Violetear Hummingbird stayed for more than a week at a feeder in Asheville, North Carolina, about 1,500 miles north of its normal Mexican range.

Northern Cardinal   Tufted Titmouse

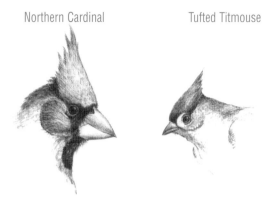

Important details: crests ("topknots")

Cardinals, some species of jays, titmice, and
waxwings have long, well-developed crests
("topknots"). Some species of flycatchers and finches
have shorter, smaller crests.

Mourning Dove   Wood Thrush

Brown Thrasher

Important details:
plain, streaked, and spotted underparts

Doves and some other species have plain, unmarked
underparts. Other species, like thrashers, have
streaked (the marks are longer than they are wide)
underparts, while thrushes and others have spotted
("round") markings.

Habitat

Most birds live in environments that meet their specific requirements for food and cover. When you see a "mystery" bird, note the type of vegetation where it is—that will give you a good clue to its identity.

Impression

First impressions of a "mystery" bird will give you clues for comparing it with birds you already know. Notice if the stranger looks like a crow, jay, robin, sparrow, wren, dove, or other common bird. Also notice its approximate size. It's hard to accurately estimate a bird's size in inches, centimeters, or feet, but you can judge whether it's sparrow size or smaller (5-6 inches), robin size (9-11 inches), crow size (17-20 inches), or larger than a crow.

Comparison

Decide whether your "mystery" bird looks like a species you already know. If so, you have a head start in identifying it. Identifying a "mystery" bird involves comparing a newcomer with other species and eliminating species whose geographic ranges and features don't match the newcomer's.

For example, you may deduce that a new bird is a woodpecker of some kind because it looks and acts like a woodpecker. Make notes about its size, field marks, and the sounds it makes, and then compare it to the descriptions of woodpeckers in this book or a birdwatching field guide.

Habits

Your "mystery" bird's habits give you important identification clues, especially if the bird looks like another species. Make notes about how the stranger behaves. Does it feed only on the ground or only on the hanging feeder? Is it solitary or does it come and go with a group of similar birds? Does it walk (like many ground-dwelling birds do) or does it hop (like many tree-dwelling species do)? If it climbs trees, does it back down the

Northern Flicker   Yellow-rumped Warbler

Identification flashes: sharply contrasting feathers

The eye-catching flash of sharply contrasting feathers will help you identify Northern Flickers and Yellow-rumped Warblers.

Rose-breasted
Grosbeak

Red-tailed
Hawk

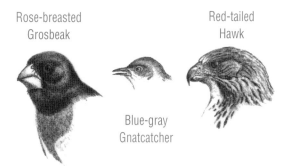

Blue-gray
Gnatcatcher

Important details: shape of the bill

Seed-eaters, like Rose-breasted Grosbeaks, have cone-shaped bills that help them crush seed coats. Insect-eaters, like Blue-gray Gnatcatchers, have small, tweezerlike bills that help them pick up their prey. Meat-eaters, like Red-tailed Hawks, have hooked bills that help them tear apart their prey.

tree in a hitching fashion like a woodpecker, walk headfirst down the tree like a nuthatch, or spiral slowly up and around the tree like a Brown Creeper? Does it cock its tail over its back like a wren or bob it up and down like a phoebe? Is it nesting in a cavity or in the open? Does it fly in a direct line or does its flight path undulate?

Identification Flashes

Many birds have colorful contrasting patches of feathers that produce eye-catching flashes of color when they are exposed. Sometimes these flash marks are enough to identify a "mystery" bird without seeing its other field marks.

Identification flashes include the white outer tail feathers of flying Eastern Meadowlarks or Dark-eyed Juncos and the white oval patches on the outer wings of flying Northern Mockingbirds and Red-bellied Woodpeckers. Other quick clues include the bright white rump patches of Northern Flickers and Red-bellied Woodpeckers, the yellow rump of the Yellow-rumped Warbler, the crimson crown of a Ruby-crowned Kinglet, and the brightly colored speculum on the trailing edge of the wings of many ducks.

Sounds

The songs male birds sing during the breeding season and the calls birds make year-round are often species specific. Professional ornithologists doing bird-census work may identify more than ninety percent of the birds in an area by sound rather than sight. Most species inhabit treetops, the darkest part of the woodlot, or other places where they may be difficult to see, but their songs and calls reveal their presence and their identity. Some species, particularly the small flycatchers in the genus *Empidonax,* are so similar in appearance that it is difficult to tell them apart with accuracy even when holding the bird in your hand, but their sounds are very different. Nothing beats listening to these vocal vertebrates, and as you learn their calls, you will be able to identify and more fully enjoy the birds in your backyard.

Sharp-shinned Hawk	American Kestrel	Eastern Kingbird

Tail and wings:
tail length, shape, and feather pattern

Some birds, like Sharp-shinned Hawks, have tails with alternating bands of color. Others, like male American Kestrels, have a subterminal band of contrasting color, while others, like Eastern Kingbirds, have a terminal band of contrasting color.

Ruby-crowned Kinglet **Eye Ring**	American Robin **Broken Eye Ring**	Golden-winged Warbler **Cheek Patch**

Important details: face patterns

Some birds, like Ruby-crowned Kinglets, have bare skin or a ring of contrasting feathers around their eyes. Others, like American Robins, have incomplete or "broken" eye rings. Some species, like Golden-winged Warblers, have distinguishing cheek patches or other face markings.

You can learn to identify the sounds of specific species by listening to the birds in your backyard, consulting descriptive phrases (mnemonics) in a birdwatching field guide, and listening to records, cassettes, CDs, and computer software available at your local library, bookstore, or bird store and through wildlife magazines.

Important Details

Try to get a good look at the "mystery" bird, and train yourself to look for details. Does it have a crest like a cardinal or titmouse? Is its breast plain, streaked, or spotted? Is its rump the same color as its back? How big is its bill? Is its bill cone-shaped like a seed-eating finch's, small and forceps-shaped like a warbler's or vireo's, or curved and hooked like a hawk's? Does it have contrasting patterns on its head like eye stripes or eye rings (complete or broken), crown stripes, or patches on its crown, cheeks, lores (the area between the base of the bill and the eye), or throat?

Tail and Wings

Your "mystery" bird's tail gives good clues to its identification. Notice the tail's length, shape, and any feather pattern. Is the tail long or short, rounded, pointed, square, notched, or deeply forked? Do the feathers have terminal or subterminal bands? Are there identification flashes along the sides, on the tip, or on the outer corners?

The newcomer's wings also give good clues. Notice if they are long or short, rounded, pointed, broad, or narrow. Also notice if the color contrasts with the bird's body color, like the black wings of a Scarlet Tanager contrast with its red body. Also notice if there are patches of color, bars, or stripes.

Using the **WHICH IS IT?** checklist will help you pay attention to detail, find field marks, and identify the birds. The more you use the checklist, the better you will become at identifying "mystery" birds. Identifying birds by their appearance and sounds is a satisfying skill you can use in your own backyard or wherever you go to watch birds.

Eastern Meadowlark   Dark-eyed Junco

**Identification flashes:
sharply contrasting tail feathers**

The flash of sharply contrasting tail feathers of a bird in flight help identify Eastern Meadowlarks and Dark-eyed Juncos.

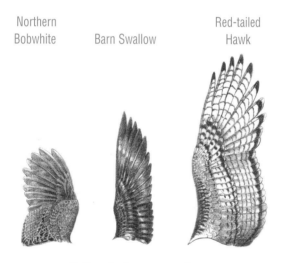

Northern   Red-tailed
Bobwhite   Barn Swallow   Hawk

Tail and wings: wing shape

The wings of different bird species have adapted to where and how they fly. Nothern Bobwhites, most songbirds, and others that live in densely vegetated areas have short rounded wings. Barn Swallows and other birds that hunt insects on the wing (while in flight) have long, narrow, high-speed wings. Red-tailed Hawks, vultures, and other soaring birds have long broad wings with slotted "fingers" for slow flight.

White-throated
Sparrow

Red-eyed
Vireo

Wilson's Warbler

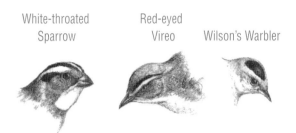

Important details: face patterns

Some birds, like White-throated Sparrows, have bold, striped crowns and eyelines. Red-eyed Vireos and other species have eyebrow (supercillary) stripes, while others, like Wilson's Warblers, have crown patches.

Red-bellied
Woodpecker

Northern
Mockingbird

Identification flashes: boldly colored wing patches

The flash of the boldly colored wing patches of Red-bellied Woodpeckers and Northern Mockingbirds, seen when the birds are in flight, provide good clues to their identities.

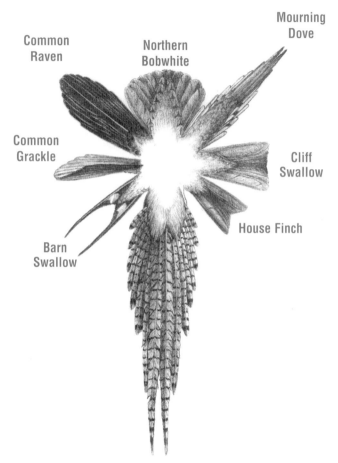

Common Raven
Northern Bobwhite
Mourning Dove
Common Grackle
Cliff Swallow
House Finch
Barn Swallow
Ring-necked Pheasant

Tail and wings: length and shape of tail

Birds' tails can be deeply forked (see Barn Swallow above), keeled (Common Grackle), rounded (Common Raven), fan-shaped (Northern Bobwhite), pointed (Mourning Dove), squared (Cliff Swallow), notched (House Finch), or wedge-shaped (Ring-necked Pheasant).

Sharp-shinned Hawk

Accipiter striatus

This slender, small-headed accipiter has a long square-tipped or slightly notched tail. Sharp-shinned Hawks are secretive, seldom-seen birds of prey that frequent woodlands.

Sharp-shinned Hawks will visit your backyard if you have pines and other conifer trees for nesting and if large insects, small mammals, or small- to medium-size birds are readily available for food.

Ron Austing

Identification Flashes and Distinguishing Features:

Sharp-shinned Hawks have small heads. Look for the square-tipped or slightly notched tail that distinguishes them from Cooper's Hawks.

Size: 10–14 inches (25–36 centimeters)
Like all North American hawks, females are larger than males.

Color: Adults have blue-gray upperparts and reddish-barred underparts, with white undertail coverts and a boldly barred square-tipped tail. Immature birds have brown upperparts and white underparts heavily streaked with dark reddish-brown.

Voice: Often silent but make a cackling *kik, kik, kik, kik* sound when defending their nests.

Range: Permanent residents from southern Maine south along the Atlantic Coast to northern Maryland, through West Virginia to central Alabama, and north to Ohio and southern Michigan; also permanent in West from Wyoming and western Colorado west to the northern Pacific Coast, and up the coast to southern Alaska. Winters throughout the U.S. between these two ranges. Summers north of permanent range into Canada.

Habitat: Frequents woodlands and usually nest in pines and other conifers and shrubs. Each year they build new bulky nests of sticks, often placing nests on large limbs against tree trunks.

Eggs: Lays 4–5 white-to-pale blue eggs with large brown patches; 1 brood per breeding season. The female incubates the eggs; incubation takes 32–35 days. Fledglings leave the nest about 23–27 days after hatching.

Food: Feeds primarily on birds ranging in size from sparrows to starlings. They also feed on large insects and small mammals.

Habits: Sits quietly on partially concealed perches and makes quick dashes to snatch up prey. Northern birds are highly migratory.

Cooper's Hawk

Accipiter cooperii

Ron Austing

Cooper's Hawks look like large versions of Sharp-shinned Hawks. You can tell the two species apart by the shape of their tails: Sharp-shinned Hawks have have square-tipped tails, while Cooper's Hawks have rounded tails. Cooper's Hawks seem to have adjusted better to the fragmentation of woodlands and are more commonly seen than Sharp-shinned Hawks. The two species do not tolerate each other's company. Cooper's Hawks are sometimes called "chicken hawks," but they rarely disturb chickens or other birds that live close to their nests.

Cooper's Hawks will visit your backyard if you have pines and other conifer trees for nesting. They will feed on available small mammals and small to medium-size birds.

Identification Flashes and Distinguishing Features:

Look for the rounded tail that distinguishes Cooper's Hawks from Sharp-shinned Hawks. The crow-size female Cooper's Hawks are much larger than male or female Sharp-shinned Hawks.

Size: 14–21 inches (35–53 centimeters)

Color: Male and female adults have slate-gray upperparts with streaked and barred reddish underparts; their tails have white coverts and 4–5 blackish bars. Immatures have brownish upperparts with heavily streaked paler underparts.

Voice: Usually silent, but when defending their nests they make noisy *cac, cac, cac, cac* clucking sounds.

Range: Permanent residents of a large portion of the U.S., excluding a small circular range from the southwestern tip of Nebraska to northern Texas and including the western arm of Oklahoma. Summers north of range into southern Canada. Winters south of range in southwestern Florida, the coast of Louisiana to the southern coast of Texas, the northwestern border of Texas and Mexico, and western Arizona.

Habitat: Frequents woodlots and stands of deciduous or conifer trees. They make bulky nests from sticks and twigs and line them with chips of the outer bark of pines and oaks.

Eggs: Lays 4–5 dirty-white eggs marked with small, pale spots; 1 brood per breeding season. Incubation takes 32–36 days. Fledglings leave the nest 27–34 days after hatching.

Food: Eats small mammals and small- to medium-size birds (meadowlarks, jays, bobwhites, and doves).

Habits: They often perch in heavy cover below the canopy of trees and fly close to the ground in woodlots, which makes them difficult to observe. They sometimes soar on their short, rounded wings and long tails.

American Kestrel
(Sparrow Hawk)
Falco sparverius

American Kestrels, which are also known as Sparrow Hawks, are the smallest falcons in North America. You can attract American Kestrels to your backyard by providing nesting boxes on poles or in trees (see Habitat, below). They will feed on available large insects, small mammals, and small- to medium-size birds.

Ron Austing

Identification Flashes and Distinguishing Features:

Look for the distinctive black vertical marks on the sides of their faces, their long, pointed wings, and long tails.

Size: 9–12 inches (23–30 centimeters)

Color: Males have brownish-red backs and tails, blue-gray wings, and streaked and spotted underparts. Females have brownish-red barred backs, wings, and tails and streaked and spotted underparts. Both males and females have black vertical marks on the sides of their faces.

Voice: When alarmed they make loud, rapid *killy, killy, killy* sounds.

Range: Permanent residents across most of the U.S. Summers across Canada to Alaska and winters in south Texas, along the Gulf Coast in Louisiana, and the eastern panhandle of Florida.

Habitat: Frequents open and semi-open country and nest in cavities and natural holes in dead trees as well as in large abandoned woodpecker holes. They will nest in suitable boxes (at least 8 x 8 x 12–15 inches with a 3–inch entrance hole) mounted about 10 feet off the ground on poles or in trees.

Eggs: Lays 3–7 white to cinnamon-colored eggs with small dark-brown spots; 1 brood per breeding season, sometimes two in the South. Both parents incubate the eggs; incubation takes 29–31 days. Fledglings leave the nest 30–31 days after hatching.

Food: Feeds primarily on grasshoppers and similar-size insects. They occasionally eat snakes, lizards, and small mammals. They also prey on birds at feeders during winter months.

Habits: Often seen perched on utility wires along highways. They sometimes raise and lower ("bob") their tails when perching. They hover with rapidly beating wings before swiftly swooping to snatch up prey.

Scaled Quail

Callipepla squamata

Called "cotton top" because of its white-tipped crest, the Scaled Quail is attracted to permanent manmade water sources throughout the Southwest. They prefer to walk and run, not fly. Flocks will run for cover when frightened.

They are attracted to stations with small feed on the ground.

Tom Vezo

Identification Flashes and Distinguishing Features:

Look for the white-tipped crest and gray, chunky, rounded body. There are dark edges on the mantle, neck, breast, and belly feathers giving it the scaled appearance it is named for.

Size: 10 inches (25 centimeters)

Color: Gray all over with a bluish gray breast and a white-tipped crest. The wings are olive-brown and there are white streaks on the sides. There are darker edges on the mantle, neck, breast, and belly feathers. The female looks like the male except for the smaller buffier crest. Juveniles appear more rufous and are more mottled than scaled. In southern Texas the male displays a dark chestnut patch on its belly.

Voice: Makes clucking notes, and a low nasal *chip-CHURR* or *pe-COS* or *wait-UP* with the inflection on the second syllable.

Range: They are native to the Southwest from southeastern Colorado to Mexico, and central Texas west through New Mexico.

Habitat: Prefer dry regions—scrub vegetation, grasslands, semidesert and desert. Their nests are sheltered by shrub or grassy tussock and softened with feathers and dry grasses; they sometimes build in open fields. The female builds the nest.

Eggs: They lay 9–16 dull white to cream-white eggs occasionally speckled heavily with small, light brown spots; 1 brood per year. The female primarily incubates with incubation lasting 22–23 days. The precocial young leave the nest soon after hatching and first flight is at 14–16 days. The young are tended by both parents.

Food: Eats insects, flower blossoms, and tender shoots. They eat seeds from desert shrubs, cacti, weeds, grasses, and flowers.

Habits: In spring and summer they travel in pairs or small groups. In fall or winter they can be seen in groups of 7 to more than 100. They make daily trips to water sources and spend hot afternoons in the shade of a shrub. Breeding is adversely affected by lack of rainfall.

Gambel's Quail

Callipepla gambelii

Gambel's Quail is the most hunted game bird in Arizona, Nevada, New Mexico, and California. Named after William Gambel, an early collector of birds in southern California, the male's pleasant call is a familiar desert sound heard in old western films.

They are attracted to stations with small seeds scattered on the ground and permanent manmade pools of water, lawn sprinklers, and cattle tanks.

Ron Austing

Identification Flashes and Distinguishing Features:

Look for the comma-shaped black head plume and black belly patch on the male. The female does not have the scaly underparts that are characteristic of other quail in the region.

Size: 11 inches (28 centimeters)

Color: The male has a black plume; chestnut crown; black face, chin, and throat with a white outline; and chestnut sides. The female has a black crest, russet crown, and sandy-buff underparts.

Voice: Makes grunting noises similar to piglets. There is a sad *quoit* or *oit* and a loud 4-note *chi-CA-go-go*. If a mate is out of sight, there is a location call.

Range: Resides in the lower Southwest, along the north, west and southern Arizona border and those states it borders, into southern New Mexico and south into northwestern Mexico.

Habitat: Frequents dry regions—desert and desert scrub vegetation. The nest is built by the female on the ground sheltered by grassy tussock or desert shrub. The nest is lined with grasses, sticks, and feathers.

Eggs: Lays 9–14 dull white, buff, or pink-buff eggs with blotches or spots of purples and browns; 1–2 broods per year. The female incubates the eggs for 21–24 days. Young leave nest soon after hatching, both parents tend them. When the family moves, the male takes the lead, the female brings up the rear.

Food: Eats plant material, but also insects, spiders, and small reptiles. Will eat from feeders with small seeds on the ground.

Habits: They leave their roosts in shrubs in the early morning. Large groups gather at water sources and feed for hours when weather permits. They rest in the midday heat. Forms large coveys in autumn and winter.

Northern Bobwhite

Colinus virginianus

Northern Bobwhites prefer brushy areas, and you will more often hear than see them. Northern Bobwhites, which are also known as "quails," are managed as a game species with designated fall hunting seasons.

You can attract Northern Bob-whites to your backyard by providing brushy cover close to food and water and brushy "safe" corridors to larger nesting and foraging areas. They will readily come to ground feeders filled with cracked corn and small seeds and grains, such as millet, wheat, and milo. They also like water in a low birdbath or ground-level container.

Ron Austing

Identification Flashes and Distinguishing Features:

The only small rufous-brown quail over its range. Note the short crest with black tips and broad blackish (males) or rufous (females) eyeline.

Size: 9–10 inches (23–25 centimeters)

Color: These small, chunky reddish-brown birds blend with ground vegetation. Both sexes have distinctively patterned faces: Males have white throats and eye stripes; females have buff-collared throats and eye stripes.

Voice: Males whistle familiar *bob-white* song mainly during spring and summer; they make whistled *boy* calls year-round.

Range: Permanent residents of the East from southern Michigan to the Gulf Coast, from Rhode Island south to Florida, west to Kansas south through Texas to Mexico, excluding the Appalachian Mountain range.

Habitat: Frequents agricultural areas, and plowing under cover crops and cleaning up fencerows may cause population declines. They prefer old fields, ungrazed grasslands, abandoned farmlands with brushy cover, and regularly burned open pinelands. They nest in hollowed-out clumps of grass; arches of grasses and weeds conceal their nesting cups.

Eggs: Lays 14–16 dull or creamy white eggs. Some nests receive clutches of eggs from more than one female and may contain 30–37 eggs; 1 brood each season. Both parents incubate eggs for 23–24 days. Fledglings are precocial (capable of a high degree of independent activity from birth) and, like baby chickens and ducks, leave the nest within hours after hatching.

Food: Eats a wide variety of seeds, insects, fruit, greens, and buds.

Habits: They travel in coveys of up to 30 birds; the coveys split up in spring to pair and nest during the breeding season. Bobwhites often rise from underfoot on rapidly whirring wings.

Rock Dove (Pigeon)

Columba livia

Rock Doves, which were introduced about 1621 by European settlers in Virginia, are now common permanent residents throughout the United States, particularly in urban areas. Almost everyone has seen pigeons in a city park, making Rock Doves one of our most easily recognized bird species.

Ron Austing

While many birdwatchers don't want to attract Rock Doves to their backyards, others find them attractive and interesting. In some inner-city neighborhoods, Rock Doves may be one of the few species that visit feeders. You can attract them by placing small seeds and table scraps (particularly breads) on the ground or in large platform feeders that have plenty of room for landings and takeoffs. They welcome water in ground-level containers or low-pedestal birdbaths. They readily accept nesting lofts.

Identification Flashes and Distinguishing Features:

Look for their pigeon shape and white rump patches.

Size: 12.5–14 inches (32–34 centimeters)

Color: Their plumage colors and patterns vary widely. Many have white rump patches, dark bands at the tip of the tail, and black inner wing bars.

Voice: Makes soft *coo-cuk-cuk-cuk-cooooo* calls.

Range: They are permanent residents across the entire U.S., southern Canada, and Mexico.

Habitat: They haphazardly build nests by placing grasses, straw, and debris on "artificial cliff" ledges, such as window ledges and crevices of tall buildings, bridges, and highway overpasses. Some live singly, while others form colonies near human habitation.

Eggs: Lays 2 white unmarked eggs; they lay eggs throughout the year and raise multiple broods. Both parents incubate the eggs; incubation takes 16–19 days. Fledglings leave the nest 27–35 days after hatching.

Food: Eats spilled grain, animal matter, insects, greenery, and direct human handouts of bread and table scraps. They will come to ground feeders for seeds and table scraps.

Habits: In urban areas they have become so tame that they will eat out of your hand. Their strong wing beat places them among the swiftest birds in flight. They often "slap" their wings together over their backs as they take flight and sometimes as display behavior.

Eurasian Collared-Dove

Streptopelia decaocto

These large doves, which are common in Europe and parts of Asia, are now well established in Florida and the Gulf Coast and are extending their range northward. Although they prefer open woodlands and scrub or brushy areas, they also live in settled areas where people regularly feed grain to other birds.

You can attract Eurasian Collared-Doves to your backyard by includng palms and other trees and shrubs in your naturescape, providing water, and offering grains either on the ground or on large platforms feeders close to the ground.

Fred J. Alsop III

Identification Flashes and Distinguishing Features:

Look for a black half-collar on the back of the neck of adult birds. Also look for the white lower half of their tails in flight.

Size: 12.5 inches (32 centimeters)

Color: Both males and females have ashy-brown upperparts and paler ashy-brown underparts, with a pinkish wash on their breasts; their wings have blackish tips; and the terminal half of their tails are black at the base and white on the terminal half. Adult birds have a black half-collar on the back of their necks.

Voice: Makes persistent *coo-cooo-cuh* sounds.

Range: Well-established permanent residents in Florida and the Gulf Coast to east Texas. They are rapidly expanding their range northward and have reached the Ohio Valley.

Habitat: Frequents palms and other trees in urban areas but sometimes builds nest on window ledge. They make fragile-looking nests of twigs with minimal lining material.

Eggs: Lays 2 creamy white unspotted eggs; several broods annually. Both parents incubate the eggs; incubation takes about 14–18 days. Fledglings leave the nest 15–20 days after hatching.

Food: Their favorite foods include cracked corn, sunflower seeds, and millet.

Habits: These tame doves often feed on the ground with other birds. They are generally seen in pairs rather than flocks. They frequent lawns, utility wires, and buildings.

White-winged Dove
Zenaida asiatica

The White-winged Dove's rounded tail and large white wing patches, seen as a bold white edge on folded wings, distinguish it from the more commonly seen Mourning Dove. The distinctive *who-cooks-for-you* coo of White-winged Doves also distinguishes them from Mourning Doves, which make mournful coos.

Fred J. Alsop III

You can attract White-winged Doves to your backyard by offering cracked corn and small grains (millet, wheat, oats, barley) and black oil sunflower seeds on the ground or in large platform feeders that have plenty of room for landings and takeoffs. Like other doves, they welcome birdbaths and other sources of water.

Identification Flashes and Distinguishing Features:

Look for the distinguishing bold white edges on the folded wings of sitting and walking White-winged Doves. Also look for the white corners on their rounded tails.

Size: 11–12 inches (28–30 centimeters)

Color: Males are larger and more highly colored than females. Both have brown upperparts with pale underparts; purplish-rose heads and necks; and red legs and feet. A blue ring of bare skin encircles their red-orange eyes; they have black marks below and behind their eyes.

Voice: Makes distinctive *who-cooks-for-you* coos.

Range: Native to desert areas of the western U. S.; increasing numbers are permanent residents along the Gulf Coast from Mississippi to Texas, and in Tropical Florida. Winters along the Alabama/Florida Gulf Coast, and summers in most of Texas, parts of Arizona, and southern New Mexico.

Habitat: Builds flimsy nests of grasses and sticks. Some nest singly, while others form colonies, especially in suitable dense thickets of shrubs and low trees.

Eggs: Lays 2 creamy white unspotted eggs; 2–3 broods per breeding season. Both parents incubate the eggs; incubation takes 13–14 days. Both feed the young birds regurgitated seeds, insects, and rich "pigeon's milk," a granular fluid produced by the lining of the adults' crops (part of their gullets). Fledglings leave the nest 13–16 days after hatching.

Food: Eats a variety of seeds and grains (wild sunflower, doveweed, and small grains, such as milo, sorghum, and millet).

Habits Often found in flocks, especially after breeding season. Some reuse their nests, while others dismantle them and "recycle" the materials in new nests.

Mourning Dove

Zenaida macroura

Mourning Doves, the most widespread and possibly best known doves in North America, have successfully adapted to a wide variety of "disturbed" habitats. The clearing of large forest blocks, opening of farmlands with grain and weed seeds, and close-cropping of grazing pastures have benefited this bird's populations. Mourning Doves are hunted as game birds during designated seasons.

You can attract Mourning Doves to your backyard by offering cracked corn and small grains either on the ground or on large platform feeders that have plenty of room for landings and takeoffs. Like other doves, they welcome birdbaths and other sources of water.

Ron Austing

Identification Flashes and Distinguishing Features:

Look for their long pointed tails and heads that are "too small" for their bodies. Listen for their distinctive mournful coo. Also listen for the shrill whistle of their wings in flight.

Size: 12 inches (31 centimeters)

Color: Both males and females have brownish bodies with a pinkish wash on the underparts. They have long, pointed, white-tipped tails.

Voice: Makes mournful calls of long and short cooing *oowoo-woo-woo-woo* sounds similar to an owl's call.

Range: Permanent residents of most of the U. S.; southern Minnesota to the Gulf Coast, from entire Atlantic Coast west to the Pacific Coast. They summer north of this range into southern Canada, and winter to the south in Mexico.

Habitat: Often nests in trees and shrubs close to houses and sometimes build on top of abandoned robin or grackle nests. They build fragile-looking nests of twigs with minimal lining material.

Eggs: May nest as early as February and lay 2 creamy white eggs; 5–6 broods in the South, 2–3 in other areas. Both parents incubate the eggs; incubation takes 14 days. Both parents feed the young birds regurgitated seeds, insects, and rich "pigeon's milk," a granular fluid produced by the lining of the adults' crops (part of their gullets). Fledglings leave the nest 12–14 days after hatching.

Food: Primarily small seeds, nuts, fruit, and berries. Will come to feeders for black oil sunflower seeds or millet.

Habits: Unlike other birds, doves drink by sucking liquid up their bills, horselike, without raising their heads. Usually mate for life. Individual pairs separate from the flock during breeding season and then rejoin the others. They fly rapidly in direct paths.

Common Ground-Dove

Columbina passerina

Hardly larger than sparrows, Common Ground-Doves are the smallest North American doves, and their small size alone distinguishes them from similar species. These stocky little doves have scaly breasts and short rounded tails.

You can attract Common Ground-Doves to your backyard by filling platform feeders with cracked corn and small seeds, such as millet, oats, and wheat. They are highly attracted to water in birdbaths and shallow pools.

Ron Austing

Identification Flashes and Distinguishing Features:

Look for the flash of chestnut-brown in their outer wings when they are in flight. Also look for the black tails of the males.

Size: 6–7 inches (15–18 centimeters)

Color: Both sexes have brown upperparts, with some black spots on their backs and wings, and pinkish-brown underparts. Dark bills have pinkish-red bases; legs and feet are pink to yellow.

Voice: Makes repeated soft, rising *coo-up* sounds.

Range: Permanent residents in southern Georgia and Alabama, and all of Florida; also reside in southern Texas, southern California and Arizona, and into extreme southwestern New Mexico.

Habitat: Prefers open, dry ground and nests on the ground or close to it. They make shallow nesting cups from small twigs, grasses, and rootlets.

Eggs: Lays 2–3 white unmarked eggs; 2–4 broods per breeding season. Both parents incubate the eggs; incubation takes 12–14 days. Fledglings leave the nest about 11–12 days after hatching.

Food: Favorite foods include millet, hemp, and cracked corn. Also feed on grass seeds, weed seeds, small berries, and insects.

Habits: May pair for life. They walk briskly on their short legs and nod their heads while walking. They are quite tame and may allow you to get within a few strides' length. They fly in a zigzag pattern on dry-sounding wings. Often seen walking on lightly traveled roadsides picking up grit and food early in the morning and late in the afternoon.

Greater Roadrunner

Geococcyx californianus

The state bird of New Mexico, the Greater Roadrunner can run up to fifteen miles per hour. They rarely fly, and instead they run on the ground in pursuit of prey. This member of the cuckoo family is a shy and solitary bird and often difficult to see.

Tom Vezo

Identification Flashes and Distinguishing Features:

Look for the large streaked body, shaggy crest, and long tail. When the tail is spread it shows white tips. When in flight, they reveal a white crescent in the primaries.

Size: 20–24 inches (50–60 centimeters)

Color: There are cinnamon, blackish, and white streaks overall, and metallic greens on tail, wings, and back. In flight, they show a white crescent on the wings.

Voice: Makes a series of dovelike *coooos*, and a low, rolling *preeet-preeet*.

Range: They are permanent residents of the southwestern states from Arkansas and the northwestern tip of Louisiana to California, and south into Mexico.

Habitat: Prefers open landscapes, semidesert, desert, scrub vegetation, and thickets. They build their nest 2–12 feet above ground in a shrub, tree, or cactus. The nest is built of twigs and lined with grass, mesquite pods, leaves, feathers, snakeskin, and horse or cattle droppings.

Eggs: Lays 2 white to pale yellow eggs; 1–2 broods per year. Though both parents incubate the eggs, the male does more; incubation takes 20 days. The fledglings leave the nest 17–18 days after hatching. The young are fed by both parents.

Food: Eats insects, snakes, lizards, rodents, small birds, some fruits, and seeds.

Habits: Lives in pairs and holds territory all year. When disturbed, they perform a distraction display to protect the nest.

Western Screech-Owl

Otus kennicottii

A nocturnal bird, this small tufted owl is more often heard than seen. Being sedentary, they frequently stay in the same home area throughout the year. They will nest in manmade nest boxes. When they catch more food than they can eat, they store it in roosting cavities.

Tom Vezo

Identification Flashes and Distinguishing Features:

Look for an overall gray appearance and the small tufted ears; Pacific Coast birds are browner.

Size: 8–10 inches (20–25 centimeters)

Color: They have gray to brown upperparts marked with wavy lines and streaks. There are large white spots on the scapulars. They have yellow eyes.

Voice: Sings repeated brief whistles that speed up in frequency like a bouncing ball coming to a stop; there is a short trill followed by a drawn out trill.

Range: Residents of the West from Northwestern British Columbia to Mexico, and from western Colorado to California.

Habitat: Uses many different habitats from desert to wooded canyons to suburban areas. Their nests are found 5–35 feet above ground in natural holes in trees and woodpecker holes; they do not line their nests. They will use manmade nest boxes.

Eggs: They lay 2–6 white eggs; 1 brood a year. The female incubates the eggs 21–30 days. Both parents feed the young. The fledglings leave the nest after about 28 days.

Food: Eats small mammals, birds, reptiles, large insects, and arachnids, but primarily feeds on insects. Small mammals are beheaded by the parents when fed to the young.

Habits: Roosts in cavities or thick vegetation during the day, becoming active at dusk. To attract a mate, the male will begin calling at night just after sunset. The calling stops when the pair bond is formed.

Eastern Screech-Owl

Otus asio

Perhaps the most common owl in the East, small Eastern Screech-Owls have distinctive ear tufts that can be raised or lowered to give them a broad, round-headed appearance. These owls are attracted to trees, including dead or partially dead ones, with suitable nesting and roosting cavities.

Ron Austing

You can attract Eastern Screech-Owls to your backyard by providing suitable nesting and roosting boxes (see Habitat, below). They will feed on available large insects and small animals.

Identification Flashes and Distinguishing Features:

Look for their distinctive ear tufts and small bodies.

Size: 8–10 inches (20–25 centimeters)

Color: Variable; an overall covering of reddish, brown, or gray; those with reddish plumage are most common in the South, while the gray occur in the northern and western part of the range. They have dark streaks below their yellow eyes.

Voice: Their call is not a screech (as their name implies) but rather a low, long trill on one pitch or a series of quavering whistles that descend in pitch.

Range: Permanent residents of the eastern two-thirds of the U.S.

Habitat: Prefers to roost in tree cavities or crevices in buildings during the day. They nest and roost in the same cavities, often choosing abandoned flicker and Pileated Woodpecker holes. They will nest in suitable boxes (9 x 9 x 16 inches with a 3-inch hole cut 3 inches below the top) mounted at least 10 feet above the ground in wooded areas. They do not build nests; they lay their eggs directly on the wood chips, leaves, and other debris on the cavity floor.

Eggs: Lays 2–8 round, white eggs at 2–3 day intervals; 1 brood per breeding season. Female incubates eggs, male may stay in the cavity with her during the day; incubation takes about 26 days. Fledglings leave the nest about 28 days after hatching.

Food: Wide variety of large insects, fish, and animals, including small rodents, small reptiles, amphibians, small birds, crayfish, and earthworms.

Habits: Nocturnal, they become active around dusk. Although not attracted to bird-feeder fare, they may hunt mice that eat at the feeders at night. You will more often hear than see Eastern Screech-Owls. By imitating their call, you may be able to get the birds to keep calling and come closer into view.

Ruby-throated Hummingbird
Archilochus colubris

Ruby-throated Hummingbirds are the smallest breeding birds in the East. They are so small and active that you may mistake them for large insects, such as bumblebees and hawk (hummingbird) moths.

You can easily attract these fearless winged "mites" to your backyard by providing water, offering nectar feeders (see Just for Hummingbirds, page 54), and including plants that bear red, orange, or yellow tube-shaped flowers in your naturescape.

Ron Austing

Identification Flashes and Distinguishing Features:

Look for the flash of iridescent green and red feathers as they dart around flowers and feeders. Listen for the humming sound of their wings, which beat up to 75 strokes per second.

Size: 3–3.75 inches (8–9 centimeters)

Color: Males are metallic green above and white below, with dusky green sides, dark forked tails, black chins, and brilliantly colored throats that flash ruby red when the sunlight catches them at the right angle and otherwise appear black. Females are metallic green above and white below, with a buffy wash on their sides. They have green tails tipped with blackish feathers; the three outermost tail feathers have white tips.

Voice: Makes excited, high-pitched squeaks and twitters.

Range: Summers throughout the East from Canada to the Gulf Coast, the Atlantic Coast to central Kansas, excluding the southern tip of Florida where a few may winter.

Habitat: Females construct nests using plant down, flower petals, fibers, and bud scales; they decorate the outside with lichens held on by spider's silk or webs from tent caterpillars' nests. Nests are attached with spider's silk to tops of gently slanted branches; completed nests resemble lichen-covered knots approximately 1.5 inches in diameter.

Eggs: Lays 2 pea-size white eggs; 1–3 broods each breeding season. The female incubates the eggs; incubation takes 11–16 days. Fledglings leave the nest 20–22 days after hatching.

Food: Flower nectar and tree sap, sugar-water nectar in feeders, and small insects.

Habits: Especially attracted to red flowers and feeders. They hover while feeding and are the only family of birds that can fly backward. They actively defend their feeding territories from other hummingbirds as well as much larger birds.

Black-chinned Hummingbird
Archilochus alexandri

The male Black-chinned Hummingbird performs a courtship ritual that includes flying in a pendulum pattern, creating a buzzing noise with his vibrating wings as he dives downward past a perched female. Similar to the Ruby-throated Hummingbird, the black throat and white collar distinguishes this bird from its cousin. They will frequent feeders offering sugar water.

Identification Flashes and Distinguishing Features:

Look for the black throat and distinctive white collar. In the light, the lower throat flashes a violet band.

Size: 3.5–3.75 inches (9–10 centimeters)

Color: The male has a greenish head and upperparts, black throat, partial white collar, and whitish underparts. The sides and flanks are dusky green. The notched greenish tail has blackish outer tail feathers. The female has greenish upperparts, a whitish throat possibly with faint green streaking, dusky sides and flanks, and whitish underparts. The female's green tail is rounded with white corners. The juveniles resemble adult females.

Voice: Makes a repetitive *teew* or *tchew*. When territorial, they combine the *teew* note with high pitched twitters and squeaks.

Range: Resides in the West from Washington to the southern tip of Texas. They are more common in the lowlands and mountain foothills. They occasionally visit the Southeast in the winter.

Habitat: Frequents open forest, scrub vegetation, grasslands with scattered trees, and gardens, often near water. The female builds the nest 4–8 feet and up to 30 feet above the ground. The nest is typically set in a fork of a small branch. It is decorated outside with small leaves and flowers.

Eggs: Females lay 1–3 white eggs; 2–3 broods per year. The female incubates 13–16 days. The fledglings leave the nest after 13–21 days. The female feeds the young.

Food: Eats nectar, pollen, and insects.

Habits: These birds are solitary. They twitch their tail when hovering. They bathe by hovering near wet foliage.

Anna's Hummingbird

Calypte anna

Anna's Hummingbird is growing both geographically and in population. They eat more spiders and insects than any other hummingbird. They are residents of the west coastal U.S. from Washington through California and into southern Arizona. In summer they may travel to Alaska, and are occasionally spotted in the East in the winter. They will visit feeders with sugar water.

Ron Austing

Identification Flashes and Distinguishing Features:

Look for the distinctive rose-red crown and throat of the male, the only North American hummingbird with this color head and throat.

Size: 3.5–4 inches (9–10 centimeters)

Color: The male's head, throat, and sides of the neck are rose-red. The underparts are grayish with a greenish tint to the sides, flanks, and belly. The female has a green crown, nape, and upperparts. There are red flecks on the throat and the underparts are gray.

Voice: Makes a sharp squeaky *chick*. When in chase, the call is a rapid high-pitched rattle. They will make coarse squeaky notes often from a perch.

Range: Resides in west coastal states from Washington south through California and into southern Arizona. In summer, they can travel as far north as Alaska; in winter, they are sometimes seen in the East.

Habitat: Frequents open forests, bushes and thorn scrub, and desert, often near water. The nest is built by the female 1.5–30 feet above ground. The nest is built on a small tree branch, on a cliff ledge, or a utility wire. They build with plant down bound with spider silk, and line with plant down and feathers.

Eggs: Lays 1–3 white eggs; 2–3 broods per year. The female incubates the eggs; incubation takes 14–19 days. The fledglings leave the nest 18–23 days after hatching. The young are fed by the female.

Food: Nectar, insects, spiders, and sap from sapsucker drill wells. They catch insects in mid-air, snatch spiders and insects from webs, and hover for nectar.

Habits: Bathes while hovering against wet foliage. The male will display for the female in a high arc with an explosive chirp at the base of a dive.

Broad-tailed Hummingbird

Selasphorus platycercus

The Broad-tailed Hummingbird is found in the Rocky Mountains and surrounding mountain ranges and spends summer in the mountains, where it defends patches of wildflowers from other hummingbirds. A distinguishing trilling sound is produced by the male when in flight. Air buzzes through slots in the tips of the male's outer primaries. When this hummingbird perches, the wings extend beyond the tail.

Ron Austing

You can attract the Broad-tailed Hummingbird to your feeder by offering sugar water.

Identification Flashes and Distinguishing Features:

The male displays the rose-red gorget and iridescent green upperparts; the female displays green upperparts, rufous sides, and bronze dots on the throat.

Size: 4–4.5 inches (10–12 centimeters)

Color: The male sports a rose-red gorget, iridescent green upperparts, green sides and underparts graduating from gray to white at the throat. The female has green upperparts, rufous sides, buff underparts, and bronze dots on the throat. The white tipped outer tail feathers have a rufous base.

Voice: They utter a repetitive *chip; chitter chitter chitter*; no song. There is a high thin slurred *szzzzzziiuu* when in display.

Range: Residents of the West in the Rocky Mountains and surrounding mountain ranges. They spend summer in the mountains and winter in Mexico, and casually to the Gulf Coast region.

Habitat: Found in open forest in mountains, often near streams. Females build the nest 4–15 feet above ground often near or over mountain streams. They build the nest on a horizontal tree branch or in a fork with the exterior constructed of lichens, bark shreds, and leaves.

Eggs: Lays 2 white elliptical-oval or subelliptical eggs; 1–2 broods per year. Female incubates eggs for 14–17 days. Fledglings leave the nest after 21–26 days. The female feeds the young.

Food: Nectar, insects, sap, and spiders; plucks insects and spiders from spider webs. They hover with tail closed to feed on nectar and catch insects in flight; also eats sap from holes drilled by sapsuckers.

Habits: They are solitary. In display flight, the male flies in a U-shaped pattern in front of the female, diving 30–50 feet. Both sexes often ascend together to 90–100 feet, 4–5 feet beneath one another, before diving again.

Rufous Hummingbird

Selasphorus rufus

Ron Austing

Rufous Hummingbirds, which breed in the Northwestern United States from Oregon, Idaho, and western Montana north to southeastern coastal Alaska, have been showing up increasingly more frequently in the Southeast as winter visitors. They often arrive in October and may stay until the following spring breeding season. If you live north of tropical Florida and see a hummingbird at your nectar feeder after the Ruby-throated Hummingbirds have departed (usually by mid-October), your visitor is probably a Rufous Hummingbird.

You can attract Rufous Hummingbirds by offering water and sugar-water nectar (see Just for Hummingbirds, page 54). Be sure to keep your feeders cleaned and filled for several weeks after your last Ruby-throated Hummingbird has departed to catch the hungry eye of the winter visitors.

Identification Flashes and Distinguishing Features:

Look for the distinguishing rufous underparts and backs of males. Listen for the low, quiet humming sound of the wings.

Size: 3.75 inches (10 centimeters)

Color: Males are the only North American hummingbirds with both rufous upperparts and underparts; they have green crowns, white breasts, and iridescent scarlet-burnished gold gorgets (throat and upper breast areas). Females have iridescent green upperparts, white underparts, and faded rust-colored sides.

Voice: Makes *chup, chup* whistles.

Range: Summer residents of the extreme Northwest, north to the southern Alaskan coast. Uncommon fall, winter, and early spring visitors in the Southeast from central Tennessee to the Gulf Coast, the southern Atlantic Coast from southern North Carolina south, west to the Texas coast.

Habitat: Females construct nests using plant down, flower petals, fibers, and bud scales; they decorate the outside with lichens held on by spider's silk or webs from tent caterpillars' nests. Nests are attached with spider's silk to tops of gently slanted branches, usually in a conifer; completed nests resemble a lichen-covered knot about 1.5 inches in diameter.

Eggs: Lays 2 white unmarked eggs; 1–2 broods per breeding season. Female incubates eggs 12–14 days. Fledglings leave the nest 20 days after hatching.

Food: Feeds on nectar and tree sap, sugar-water nectar in feeders, and small insects.

Habits: Especially attracted to red flowers and feeders. They hover while feeding and are the only family of birds that can fly backward. They actively defend their feeding territories from other hummingbirds as well as much larger birds.

Red-headed Woodpecker

Melanerpes erythrocephalus

These medium-size woodpeckers have suffered population declines where aggressive European Starlings have caused them to abandon their nesting cavities. Their reduced populations and patchy distribution makes them relatively uncommon, but their habit of feeding along roads makes them the woodpecker most frequently killed by vehicles.

Ron Austing

You can attract them by providing dead snags or nesting boxes (see Habitat, below) and offering sunflower seeds, raisins, or suet.

Identification Flashes and Distinguishing Features:

The contrast between their red heads, white underparts, and black backs makes it hard to miss these adults.

Size: 8.5–9.25 inches (22–24 centimeters)

Color: Both sexes have bright scarlet-red head, neck, and throat areas; juveniles have ashy-brown heads. They have snowy white underparts, rumps, wing patches, and secondary wing feathers; jet-black backs, tails, and wings.

Voice: Makes loud *queer, queer, queer* or *queark* sounds.

Range: Permanent residents of the Southeast from the Atlantic coast west to central Indiana and northeastern Texas (excluding the Blue Ridge Mountains), and south to the Gulf Coast, excluding tropical Florida. Summers north and west of this range. Winters in southern Louisiana west to central Texas.

Habitat: Prefers open stands of trees with little undergrowth. Both parents excavate the nesting cavity, in a dead tree, dead stub of a live tree, utility pole, or fence post. Occasionally nest in manmade boxes (5 x 7 x 16 inches with a 2-inch hole cut 3 inches below the top) mounted 10 feet above the ground in a wooded area and filled with sawdust, allowing the birds to "excavate" their cavity.

Eggs: Lays 4–7 oval white eggs; 1–2 broods per breeding season. Both parents incubate eggs 12–14 days. Fledglings leave the nest 27–31 days after hatching.

Food: Drills for wood-boring grubs and insects; forages on the ground for insects, and fallen seeds. Like flycatchers, they also perch and wait for flying insects. Feeds on fruit, berries, and large nuts in fall, and stores winter foods, especially acorns, beechnuts, and corn. Will come to feeders for cracked corn, sunflower seeds, raisins, suet, and suet mixes.

Habits: Frequents parklike stands of large trees in rural and urban areas, large scattered deciduous trees in open grasslands and agricultural areas, and dead trees in swampy or burned-over areas. They catch insects in midair, flycatcher style.

Acorn Woodpecker

Melanerpes formicivorus

This noisy woodpecker is a resident of the Southwest and is found along the Pacific Coast from Washington to Baja, California. Its distinctive face is painted with white, black, red, and yellow splashes setting off pale yellow-white eyes. It is drawn to areas ripe with oaks.

Ron Austing

Acorn Woodpeckers will come to nectar feeders that are large enough to provide a perch, and to feeders with sunflower seeds or suet.

Identification Flashes and Distinguishing Features:

Look for the distinctive face pattern with splashes of white, black, red and yellow. The wing and rump display white patches in flight.

Size: 9 inches (23 centimeters)

Color: The crown is red. There is white across the forehead, in front of the eye, and forming a bib across the throat. The breast and sides are black and there is a black patch at the base of the bill. The flanks and sides are white with black streaks. There are white undertail coverts. The female's crown is black in front and red in back.

Voice: They make a repeated *waka, waka, waka.*

Range: Resides along the Pacific Coast from Washington to Baja, California, and from mountains of southern Arizona, New Mexico, and west Texas south through Central America.

Habitat: Frequents forests in mountain valleys. Both sexes and members of the social group build the nest from 5–60 feet above ground. The nest is built of wood chips in the base of a cavity.

Eggs: Females lay 3–7 white eggs; 1–2 broods per year. Both sexes and helpers incubate the eggs; incubation takes 11–14 days. The fledglings leave the nest after 30–32 days. Both sexes and helpers feed the young.

Food: Eats insects caught in flight and tree sap from drill wells it excavates. Members of the social group store acorns in holes drilled in a tree trunk for a winter food supply. The group defends the stored food from other animals and birds.

Habits: Forms and works in small groups, called clans, of up to 16 members. There are several females per nest.

Red-bellied Woodpecker

Melanerpes carolinus

They are perhaps the most common medium-size woodpeckers found in the East, and their noisy tappings and frequent calls announce their presence. They are often mistakenly called "red-headed woodpeckers" (see page 110) because their heads have a lot of red and their namesake red belly patches are often hidden from view.

You can attract Red-bellied Woodpeckers to your backyard by filling feeders with black oil sunflower seeds, corn, suet, or peanut butter-suet mixes.

Fred J. Alsop III

Identification Flashes and Distinguishing Features:

Look for the distinguishing "zebra-striped" bars on their backs and their bold white rumps and wing spots when they're in flight.

Size: 9–10.5 inches (23–27 centimeters)

Color: Males have red foreheads, crowns, and napes. Females have only red napes; the rest of their head areas are pale gray. Both sexes have pale gray on the sides of their faces; black-and-white barred wings, upperparts, and central tail feathers; and a reddish wash on their lower bellies in front of and between their legs. Their white rumps and wing patches are conspicuous in flight.

Voice: Makes rolling *churrrrr, churrrrr* and abrupt *chuck, chuck, chuck* sounds.

Range: Permanent residents of the eastern half of the U.S.

Habitat: Frequents lawns and gardens wherever there are shrubs and trees. Common in woodlands, swamps, pinelands, areas of mixed pines, and hardwoods with large trees. Also common in urban areas with large trees and wooded farmlands. Both parents excavate the nesting cavity in a dead stub or soft-wooded deciduous tree. They sometimes nest in utility poles, fence posts, or abandoned cavities of other woodpeckers.

Eggs: Lays 3–8 unspotted white eggs; 1 brood in North, 2–3 in the South. Both parents incubate the eggs—the female during the day and the male during the night—for 12–14 days. Fledglings leave the nest 22–27 days after hatching.

Food: Drills for wood-boring insects and larvae and forages on the ground for beetles, ants, and grasshoppers. Also feeds on nuts, berries, and fruit. Will come to feeders for sunflower seeds, corn, suet, and peanut butter-suet mixes.

Habits: They make noisy, loud tappings and frequent calls that seldom go unnoticed.

Yellow-bellied Sapsucker
Sphyrapicus varius

Before you see these medium-size woodpeckers, you may notice neat horizontal rows of 1/4-inch feeding wells in trees in your backyard—sure signs that a sapsucker has been at work. While people in the timber business may not like the small regular holes left by sapsuckers, they probably do appreciate the fact that sapsuckers feed on many insects that are injurious to trees. Unlike other woodpeckers, sapsuckers have brushlike tongues that are adapted to licking tree sap. Other birds feed at the sap wells that are drilled and maintained by sapsuckers.

Ron Austing

You can attract Yellow-bellied Sapsuckers to your backyard by including sugar maple, apple, and pear trees in your naturescape and by filling feeders with suet or suet mixes.

Identification Flashes and Distinguishing Features:

Look for their straw-yellow underparts; white rumps and shoulder patches; and black breast bibs, wings, and tails.

Size: 8–9 inches (20–23 centimeters)

Color: Males have red chins and throats; females have white chins and throats. Both sexes have black breast bibs, wings, and tails; and large, white shoulder patches readily seen on their folded wings. Their backs are mottled white, brown, and black in a lichenlike pattern; their bellies have a yellowish wash.

Voice: Most often they make catlike, nasal mewing sounds.

Range: Summer breeding birds in the Southern Blue Ridge area of eastern Tennessee, northward through central Pennsylvania to the north Atlantic Coast, and across most of Canada. Winters throughout the mid-Atlantic and Southeast from Rhode Island south through Florida and west across southern Missouri through most of Texas south to Mexico.

Habitat: Frequents both deciduous and coniferous trees. Both parents excavate a gourd-shaped cavity in a soft northern hardwood tree, such as yellow birch.

Eggs: Females lay 4–7 white eggs; 1 brood per breeding season. Both parents incubate the eggs—the female during the day, the male during the night; incubation takes 12–13 days. Fledglings leave the nest 25–29 days after hatching.

Food: Licks tree sap, a major part of its diet, with its brushlike tongue. Feeds on insects attracted to their sap wells. Also feeds on fruit and berries. Will come to feeders for suet, suet mixes, or sugar-water nectar.

Habits: Drills feeding-wells in more than 275 species of trees and returns frequently to lick the sap. Also catches insects on the wing, flycatcher style.

Red-naped Sapsucker

Sphyrapicus nuchalis

The Red-naped Sapsucker is taught to eat sap by its parents just after fledging. Parents store sap in their crops to feed their young. These woodpeckers provide holes that house other species in their habitat, often being the only woodpecker in the region.

This sapsucker, residing west of the Rocky Mountains, resembles its eastern counterpart, the Yellow-bellied Sapsucker. They will visit feeders offering a mixture of sugar and suet.

Tom Vezo

Identification Flashes and Distinguishing Features:

Look for the red forehead, forecrown, and nape, the two white stripes on a black face, and white shoulder patches. Notice also the white patch on the rump when in flight.

Size: 8–9 inches (20–23 centimeters)

Color: They have a red forehead, forecrown, and nape, two white stripes on a black face, and black and white barring on the back and wings. There are two rows of spotting on the back. The white underparts have a yellow wash on the breast and belly. A white patch on the rump is displayed when in flight, and there are white patches on the shoulders.

Voice: Often are silent, but occasionally, make a low growling *meeah*, similar to the Yellow-bellied Sapsucker. Males make a soft, rapid drumming sound.

Range: In the summer, they reside in the West from southern British Columbia to northern Arizona, and central Colorado west through Nevada. They winter south of this range and into Mexico.

Habitat: Prefers forests and forests' edge, primarily deciduous. Both sexes build the nest 10–35 feet above ground. They rarely use materials, only a few bark chips as they build in a dead or live tree. The nest is gourd-shaped, and is 5 x 14 inches large.

Eggs: They lay 5–6 white eggs; 1 brood per year. Both parents incubate the eggs. The male incubates at night; incubation takes 12–13 days. The fledglings leave the nest 25–29 days after hatching. The young are fed by both sexes.

Food: They eat sap, pine pitch, cambium, and some insects and berries.

Habits: Lives as solitary individuals or in pairs. Couples perform drumming duets during courtship, as well as ritual tapping at the nest hole.

Ladder-backed Woodpecker

Picoides scalaris

The Ladder-backed Woodpecker inhabits the dry scrublands and woodlands of the Southwest. It is the smallest woodpecker in this region, and is suited to the native woody plants in this range—the smaller trees, shrubs, and cacti.

They are often encountered in towns and rural areas. Birdbaths and pools will attract this woodpecker, as well as feeders filled with suet, peanut butter, corn, and sunflower seeds.

Tom Vezo

Identification Flashes and Distinguishing Features:

Look for the black-and-white barred back, the white spotting and barring on the wings and shoulders, and the buffy gray underparts.

Size: 7.25 inches (19 centimeters)

Color: The male has black and white barred upperparts, shoulders, and wings. He sports a red crown and a buffy gray face outlined with a black triangle. The underparts are buffy gray with black spots. The female has a black forehead, crown, and nape; the face is whitish gray outlined with a black triangle.

Voice: The call is a clear high-pitched *pik,* and a descending whinny.

Range: They are residents of the Southwest, from North Texas south to Mexico, and from eastern Texas to southeastern California.

Habitat: Frequents deserts, scrublands, and riparian woodlands. They nest in cavities lined with chips in the upper part of a large cactus, in dead trees or branches, or in the top of woody shrubs. Nests are from 3–30 feet above ground. It is not known which sex builds the nest.

Eggs: They lay 2–7 white eggs, oval to elliptical; 1 brood per year. Both sexes incubate; incubation takes 13 days. Both sexes feed the young. Fledglings leave the nest 20–25 days after hatching.

Food: Eat insects and the fruit of cactus. From feeders they will eat suet, peanut butter, corn, and sunflower seeds.

Habits: Lives solitary or in pairs. The males forage differently from the female, lower on the ground, searching for insects, especially ants. Females forage higher in vegetation, picking insects from the bark.

Downy Woodpecker

Picoides pubescens

Ron Austing

Downy Woodpeckers, the smallest and most common woodpeckers in North America, look like small Hairy Woodpeckers with sparrow-size bills. Their fondness for small broken woodlots makes them at home in cities as well as in suburbs and rural settings.

You can attract Downy Woodpeckers by providing nesting boxes (see Habitat, below) and by offering black oil sunflower seeds, suet, peanut butter, nuts, and table scraps, especially cornbread and doughnuts.

Identification Flashes and Distinguishing Features:

Look for their small size, stubby bills, and white backs, which help distinguish them from other woodpeckers.

Size: 6.75–7 inches (17–18 centimeters)

Color: Adults have black-and-white heads, but males have a red patch on the back of their heads. Both have black wings with many white spots, black tails with white outer tail feathers marked by blackish dots, and white underparts and backs.

Voice: Makes sharp *plik* calls and a downward whinnying that sounds like a small horse.

Range: Permanent residents across most of the U. S. and Canada, excluding the Southwest from western Texas across to southern California and Nevada.

Habitat: Frequents small saplings (especially males) and smaller branches of trees that won't support the weight of larger woodpeckers. Both parents dig a gourd-shaped nesting cavity with a 1¼–inch entrance hole. Usually nest in dead stubs, but sometimes in living trees or fence posts. Occasionally use manmade boxes (5 x 5 x 10 inches with 1¼–inch hole cut 2 inches below the top) mounted at least 8 feet above the ground in a wooded area and filled with sawdust, which allows the birds to "excavate" their nesting cavity.

Eggs: Female lays 3–7 oval white eggs; 1–2 broods per breeding season. Both parents incubate the eggs—the female during the day, the male during the night—for about 12 days. Fledglings leave the nest 20–25 days after hatching.

Food: Feeds on wood-boring, fruit-boring, and nut/seed-boring insects as well as grasshoppers, spiders, and snails. Also feeds on fruit and small berries, including poison ivy berries. Will come to feeders for sunflower seeds, suet, cornbread, cracked walnuts, peanuts, and doughnuts.

Habits: Frequently joins mixed-species foraging flocks in fall and winter and are often seen in the company of chickadees, titmice, nuthatches, and kinglets.

Hairy Woodpecker
Picoides villosus

Hairy Woodpeckers look like larger versions of Downy Woodpeckers (see page 116). Since they are only two inches larger, however, the best way to distinguish them is by the length of their bills: Downy Woodpeckers have short, stubby bills, while Hairy Woodpeckers have bills that are as long as the depth of their heads. Also, Downy Woodpeckers have dark spots in their white outer tail feathers—Hairy Woodpeckers do not.

Ron Austing

Although Hairy Woodpeckers do not frequent feeders, you can still attract them by offering suet and peanut-butter suet mixes. Also leave or "plant" some dead snags in your backyard to provide roosting sites.

Identification Flashes and Distinguishing Features:

Look for their larger bills to help distinguish them from the similar but smaller Downy Woodpeckers.

Size: 8.5–10.5 inches (22–27 centimeters)

Color: Both sexes have black upperparts, tails, and wings with white bars and dots; they have white underparts, backs, and outer tail feathers. Both males and females have white faces with black ear patches and crowns; males have a red patch on the back of their heads.

Voice: Makes sharp, metallic *peek* sounds that are higher in pitch than similar Downy Woodpecker sounds. They also make descending, loud kingfisher-like rattles and drumming, rolling tattoo sounds.

Range: Permanent residents throughout much of the U. S. excluding a small pocket in the south central U.S. from the border of Kansas and Colorado south through western to central Texas, where they do spend winter.

Habitat: Frequents deciduous and pine forests, parks, orchards, and woodlots. Both parents excavate a nesting cavity with a 1½-inch opening in a dead limb on a dead or dying tree.

Eggs: Lays 3–6 pure white eggs; 1 brood per breeding season. Both parents incubate the eggs—the female during the day, the male during the night; incubation takes 11–15 days; fledglings leave nest 28–30 days after hatching.

Food: More than 75 percent of diet is insects, especially pine borers and spruce bark beetles; also eats ants, millipedes, spiders, and stag beetles. Occasionally feeds on berries, nuts, and sap at sapsucker feeding-wells. Will come to feeders for suet and suet mixes, sunflower seeds, peanut butter, nut meats, cheese, and apples.

Habits: Appears to stay paired throughout the year and remain in the same area. These noisy woodpeckers regularly call to their mates while foraging.

Northern Flicker

Colaptes auratus

There are two different regional groups of Northern Flickers; one is the Yellow-shafted Flicker in the East and Northwest, and the Red-shafted Flicker in the West. Like most woodpeckers, they seek drumming perches in the spring that provide good sounding boards.

Red-shafted

Yellow-shafted

You can attract Northern Flickers by providing nesting boxes (see Habitat, below) and by filling feeders with peanut butter, suet, and suet mixes.

Identification Flashes and Distinguishing Features:

Look for a brown woodpecker with yellow underwings, undertail, and black mustache (East and Northwest); and in the West, bright orange-red underwings, undertail, and red mustache. Females lack mustaches.

Size: 12.75–14 inches (32-35 centimeters)

Color: Brown upperparts with dark brown barring, black crescent bib, black spotting on underparts, and a white rump patch. Yellow-shafted form has tan face, gray crown and forehead, and red crescent on nape. Red-shafted form has a reversed head pattern with gray face, brown forehead, crown, and nape with no red crescent. White rump patches, underwings, and undertail surfaces are conspicuous in flight.

Voice: Makes loud *clearrer* sounds as well as series of identical *wick-wick-wick-wick-wick* or *wick-er, wick-er, wick-er, wick-er* sounds that, unlike the Pileated Woodpecker's sounds, don't change in pitch, loudness, or cadence.

Range: Permanent residents throughout most of the U.S. and in summer over most of Canada and Alaska.

Habitat: Frequents open areas, including lawns, farm clearings, roadsides, and open woodlots. Both parents excavate a nesting cavity in a living tree, dead snag, utility pole, or fence post. Sometimes use a nesting cavity from previous year and will accept boxes built from 1½-inch cedar boards (4½ x 7½ x 24 inches with a 2¼-inch hole cut 3 inches below the top) mounted at least 4 feet above the ground and filled with sawdust, which lets the birds "excavate" a cavity.

Eggs: Lays 3–12 white eggs; 1–2 broods. Both parents incubate the eggs—female during day, male at night—for 11–16 days. Fledglings leave nest 25–28 days after hatching.

Food: About half of diet is ants; also feeds on beetles, grubs, and wasps, as well as fruit and small berries. Will come to feeders for peanut butter, suet, and suet mixes.

Habits: Usually seen either in undulating flight that is typical of most woodpeckers or on the ground foraging for ants. Gives conspicuous vocal and bowing displays in spring as part of their courtship behavior.

Pileated Woodpecker

Dryocopus pileatus

These crow-size birds are the largest woodpeckers commonly seen in North America; only the Ivory-billed Woodpecker is larger, and is probably extinct. This woodpecker's loud, jungle-birdlike calls, large size, and loud raps it makes when drumming on trees will command your attention.

You can attract Pileated Woodpeckers to your backyard by filling feeders with sunflower seeds, cracked corn, suet, or suet mixes.

Ron Austing

Identification Flashes and Distinguishing Features:

Look for their large size and crest, which easily distinguish them from other woodpeckers.

Size: 16–19.5 inches (42–49 centimeters)

Color: Both sexes have mostly black bodies, white chins and throats; white stripes extend from their faces along their necks and sides into the pit of their wings. Males have red mustaches and crowns, including their crests. Females have black mustaches and foreheads and red-crested crowns.

Voice: Makes loud, flickerlike *yucka-yucka-yucka* and *cuk-cuk-cuk-cuk* and *wick-wick-wick-wick* sounds that, unlike the sound of flickers, change in pitch, loudness, and cadence.

Range: Permanent residents in the eastern half of the U.S.; also in the West in northern Idaho and eastern Montana west along the border with Canada to the Pacific Coast, and south along the coast to central California.

Habitat: Prefers mature woodlots and riverbottom hardwoods, mature pine stands, cypress swamps, and woodland borders. Most often chooses dead trees or dead stubs of living trees. Each year they excavate a new nest cavity with a 3½-inch oval to triangular entrance hole.

Eggs: Lays 3–8 oval to elliptical white eggs; 1 brood per season. Both parents incubate the eggs for 15–18 days. Fledglings leave nest 26–28 days after hatching.

Food: Favorite food is Carpenter Ants, which they dig out of the deep heartwood of trees. Also eats other wood-boring beetle larvae and insects. Feeds on fruit, berries, and seeds (wild grapes, poison ivy, sour gum, cherries, sumac, and beechnuts). Sometimes come to feeders for sunflower seeds, cracked corn, suet, and suet mixes.

Habits: These birds are more often heard—by their loud rappings on trees—than seen. They forage on the ground as well as on fallen timber, logs, and stumps in deep woodlots. Pairs often frequent the same woodlots for years, nesting and roosting near nests used in previous years.

Black Phoebe

Sayornis nigricans

The Black Phoebe resides in the Southwest and is found near bodies of water—streams, rivers, lakes, ponds, etc. Artificial ponds in this region have contributed to its increasing population. Phoebes watch for prey from fences and low shaded perches, while pumping their tails.

Ron Austing

You can attract this bird by providing a water element. They also use man-made structures with sheltering overhangs and ledges for nesting.

Identification Flashes and Distinguishing Features:

Look for the black body, white belly, and white undertail coverts.

Size: 6–7 inches (15–18 centimeters)

Color: The body and tail are black, and the belly and white undertail coverts are white. Juveniles are browner with a cinnamon rump and 2 indistinct cinnamon wing bars.

Voice: Makes a sharp *seek!* The typical song, repeated primarily at dawn, begins with an ascending scale followed by 2 descending notes, *pee-wee, pee-wee*. They sometimes make a loud *tseee*.

Range: Resides in the West to Southwest from northern California down to southern Texas and into Mexico.

Habitat: Found near water, rocky places or cliffs, open areas with scattered trees, and near human habitation and buildings. The female builds the nest attached to a vertical surface and made of mud pellets and moss. The nest is lined with grass, weeds, roots, bark, and hair.

Eggs: Females lay 3–6 white eggs with occasional reddish brown spots; 2–3 broods per year. The female incubates the eggs; incubation lasts 15–17 days. The fledglings leave the nest 14–21 days after hatching. Both parents feed the young.

Food: Eats insects; sometimes small fish caught at the water's surface.

Habits: Hunts from low, shaded perches. They live as solitary individuals or in pairs.

Eastern Phoebe

Sayornis phoebe

These tail-wagging birds are the hardiest of the eastern flycatchers, and they winter much farther north than any of their other family members. Eastern Phoebes have adapted well to nesting on manmade structures and are frequently seen near homes and farmsteads where flying insects and nesting ledges are plentiful.

Ron Austing

You can attract Eastern Phoebes by providing nesting ledges (see Habitat, below) and water. They especially like moving or dripping water.

Identification Flashes and Distinguishing Features:

Eastern Phoebes wag their tails from side to side and up and down, a habit that distinguishes them from other flycatchers. Also, they are the only flycatchers that winter in the Southeast.

Size: 7 inches (18 centimeters)

Color: Both males and females have brownish-gray upperparts, with the darkest feathers on their heads, wings, and tails; whitish underparts with an olive to yellowish wash on their breasts and sides; and dark mandibles.

Voice: Sings distinctive raspy *FEE-bee* songs. In spring and early summer they frequently give sharp *chip* calls.

Range: Permanent residents in a narrow swath from the mid-Atlantic Coast, south and west to central Texas. Summer breeding season is spent north of this range into Canada, west to the Northwest Territory. They winter south of their permanent range from the Atlantic Coast west to southern Texas.

Habitat: Historically nested on ledges in rock walls; now they nest on manmade structures, including bridges and culverts, window shutters, eaves, rafters, and doorsills. Attract them by mounting (with contact cement) 5-inch sections of 2 x 4 lumber to the sides of buildings 10–12 inches below the roof overhang. Although the female does most of the work, both parents gather grasses, fibers, weeds, and mud and form a 4½-inch nesting cup. They cover the nesting cup with mosses and line it with finer grasses, hair, and feathers.

Eggs: Lays 2–8 white eggs (a few eggs in the clutch may be brownish near larger end); 2–3 broods per breeding season. The female incubates the eggs; incubation takes 14–16 days. Fledglings leave nest 15–16 days after hatching.

Food: Feeds mainly on flying insects (beetles, flies, mosquitoes, ants, wasps, grasshoppers, crickets, dragonflies, and moths).

Habits: They have a telltale habit of wagging their tails. Cowbirds sometimes lay their eggs in Eastern Phoebe nests, and the phoebes will often raise the young cowbirds at the expense of their own young (see Brown-headed Cowbird, page 189).

Say's Phoebe

Sayornis saya

Say's Phoebe lives year-round in the Southwest, migrating in summer as far north as Alaska. Although it superficially resembles the American Robin, its upright posture and aerial expertise distinguish it as a flycatcher. An active bird, it is often seen chasing insects or wagging its tail.

This flycatcher is attracted to water in birdbaths, pools, ditches, etc., and to manmade structures that provide niches for nesting and roosting.

Brian E. Small

Identification Flashes and Distinguishing Features:

It resembles the American Robin with its brownish gray upperparts and tawny belly and undertail coverts.

Size: 7.5 inches (19 centimeters)

Color: Brownish gray upperparts, pale grayish brown throat and breast, and a tawny belly and undertail coverts.

Voice: Sings at dawn, with an often repetitive, plaintive, downslurred whistled *phee-eur* or *chu-weer*. When in flight they utter a sudden *pit-tse-ar*.

Range: Residents from southwest Texas to southern California, migrating as far north as Alaska in the summer.

Habitat: At home in dry areas—savannas, farmlands, and open brushlands. The female builds the nest attached to vertical surfaces. The nest is built with mud pellets, moss, and grass; it is lined with grass, weeds, moss, spider webs, and wool.

Eggs: Females lay 3–7 white eggs with occasional brown or reddish spots; 1–2 broods a year, sometimes up to 3 in the lower Southwest. The female incubates the eggs; incubation takes 12–14 days. The fledglings leave the nest 14–16 days after hatching. The young are fed by both sexes.

Food: Catches insects in midair with a loud snap of the bill. They take off from fairly low perches on branches, large rocks, fences, etc. Rarely eats berries.

Habits: Phoebes travel alone or in pairs. Not sedentary, this bird hovers in the air looking for insects, and wags its tail.

Great Crested Flycatcher
Myiarchus crinitus

These large, colorful birds will get your attention with their loud calls. They dash from conspicuous treetop perches and take insects on the wing. They are the only eastern fly-catchers that nest in cavities; they decorate their nests with a snake skin—or cellophane, if a castoff reptile skin isn't available.

You can attract them to your backyard by leaving or planting dead snags or providing nesting boxes (see Habitat, below). They will feed on available insects and berries.

Ron Austing

Identification Flashes and Distinguishing Features:

Look for their bright rufous-red tails, gray throats and upper breasts, and yellow underparts. Also look for their short, bushy crests. Listen for their loud calls.

Size: 8½ inches (21 centimeters)

Color: Both males and females have olive-brown upperparts, yellow underparts, gray throats and breasts, cinnamon-brown wings, bright rufous-red tails, and short, bushy crests.

Voice: Makes loud *wheeeep!* or *creeeep!* whistles and sometimes combine notes into *wheep, wheep, wheep, preeeep!* calls.

Range: Spends summer breeding season primarily in the East from southern Canada to the Gulf Coast, and west to extreme eastern Colorado.

Habitat: Frequents woodlots, wooded lake and stream borders, farmlands, and urban areas with large shade trees. Both parents build a nesting cup from twigs, leaves, mosses, hair, bark fibers, string, plant fibers, feathers, onion skins, snake skins, or cellophane. Occasionally nest in suitable boxes (6 x 8 x 10 inches with a 2-inch hole cut 7 inches above the bottom) mounted 8–20 feet above the ground in wooded areas. They fill their nesting cavities with leaves and debris.

Eggs: Females lay 4–8 pinkish or yellowish-white eggs blotched, streaked, and dotted with brown and purple; 1 brood per breeding season. The female incubates the eggs; incubation takes 13–15 days. Fledgings leave the nest 12–21 days after hatching.

Food: Feeds primarily on large insects taken in flight or gleaned from the ground or tree crevices (dragonflies, moths, bees, wasps, beetles, grasshoppers, crickets, katydids, spiders, and caterpillars). They also eat berries, cherries, and grapes.

Habits: They usually perch high in trees and make swift, hawking feeding sallies, often returning to the same conspicuous perch. Sometimes they feed in the lower canopy or close to the ground. The territorial males engage in aerial combat, often tangling claws and pulling out their opponents' feathers.

Western Kingbird

Tyrannus verticalis

The Western Kingbird has adapted and taken advantage of human development of its habitat, using telephone poles and other structures to nest, and fences and utility wires as hunting perches. It is aggressive and chases larger birds, including hawks and crows, from places where it nests. This flycatcher is very common and conspicuous.

Ron Austing

Identification Flashes and Distinguishing Features:

Look for the black tail with white edging on the sides and the bright lemon-yellow underparts.

Size: 8.75 inches (22 centimeters)

Color: The head, neck, and breast are pale ashy gray. There is a dark thin gray eye patch. The back is olive-green tinted, and the underparts are bright lemon-yellow. The tail is black and squared, with white edges. A red-orange patch on the crown is usually concealed.

Voice: They call with a quiet clipped *bek*, and make an abrasive chatter of *ker-er-ip, ker-er-ip, pree pree pr-prrr*.

Range: Establishes breeding populations from Minnesota south to Texas and west to the Pacific Coast.

Habitat: Frequents open landscapes with little rainfall. Both parents build the nest 8–40 feet above the ground near the trunk on a tree limb or fork, or on the brace arm of a utility pole, or other manmade structure. The nest is constructed of grass, weeds, and twigs; the inside is softened with hair, plant down, or cotton.

Eggs: Females lay 3–7 whitish eggs marked with brown, lavender, and black; 1–2 broods per year. The female incubates the eggs for 18–19 days. The fledglings leave the nest after 16–17 days. The young are fed by both parents.

Food: Insects, fruit, and berries; they hover over foliage or the ground and dip to pick up food.

Habits: Hunts from perches on low, middle and high levels. They fly out to catch their prey and then return to perch. There is a hectic courtship flight by the male—darting up, fluttering, vibrating feathers, and singing a trilling song.

Red-eyed Vireo
Vireo olivaceus

Ron Austing

Once considered the most abundant eastern woodland bird in the summer, the Red-eyed Vireo, like so many migratory songbirds, is declining in numbers. These birds are not noted for the beauty of their song but rather for the persistence of the singers, who serenade from dawn through the hottest part of summer days and into dusk. These long sermons have earned them the name "preacher birds."

You can attract Red-eyed Vireos to your backyard by including large deciduous trees in your naturescape and providing water.

Identification Flashes and Distinguishing Features:

The dark line "through" their eyes, the white line above their eyes, and the lack of wing bars help distinguish from other birds. Within close range, look for their red eyes.

Size: 6 inches (15 centimeters)

Color: Olive-green upperparts and white underparts with yellow tints on their undertail coverts; there are no bars on their wings. They have white stripes over their eyes and black stripes "through" their eyes and along their gray crowns.

Voice: Makes nasal *jmew* notes and sings long series of phrases and pauses, mostly in middle tones, in the pattern of *look up, see me? over here, this way, higher still,* etc.

Range: Summer breeding season is spent from Canada south to the Gulf Coast, except peninsular and Tropical Florida, and from the Atlantic Coast west to central Kansas; gradually west and north through Nebraska, eastern Wyoming, and Washington, north to the Northwest Territories.

Habitat: Frequents open deciduous woodlands with thick sapling undergrowth, wooded clearings, and wooded residential areas. Females build hanging nesting cups in the forks of slender horizontal tree branches. They bind together grasses, vine tendrils, bark strips, rootlets, and paper from wasp's nests with spider and tent caterpillar silks. Finished nesting cups are decorated with lichens.

Eggs: Lays 3–5 white eggs sparsely marked on the large end with black and brown dots and spots; 1–2 broods per year. The female incubates the eggs; incubation takes 11–14 days. Fledglings leave the nest 10–12 days after hatching.

Food: Feeds mostly on insects gleaned from trees (bees, wasps, ants, caterpillars, moths, webworms, beetles, and spiders). Also take some fruit and berries (elderberry, spicebush, magnolia, dogwood, and sassafras).

Habits: Except for nesting, Red-eyed Vireos stay in the treetops, but once you learn their song, you will be able to spot them. During summer they will be almost anywhere there are trees.

Steller's Jay
Cyanocitta stelleri

Stellar's Jay, discovered by and named after explorer Georg Wilhelm Steller on the Alaska coast in 1741, is the only crested jay in the West. Steller's Jay has a black head and crest with the amount of black varying among populations. The blue and white striping on the head or throat also varies.

Family groups will frequent feeders in the winter.

Ron Austing

Identification Flashes and Distinguishing Features:

Look for the black crest and head, the smoky blue belly and underparts, and the cobalt or purple upperparts.

Size: 11.5 inches (29 centimeters)

Color: Both sexes have a black crest and head and a sooty black neck, breast, and back. The underparts and belly are smoky blue. The upperparts are cobalt or purple. There is a narrow black-barred "ripple" on the wings and tail.

Voice: The calls are various and include *shaack, shaack, shaack; shooka, shooka* notes; and a mellow *klook, klook, klook*. They are known to mimic other birds such as loons and hawks.

Range: They are residents of the West from the south coast of Alaska to the southern New Mexico/Arizona border, and from mid-Colorado west to California.

Habitat: Prefers woodlands, pine-oak and coniferous. Both sexes build the nest with various pine needles, twigs, dry leaves, roots, and grass, securing the nest with mud. They build 8–100 feet above ground on limbs near the trunk, in the crotch of a conifer, and occasionally in a deciduous tree.

Eggs: They lay 2–6 eggs, but usually 4, that are pale greenish blue or bluish green with brown markings; 1 brood per year. The female incubates; incubation lasts 16–18 days. Fledglings leave the nest 17–21 days after hatching. Both parents feed the young.

Food: Omnivorous, they eat frogs; snakes; eggs and young of other birds; insects; and carrion. In winter, however, they eat pine nuts, acorns, and fruit. They are known to store seeds and acorns for winter.

Habits: Frequently travel in flocks of more than a dozen, including family groups after breeding season. They are monogamous. Courtship feeding is performed by the male.

Blue Jay

Cyanocitta cristata

Ron Austing

Although almost everyone recognizes these highly intelligent, colorful birds, not everyone welcomes them. They are noisy, generally have their way at feeders, and occasionally take young birds from other birds' nests—all of which give them a generally undeserved bad reputation. On the plus side, Blue Jays are often the first to sound the alarm note that sends other birds diving for cover.

You can attract them by providing water and offering sunflower seeds, corn, nuts, suet, or suet mixes in platform, hopper, and hanging feeders.

Identification Flashes and Distinguishing Features:

They are the only crested blue-and-white birds in their range.

Size: 11 inches (28 centimeters)

Color: Bright-blue upperparts, crests, and napes; white underparts and faces, with a black necklace around their necks; black bars and white patches on wings; black bars on their tails; and white tips on all but their center tail feathers.

Voice: Makes loud *jay, jay, jay, thief, thief, thief,* and double-noted *tull-ull* calls that sound like a squeaking pump handle. They also make loud hawklike calls and softer vocalizations.

Range: Permanent residents through eastern two-thirds of the U.S., west to eastern Colorado, Wyoming, and Montana. Spends summer north of this range into Canada; some winter as far west as southern Idaho.

Habitat: Historically prefered large woodlands but have adapted well to urbanization and forest fragmentation. Nests in deciduous or conifer trees on a large branch or where a limb joins the trunk. Both parents build bulky nest from grasses, twigs, string, mosses, rags, and other natural and manmade materials. Line nesting cups with softer, finer materials.

Eggs: Lays 3–7 olive, buff, or greenish-bluish gray eggs that have gray or brown dots and spots; 1–3 broods per breeding season. The female incubates the eggs; incubation takes 16–18 days. Fledglings leave the nest 17–21 days after hatching.

Food: Eats an omnivorous diet that is 75 percent vegetable (seeds, berries, and nuts from a variety of plants); prefers acorns, beechnuts, corn, and palmetto seeds. Also eats insects, worms, snails, frogs, salamanders, small fish, small rodents, small bats, and occasionally eggs and young of smaller birds. Will come to feeders for suet, peanut butter, peanuts, or sunflower seeds.

Habits: Clever learners, they can be easily tamed to take peanuts from your hand. Frequents birdbaths for drinking and bathing. Stores beech and oak seeds for winter; seeds not retrieved by the birds play an important role in seed distribution and "replanting" of woodlands.

Western Scrub-Jay

Aphelocoma californica

The Western Scrub-Jay was once considered a race of the species Scrub Jay. Because it saves acorns in the ground for winter, it has helped to widely disperse oak forests. This jay is tame and will sometimes take food from a human's hand.

You can attract the Western Scrub-Jay to your backyard with nuts, sunflower seeds, and fruit.

Ron Austing

Identification Flashes and Distinguishing Features:

Look for the dark blue upperparts and the white throat outlined with a blue necklace. There is a white eyebrow over a dark eye patch.

Size: 11 inches (28 centimeters)

Color: Dark blue upperparts and a smoky brown back. The tail is long and blue. The underparts are white, buff, and gray. The throat is white outlined with a blue necklace and there is a blue band on the chest. There is a white eyebrow over a dark eye patch.

Voice: Makes a noisy, hoarse, repetitive *shreep*, or *quay-quay-quay*.

Range: These jays are residents of the West and Southwest from Washington down the coast of California, across to New Mexico and into Texas.

Habitat: Prefers pine-oak-juniper woodlands and areas of scrub vegetation. Both sexes build the nest 5–30 feet above the ground in a tree or a shrub. The nest is built of twigs, grass, and moss, and softened on the inside with fine roots and animal hair.

Eggs: They lay 2–7 light green or gray eggs, with brown, reddish brown, or olive spots; 1 brood per year. The female incubates; incubation lasts 15–17 days. The male feeds the female during incubation. The fledglings leave the nest 18–19 days after hatching. The young are brooded by the female. Both parents feed the young.

Food: Omnivorous, they eat insects, grains, small lizards, frogs, fruits, and eggs and young of other birds.

Habits: Often travels in pairs and small flocks. Conspicuous, they perch in the open on trees, shrubs, or wires.

Pinyon Jay
Gymnorhinus cyanocephalus

These jays are often seen in large flocks, numbering in the hundreds. They are reliant on piñon-juniper woodlands for piñon nuts and other food. When they travel up mountains in search of places to feed, several birds in the group will keep watch, warning the others when intruders are spotted.

Brian E. Small

Identification Flashes and Distinguishing Features:

Look for the long pointed black bill and overall blue coloring with white streaks on the throat.

Size: 10.5 inches (27 centimeters)

Color: Blue overall with white streaks on the throat.

Voice: Warning call of *crauk-crauk-crauk*. They make a high nasal caw, *kaa-eh*, with a lower second note; also noisy with various other jaylike caws, and chatter.

Range: Residents of the West, from southern Montana to the southern New Mexico/Arizona border, southeastern Colorado west to northeastern California.

Habitat: Prefers high plateaus and interior mountains with piñon-juniper, 3,000–8,000 feet in elevation. Both sexes build the nest on the branch or fork of a tree 3–25 feet above the ground. There are sometimes 3 nests in 1 tree. The nest is built of sticks, bark chips, grasses, stems, roots, bits of hair, and paper.

Eggs: Lays 3–5 bluish white or greenish white eggs; 1–2 broods per year. The female incubates the eggs; incubation takes 16–17 days. The fledglings leave the nest 21 days after hatching. Both parents feed the young.

Food: They eat piñon nuts and other pine seeds, grass seeds, berries, fruit, grain, insects, and eggs and young of small birds.

Habits: Crowlike; they walk, hop, and forage on the ground and in trees. They travel in extremely large flocks, roost communally in the non-breeding season, and will nest in large colonies of up to 150 birds.

Black-billed Magpie

Pica hudsonia

The Black-billed Magpie is a songbird known for its long tail, more than half the length of its body. Only three other songbirds carry a tail as long. The male and female build large nests from mud and sticks, which they often use from year to year. Other birds have been known to use magpie nests for shelter.

Brian E. Small

Identification Flashes and Distinguishing Features:

Look for the long, iridescent blackish green tail that can be over 9 inches long, and the black and white appearance. Shows large, white wing patches in flight.

Size: 17.5–22 inches (43–55 centimeters)

Color: Male and female look alike with black head, breast, back, and rump. The wing patches, sides, and belly are white. The lengthy tail is an iridescent blackish green. When in flight, the bird appears black and white with the long green tail trailing.

Voice: Quite noisy with a plaintive nasal *mag*, they make a melodic whistle and a repetitive *chuck-chuck-chuck*.

Range: Permanent residents of the West, from central Alaska south to northern New Mexico, and in the central Dakotas west to central Oregon.

Habitat: Prefers to be near water in open woodlands, scrublands, and thickets. They typically build their nests on tree limbs or in shrubbery 25 feet above ground or less; occasionally up to 50 feet. Their nests are a large outer structure, up to 4 feet tall, made of sticks and mud; inside is a small bowl made of roots and stems.

Eggs: They lay 7–13 greenish gray eggs marked with brown; 1 brood per year. The female incubates; incubation takes 16–21 days. Fledglings leave the nest 25–32 days after hatching.

Food: Eats primarily insects, larvae, and carrion which they forage on the ground.

Habits: A breeding pair may stay together throughout a year and form evens longer bonds. They are nonmigratory and travel in flocks of 6–10, except in winter when flocks can reach 50 or more. They roost communally.

American Crow

Corvus brachyrhynchos

Even though American Crows are smaller than ravens, they are the largest crows in North America. They are also some of the best known and most easily recognized birds, and "crow-size" has become a useful reference in describing other birds. They live in many different habitats and have made positive adjustments to increased human populations.

You can attract crows by providing water and offering corn, sunflower seeds, peanuts, or suet either on the ground or in feeders.

Ron Austing

Identification Flashes and Distinguishing Features:

Look for the large, all-black appearance and the distinctive flight that has deep, steady wingbeats and resembles rowing motions.

Size: 17.5–19 inches (45–48 centimeters)

Color: Completely black bodies. The glossy metallic black feathers on their backs and heads shimmer with sheens of deep purple, green, and blue.

Voice: Their nasal *caw, caw, caw* is one of the most-recognized wild bird sounds. They also produce more melodic notes as well as imitations of human and other animal sounds.

Range: Permanent residents in most of the U.S. except extreme Southwest; from southwestern Texas to eastern California, and northwestern Washington.

Habitat: Frequents deciduous or conifer trees, open areas, agricultural land, and near human habitation. Both parents build bulky, 2-foot nesting cup in a tree crotch or the fork of a large limb. Uses sticks to make nest and lines it with leaves, vines, grass, feathers, hair, and other natural and manmade materials.

Eggs: Lays 3–7 blue-gray or green eggs spotted with browns and grays, sometimes on a reddish background; 1–2 broods per breeding season. Both parents incubate the eggs; incubation takes 18 days. Fledglings leave nest 28–35 days after hatching.

Food: Eats a variety of vegetable and animal fare (cultivated fruit, corn and other cultivated grains, large insects, small reptiles, small mammals, carrion, earthworms, and eggs and young of other birds). Also eat crabs and sea urchins, which they carry aloft and drop from considerable heights to break open.

Habits: In winter they sometimes roost in large flocks that number into the thousands. Their distinctive flight has deep, steady wingbeats that resemble the motions of rowing a boat.

Fish Crow

Corvus ossifragus

Fred J. Alsop III

Fish Crows, which look like small American Crows (see page 131), frequent tidewater marshes, beaches, mudflats, and inland reaches of slow, meandering rivers. They are often found in small flocks and family groups, but wintering flocks may number into the thousands.

You can attract them to your backyard by filling feeders with suet or peanut butter-suet mixes and by offering sunflower seeds either on the ground or on platform feeders. They will nest and perch in available large trees.

Identification Flashes and Distinguishing Features:

Their smaller size, narrower bills, and more pointed wings distinguish them from American Crows. Listen for their distinctive nasal, froglike, falsetto calls.

Size: 15 inches (38 centimeters)

Color: They have all-black bodies, including bills, legs, and feet.

Voice: Makes nasal, froglike, falsetto *ah-ah, ah-ah, ah-uk* calls.

Range: They are permanent residents from the Mississippi River Alluvial Plain to northwest Tennessee, the East Gulf Coastal Plain, Florida, and the South Atlantic and Mid-Atlantic Coastal Plains. Some of them move inland during summer months.

Habitat: Frequents coastal, tidewater, and freshwater marshes, swamps, mudflats, beaches, lakes, and rivers. They nest in small loose colonies in tree groves, each pair nesting in a separate tree. Both sexes build their nest using sticks, twigs, and bark fibers; they line the finished nest with pine needles, bark strips, grasses, roots, vines, hair, and feathers.

Eggs: Females lay 4–5 bluish, greenish, or grayish-green eggs liberally blotched and spotted with brown and gray; 1 brood per breeding season. Both parents incubate the eggs; incubation takes 16–18 days. Fledglings leave the nest 21 days after hatching.

Food: Eats primarily animal fare taken in or near water (shrimp, crabs, crayfish, tubeworms, and carrion). Occasionally they take the eggs of waterbirds; they also take turtle eggs and young. They pick grasshoppers, ants, and ticks off the backs of cattle. They occasionally feed on apples, corn, berries, and seeds (cedar, holly, dogwood, palmetto, magnolia, and other trees and shrubs).

Habits: These social, gregarious crows almost never travel or forage singly. They soar and hover more frequently than American Crows do.

Purple Martin

Progne subis

Ron Austing

Purple Martins, the largest swallows in the North America, are familiar favorites and widely beloved for their insect-eating habits, social behavior, and pleasing songs.

You can attract Purple Martins to your backyard by providing nesting boxes and gourds (see Habitat, below), and you can establish nesting colonies that will return annually. You may have to discourage House Sparrows and European Starlings from nesting in the boxes or gourds before the martins arrive in the spring.

Identification Flashes and Distinguishing Features:

Look for their notched tails. From a distance, male Purple Martins appear to be a solid dark color.

Size: 7.25–8.5 inches (18–21 centimeters)

Color: Males appear all black at a distance, but show dark, glossy purplish-black plumage in bright light. Females and juveniles have dark bluish-brown and gray upperparts, including chins, throats, and breasts. They have whitish bellies and lower breasts. Males and females have moderately forked tails.

Voice: During flight they make a loud, rich chirruping song of low-pitched, liquid, guttural notes. Males often sing at night.

Range: Breeding summer residents of the East from central Dakotas south to southern Texas and east to the Atlantic Coast. Also visit various areas of the West during the summer—along the Pacific Coast, central to southeastern Arizona, northwestern New Mexico, northwestern Utah; and isolated spots in Montana, Idaho, Wyoming, Colorado, and southern California.

Habitat: Prefers river valleys, lake shores, coastal areas, farmlands, and grasslands. Historically nested in natural and abandoned woodpecker holes in trees, on cliffs, among rocks, and in gourds. Most now live in colonies in gourds and nesting boxes (6 x 6 inches inside with a 2½-inch entrance hole). Both parents build nest from grasses, twigs, bark, string, rags, paper, and leaves; they line nesting cups with finer grasses and leaves and sometimes form a mud rim at the entrance.

Eggs: Lays 3–8 pure white eggs; 1–3 broods per breeding season. The female incubates the eggs, but the male guards the nest whenever she leaves; incubation takes 15–18 days. Fledglings leave the nest 26–31 days after hatching.

Food: Feeds primarily on insects (beetles, moths, butterflies, horseflies, mosquitoes, grasshoppers, and dragonflies). Will come for broken chicken eggshells placed on ground.

Habits: Takes insects in flight, flycatcher style; also forages while walking on the ground. One of the most domesticated wild birds, they have almost completely abandoned their original natural nesting sites for manmade homes. They nest in large active colonies in open areas, usually near water.

133

Tree Swallow

Tachycineta bicolor

They are the only swallows that normally winter in the Southeast, and thousands of them can be seen along the Gulf Coastal Plains and across Florida. They effectively reduce flying-insect populations. They are the first swallows to arrive in northern areas in the spring, and when insects are not readily available, they feed on berries and seeds.

Ron Austing

You can attract Tree Swallows by providing nesting boxes (see Habitat, below).

Identification Flashes and Distinguishing Features:

Look for their slightly notched tails, white underparts, and metallic-green upperparts.

Size: 5.75 inches (15 centimeters)

Color: Adults have glossy greenish-black or blue-black upperparts; females are paler than males and have a brown wash on their heads and backs. Their underparts, including their chins and the sides of their faces below their eyes, are snowy white. Juveniles have brownish-gray upperparts and white underparts, sometimes with a grayish-brown breast band.

Voice: Often makes a sweet liquid chatter of rapidly repeated *silip* notes while in flight.

Range: Permanent residents of the central Pacific Coast and North Carolina and Virginia coasts. Summers throughout the northern two-thirds of the U.S. and into Canada. They winter in the Atlantic and Gulf Coastal Plains and Florida, as well as extreme southwestern Arizona south to Mexico.

Habitat: Frequents wooded areas near water. As secondary-cavity nesters, they nest in natural cavities, abandoned woodpecker holes, holes in buildings, and nesting boxes (5½ x 4 x 6 inches with a 1½-inch hole cut 1⅛ inches from the top) mounted 4–6 feet off the ground on posts spaced 100 yards apart in open areas near water. They nest in single pairs or loose colonies. Females build nests from grass and straw and line them with feathers.

Eggs: Lays 4–6 white eggs; 1 brood per breeding season. The female incubates the eggs; incubation takes 13–16 days. Fledglings leave the nest 16–24 days after hatching.

Food: Feeds primarily on insects taken in flight (flies, wasps, beetles, spiders, ants, grasshoppers, and crickets). They also land on beaches and feed on the small crustaceans known as "beach fleas." In cold weather they eat small seeds (smartweed, bulrush, sedges, and bayberry fruit).

Habits: They readily accept nesting boxes scattered in open areas near water. Fall migrating flocks may number into the thousands.

Violet-green Swallow

Tachycineta thalassina

This swallow is distinguished by the brilliant green and purple reflected from its head, back, and rump, and the white patches on the sides of its rump that are visible in flight. The Tree Swallow is a closely related species to which the Violet-green Swallow is often compared. They have been known to help feed Western Bluebird nestlings and then take over the nest when the bluebirds fledge.

You can attract the Violet-green Swallow to your back yard with nesting boxes.

Mike Danzenbaker

Identification Flashes and Distinguishing Features:

Look for the bright greens and purples on the male's head, back, and rump; and the white patches on the sides of its rump which display in flight, distinguishing it from the Tree Swallow.

Size: 5–5.25 (13–14 centimeters)

Color: The male sports brilliant greens and purples on its head, back, and rump and white patches on the sides of its rump which display in flight. They have white cheeks that extend above the eye. The underparts are white, and the wings and tail are greenish black. Females have duller upperparts and the juveniles have gray-brown upperparts. Their underparts are grayish or mottled.

Voice: Makes a progression of buzzing *chi-chit* notes. The courtship song is performed in flight before daylight, a repeated *tsip, tseet, tsip.*

Range: Permanent residents of the mid coastal region of California and Mexico, they spend the summer breeding season in the West, from Alaska south to Mexico. They are often found at higher elevations.

Habitat: Prefers woodland, open woodland, grassland, and mountainous habitats near lakes or rivers. Both sexes build the nest in either a natural cavity, an abandoned woodpecker hole, on rock ridges, or in a nesting box. The nest is built with grass and with weed stems and lined with feathers. They defend their nests from other swallows.

Eggs: They lay 4–6 unmarked eggs; 1 brood per year. The female incubates 13–14 days. The fledglings leave the nest after 16–24 days. The female feeds the young with some help from the male.

Food: Eats insects that are most often caught in the air either when flying close to the ground or water. They feed in flocks.

Habits: Perches in trees, on fences, or on utility wires. They are found in loose colonies of up to 20 pairs.

Barn Swallow

Hirundo rustica

Barn Swallows have been well-known backyard birds, especially on farmsteads, since colonial times. They are the familiar swallows we see flying low over agricultural fields and in and out of barns, where they nest on beams in small colonies.

Barn Swallows will come to your backyard if you have an open building with exposed interior beams or rafters or overhangs with suitable ledges/shelves for nesting.

Ron Austing

Identification Flashes and Distinguishing Features:

Look for the deeply forked tail that distinguishes Barn Swallows from all other North American swallows. Also look for the large white "flash" spots near the base of their tails.

Size: 6.75–7.5 inches (17–19 centimeters)

Color: Males and females look alike, but the males are often richer in color. They have metallic blue upperparts, reddish foreheads and throats, and buffy to white underparts. Their tails, which are the most deeply forked of all North American swallows, have large white spots near the base.

Voice: Constantly twitters, making bubbly liquidlike *wit-wit-wit* notes.

Range: Summer residents of most of the U. S. including southern Alaska; excluding the southern tip of Florida, and most of Arizona and the southern tips of California, Nevada, and Utah, bordering Arizona. They winter in South America.

Habitat: Prefers open areas. Historically nested on cliffs and in cave entrances and rock niches; now they nest primarily in and on manmade structures, including barns, bridges, dams, wharves, docks, and porches. They nest in pairs, either singly or in colonies of 50 or more pairs. Both parents build an open nesting cup by plastering mud and straw to a ledge. They line their nests with fine grasses and usually with feathers.

Eggs: Female lays 4–7 white eggs with brown spots and dots; 1–2 broods per breeding season. Both parents incubate the eggs during the day, and female incubates them at night; incubation takes 13–17 days. Fledglings leave the nest 18–23 days after hatching, but they may return for several nights before leaving it for good.

Food: Feeds primarily on insects.

Habits: Bathes and drinks by skimming standing water. In spring and summer they can be seen following farm machinery, catching insects in swift continuous flights over open ground. Individual Barn Swallows may migrate the greatest distance of any New World land birds, traveling more than 7,000 miles twice annually from their wintering grounds in Argentina to their breeding sites in Alaska.

Carolina Chickadee

Poecile carolinensis

Many people mistakenly think the Carolina Chickadees they see at their feeders are the larger Black-capped Chickadees. The only place in the Southeast where Black-capped Chickadees are found at any time of the year is the Southern Blue Ridge mountains in eastern Tennessee and western North Carolina.

Ron Austing

You can attract Carolina Chickadees to your backyard by providing suitable nesting boxes (see Habitat, below) and by filling feeders with sunflower or thistle seeds, suet, or suet mixes.

Identification Flashes and Distinguishing Features:

Look for their distinctive white faces and black caps and bibs. Where you see them will help you distinguish Carolina Chickadees from Black-capped Chickadees; their ranges only cross in the Southern Blue Ridge mountains.

Size: 4.75 inches (12 centimeters)

Color: Ashy-gray upperparts; pale whitish-gray underparts with buffy flanks; white faces; and black caps and bibs.

Voice: Males whistle a clear *fee-bee, fee-bay* during breeding season. Males and females sing familiar *chick-a-dee-dee-dee* year-round. When disturbed, incubating birds hiss like a snake.

Range: Permanent residents of the Southeast, as far north as New Jersey west through southern Illinois, southwest to Oklahoma; south to the lower Texas coast, east across the Gulf Coast states to the Atlantic Coast, excluding southern Florida.

Habitat: Frequents coniferous, deciduous, and mixed-hardwood woodlots. As secondary-cavity nesters, they nest in natural tree cavities, abandoned woodpecker holes, fence posts, and suitable nesting boxes (4 x 4 x 8 inches with a 1⅛-inch hole cut 2 inches below the top) mounted 5–15 feet above the ground on posts or in trees. Nests have a thick foundation of moss and are lined with hair, thin grasses, and plant down.

Eggs: Females lay 5–8 white eggs rather evenly dotted with reddish brown; 1–2 broods per breeding season. Both parents incubate the eggs; incubation takes 11–12 days. Fledglings leave the nest 13–17 days after hatching.

Food: In summer they primarily eat moths and caterpillars. They also eat seeds and small berries. They will come to feeders for black oil sunflower seeds, thistle seeds, or suet.

Habits: Pairs stay together for several years. They are often seen in mixed-species feeding flocks with Downy Woodpeckers, nuthatches, Tufted Titmice, wrens, kinglets, and warblers. They take one sunflower seed at a time, fly to a perch, hold down the seed with their feet, and peck open the seed coat.

Black-capped Chickadee
Poecile atricapilla

The Black-capped Chickadee visits bird feeders from the northern half of the U.S. to Canada south of the Northwest Territory. On rare occasions, during autumn, large numbers can be seen south of this region.

The Black-capped Chickadee frequently mixes with other foraging species. When foraging for insects, it can be seen clinging to limbs upside down.

Feeders with doughnuts, peanut butter-and-cornmeal mixture, and sunflowers seeds will draw them in numbers to your backyard.

Ron Austing

Identification Flashes and Distinguishing Features:

Look for the black cap; white cheeks; and white underparts with olive-buff wash on sides, flanks, lower belly, and crissum; this combination distinguishes the Black-capped Chickadee from other North American chickadees.

Size: 5.5 inches (14 centimeters)

Color: Males and females look alike with the black cap; white cheeks; and light gray upperparts, tertials and secondaries with broad whitish edges. The underparts are white with olive-buff wash on the sides, flanks, lower belly, and crissum.

Voice: There is a low, husky, exaggerated *chick-a-dee-dee-dee*, with a clear fluted *fee-bee* or *fee-bee-be*.

Range: Found from the treeline from Alaska to Newfoundland, and south over the northern half of the U.S., reaching further south in the Rocky and Appalachian mountians. They rarely travel past the southern realm of their range and are nonmigratory.

Habitat: Nests in deciduous or mixed deciduous-conifer woodlands. Both parents build the nest in a cavity, which can be from 4–40 feet above ground and is lined with vegetation, feathers, hair, and insect cocoons. They will nest in birdhouses.

Eggs: Females lay 5–10 white eggs with reddish brown markings; 1 brood per breeding season. The female incubates the eggs for 11–13 days. Fledglings leave the nest in 14–18 days.

Food: Eats insects, insect eggs, and seeds from conifers, bayberries, and other fruit. They will come to feeders.

Habits: Lives in pairs, and often joins with other species to forage. They are seen clinging upside down when foraging for insects. They will hold a large seed down with their feet and peck the seed coat open. The female hisses like a snake when the nest is threatened.

Chestnut-backed Chickadee

Poecile rufescens

The Chestnut-backed Chickadee resides along the Pacific Coast in moist coniferous forests. Although territorial, pairs typically reside with other pairs and form loose colonies. They feed in these pairs and small family groups high in trees. You can attract them to your feeder with baby chick scratch feed, sunflower seeds, and suet.

Brian E. Small

Identification Flashes and Distinguishing Features:

Look for the sooty brown cap, white cheeks, black bib, chestnut back and rump, and whitish gray underparts.

Size: 4.75 inches (12 centimeters)

Color: They have a sooty brown cap, white cheeks, black bib, chestnut back and rump, and whitish gray underparts. The wings are edged white on the tertials and secondaries. The flanks, sides, and crissum are a chestnut wash. Along the California coast from San Francisco southward, this bird shows little chestnut, with mostly gray underparts.

Voice: The song is sparrowlike with a *chip-chip-chip-chip*. It is not whistled like other chickadees. The call is a brusque rapid *tseek-a-dee-dee*.

Range: They are residents of the Pacific Coast from southern Alaska to central California. They have only recently spread in Sierra Nevada and central California.

Habitat: Prefers forests, humid conifer and mixed conifer. The cavity nest is usually built 1.5–12 feet above ground, but can be 80 feet above ground, in a tree. The nest is lined with animal hair, feathers, and vegetation.

Eggs: Lays 5–9 white eggs with a few reddish brown marks; 1 brood per year. Little is known of the breeding biology. The females incubate; incubation is estimated at 11–14 days. The young are brooded by the female. The fledglings are estimated to leave the nest at 14–18 days. The young are fed by both parents.

Food: Food is found in treetops or on the ground in jumbled logs. They eat insects and larvae, spiders and their eggs, and fruit pulp and seeds from conifers. They will visit feeders with baby chick scratch feed, sunflower seeds, and suet.

Habits: After breeding season, they join mixed-species feeding flocks. The female hisses like a snake and flutters her wings when her nest is threatened.

Oak Titmouse

Baeolophus inornatus

The Oak Titmouse and the Juniper Titmouse are recently named species split from the Plain Titmouse. The Oak Titmouse resides primarily in the dry oak woodlands of sunny California. Except for the female Phainopepla, it is the only crested gray-brown bird in the region. You can attract this titmouse to your backyard with nestboxes and feeders with sunflower seeds and suet.

Brian E. Small

Identification Flashes and Distinguishing Features:

Look for the plain gray-brown appearance and a short crest.

Size: 5.25 inches (13 centimeters)

Color: They have medium gray-brown upperparts with a lighter gray face and underparts. The wings and tail are medium gray-brown.

Voice: The call is a raspy *tschick-a-dee*. Their song is a repeating *pee-chee, pee-chee, pee-chee*, with alternating high and low notes.

Range: They reside primarily in central California and west to the coast.

Habitat: Prefers open oak woodlands and the edge of forests. Both sexes build the nest in a natural cavity, either they excavate or they use an abandoned woodpecker hole or a nest box. The nest is moss-lined with bark pieces, feathers, and animal hair.

Eggs: They lay 6–8 white eggs sometimes spotted with reddish brown; 1–2 broods per year. The female incubates; incubation takes 14–16 days. The young are brooded by the female. The fledglings leave the nest 16–21 days after hatching. Both parents feed the young.

Food: The diet consists of a variety of seeds, acorns, and insects. They catch insects in mid-air and forage from trunks, branches, and foliage.

Habits: Travels in pairs or small groups, never large flocks. They sometimes cling to branches or cones when foraging. They hold seeds with their feet to jab them open with their bill.

Juniper Titmouse
Baeolophus griseus

Only recently has the Juniper Titmouse been named a separate species, paired formerly with the Oak Titmouse and called the Plain Titmouse. As the name implies, this titmouse is found in juniper or piñon-juniper woodlands and in riparian woodlands and suburban shade trees. You can attract these titmice to your birdfeeder with suet, peanut butter, and sunflower seeds.

Brian E. Small

Identification Flashes and Distinguishing Features:

Look for the gray crest and all over gray body with a white patch above the bill and darker gray wings and tail.

Size: 5.5 inches (14 centimeters)

Color: Both sexes are entirely gray with paler whitish gray underparts and a darker gray wing and tail. There is a distinguishing white patch above the bill.

Voice: The call is a raspy *tschick-adee*. The song is sung in one tone with a variable rolling series of notes with similar phrases.

Range: They are residents of the Southwest from the southeastern tip of Idaho to Mexico, northeast New Mexico to northeast California.

Habitat: Preferring woodland areas, especially juniper or piñon-juniper woodlands, often near lakes or rivers, they are also found in the suburbs in shade trees. They nest in tree cavities, abandoned woodpecker holes, or nest boxes. Both sexes build the nest, softening it with moss, grass, weeds, bark, feathers, and hair.

Eggs: They lay 3–9 white eggs, with occasional reddish brown marks; 1–2 broods per year. The female incubates; incubation takes 14–16 days. The young are brooded by the female but fed by both sexes. The fledglings leave the nest 16–21 days after hatching.

Food: Insects are foraged from trunks, branches, and foliage. They eat berries and seeds from twigs and the ground. They will cling under limbs or cones to get seeds and pound open seeds or nuts with their bill.

Habits: Couples will stay together throughout the year. They gather in smaller groups and pairs. They will mix with other foraging flocks after breeding season.

Tufted Titmouse
Baeolophus bicolor

These perky little gray birds are easily recognized by their rusty flanks, button-black eyes, and crested heads. You can easily draw titmice (and chickadees) to you by making loud, squeaking noises by kissing the back of your hand or imitating Eastern Screech-Owl calls. When they sound the alarm, other birds will come to the scene.

Ron Austing

You can attract Tufted Mice by providing water and nesting boxes (see Habitat, below) and by offering sunflower seeds or suet.

Identification Flashes and Distinguishing Features:

Look for their gray bodies, rusty flanks, button-black eyes, and crested heads.

Size: 6.5 inches (17 centimeters)

Color: They have grayish upperparts, including gray crests; black foreheads; and whitish to pale-gray underparts, with a rusty wash on their sides and flanks.

Voice: Makes loud, clear *peter, peter, peter* whistles and sometimes *peto, peto, peto* sounds.

Range: Permanent residents from Michigan south to the Gulf Coast; New Hampshire west to southern Wisconsin; southwest to western Texas; south to Mexico. They do not reside in extreme southern Florida.

Habitat: Prefers woodland habitats, especially bottomland hardwoods and low-elevation mixed-hardwood and hardwood forests; they also reside in wooded residential areas. Secondary-cavity nesters, they nest in natural cavities, abandoned woodpecker holes, fence posts, and suitable nesting boxes (4 x 4 x 8 inches with a 1⅜ hole cut 2 inches below the top) mounted 5–15 feet above the ground in trees or on poles in or near wooded areas. Makes nest from mosses, leaves, bark fibers, plant down, snake skin, hair, and other natural materials.

Eggs: Lays 4–8 white eggs that have dark brown dots and spots clustered at the large end; 1–2 broods per breeding season. The female incubates the eggs, and the male feeds her while she is on the nest; incubation takes 13–14 days. Fledglings leave the nest 15–18 days after hatching.

Food: In summer eats primarily insects (caterpillars, treehoppers, ants, beetles, and wasps). Also eats berries (poison ivy, blueberries, blackberries, and others) and seeds (acorns, beechnuts, tulip poplar, sunflower, and sumac). Will come to feeders for sunflower seeds, peanuts, nuts, suet, and mixes.

Habits: They hold large seeds between their feet and hack them open with their beaks. In winter they often travel in mixed-species foraging flocks with chickadees, nuthatches, kinglets, Downy Woodpeckers, and other small birds.

Black-crested Titmouse

Parus atricristatus

The Black-crested Titmouse is a newly named species, split from the Tufted Titmouse. As its name implies, the Black-crested Titmouse wears a black crest with the crest higher than the Tufted Titmouse. The song is also distinct.

The Black-crested Titmouse resides from southwestern Oklahoma south through Texas, with Oklahoma becoming slightly more populated in the winter.

These birds will visit feeders for sunflower seeds and suet, and will nest in nest boxes.

Tom Vezo

Identification Flashes and Distinguishing Features:

Look for the high black crest, white to brownish forehead, and stout, black bill.

Size: 6 inches (15 centimeters)

Color: High black crest and a light or brown patch over the bill. The upperparts are gray, the underparts are whitish, and the sides are rust colored. Females and juveniles have gray-tipped crests.

Voice: Makes a repetitive, whistled and varied *peter, peter, peter, peter* and a monotone *pete, pete, pete* or *hew, hew, hew*.

Range: They are found from southwestern Oklahoma south to southeastern Texas and east central Mexico.

Habitat: Prefers oak-juniper woodland, scrub habitat, and areas of human habitation. They nest in holes in trees from 3–22 feet above the ground, and in man-made structures such as posts, iron pipes, and nesting boxes. The nest is built with soft, natural materials including hair, grasses, leaves, and moss, and often includes snakeskin.

Eggs: Lays 4–7 white eggs with brown speckles; 1 brood per year. The female incubates the eggs for 12–14 days. Fledglings leave the nest 15–17 days after hatching and are fed by both parents.

Food: They eat seeds, insects, berries, fruit, spiders and spider eggs, and some snails. In the winter they eat acorns.

Habits: Flies in mixed species flocks after breeding season. They are active, noisy, and confiding.

Bushtit

Psaltriparus minimus

The Bushtit travels in flocks numbering from a half dozen to thirty or more individuals. These lively, twittering groups energetically brush through foliage as they forage. Tame, these little, long-tailed birds often huddle in groups on their roost to stay warm on cold desert nights. Their appearance varies slightly regionally and the black-masked adult males of the southwestern populations were once considered to be a separate species, called the Black-eared Bushtit. You can attract Bushtits by providing a birdbath and plantings of trees and shrubs.

Brian E. Small

Identification Flashes and Distinguishing Features:

Look for the ashy gray upperparts, whitish gray underparts, and short, black bill. The crown varies geographically—brown on the coast and gray in the interior regions. Southwestern males wear a black mask.

Size: 4.5 inches (11 centimeters)

Color: Ashy gray upperparts and whitish gray underparts. Their belly is sometimes light orange-yellow. The crown is brown on the coast and gray inland. Inland birds have brown cheeks and southwestern birds have a black mask. Females have yellowish eyes; males and juveniles have dark brown eyes.

Voice: Makes a high, thin, buzzy twittering and a thin, trilled *sir-r-r-r-rrrrrr*.

Range: Residents of the West and Southwest from Washington south across to Texas and on to Mexico. They winter in southern and eastern New Mexico.

Habitat: Frequents open forests, scrub vegetation, and semidesert areas. Both sexes build the nest 4–25 feet above ground in a deciduous tree or shrub. They build a hanging pouch lined with plant materials, hair, and feathers. They often bind it with spider web silk.

Eggs: 5–7 white eggs; 2 broods per year. Both parents incubate eggs, both roosting on nest at night; incubation takes 12 days. Young are brooded by the female. Fledglings leave the nest 14–15 days after hatching. Both parents feed the young.

Food: Eats insects, their larvae and eggs, spiders, some fruit, and berries.

Habits: If a pair is alarmed when building their nest, or laying or incubating eggs, they will sometimes abandon the nest, possibly change mates, and build a new nest.

Red-breasted Nuthatch

Sitta canadensis

The bird's colloquial name "nuthack" has been altered through the years to "nuthatch." They live in northern coniferous forests but will travel south when winter food supplies weaken. Red-breasted Nuthatches, like other nuthatches, do not typically migrate.

You can attract visiting Red-breasted Nuthatches by filling feeders with sunflower seeds, suet, or suet mixes.

Ron Austing

Identification Flashes and Distinguishing Features:

Their ability to walk down trees headfirst distinguishes nuthatches from all other birds. Look for the distinctive reddish underparts and black eye lines.

Size: 4.5 inches (11 centimeters)

Color: Males and females look alike, but females have paler underparts and heads. Their backs, wings, and tails are bluish-gray; their underparts are rusty red. They have white faces with a black line "through" their eyes and black caps.

Voice: They make *waa-waa-waa-waa-waa* songs that sounds like a toy tin horn. They also make *ank, ank, ank* calls.

Range: Permanent residents of the Blue Ridge Mountains, New England, Great Lakes; from the southern border of Arizona/New Mexico north to Idaho and west to the Pacific Coast, south to the mid-California coast. They winter south of their range, throughout the U.S., excluding central and southern Florida and the southern tip of Texas.

Habitat: Prefers conifers, particularly spruce, pine, and hemlock. They usually dig holes in the soft wood of rotting tree stubs; sometimes use natural cavities, abandoned woodpecker holes, or nesting boxes (4 x 4 x 8 inches with a 1¼-inch hole cut 2 inches below the top) mounted 10–20 feet above the ground in wooded areas. They build nests from mosses, grasses, rootlets, and shredded bark fibers. They gather pitch from conifers and smear it around the entrance holes.

Eggs: They lay 4–7 white eggs peppered with red-brown dots or spots; 1 brood per breeding season. Both parents incubate the eggs; incubation takes about 12 days. Fledglings leave the nest 14–21 days after hatching.

Food: Feeds primarily on seeds, particularly conifer seeds. In summer, eats some insects (spruce budworm, beetles, wasps, and caterpillars). Will come to feeders for sunflower seeds, hulled walnuts, or suet.

Habits: When foraging, they walk down trees headfirst. They wedge large seeds and nuts into crevices in tree bark and then hack open the seed coats. They often store seeds for winter food.

White-breasted Nuthatch

Sitta carolinensis

White-breasted Nuthatches are the largest North American nuthatches. They remain together in pairs all year and roam over large winter territories (twenty-five to fifty acres). They are often seen walking headfirst down trees. Their colloquial name "nuthack" has been altered through the years to "nuthatch."

You can attract nuthatches to your backyard by providing suitable nesting boxes (see Habitat, below) and by filling feeders with sunflower seeds or suet and suet mixes.

Ron Austing

Identification Flashes and Distinguishing Features:

Their ability to walk down trees headfirst distinguishes nuthatches from all other birds. Look for their distinctive, handsome blue-gray upperparts, and white underparts.

Size: 5–6 inches (13–15 centimeters)

Color: Males and females look alike, but females may have paler crowns. They have blue-gray upperparts, black caps and napes, white faces, white underparts, white tail patches, and a rusty wash on their flanks and undertail coverts.

Voice: They make nasal *yank* sounds. They also sing 6–8 *yank* running notes that sound a bit like an old car trying to start.

Range: Permanent residents over most of the U.S. Not found in the western Arizona/southern California/southern Nevada area, southwestern Idaho, or some pockets of Oregon and Washington, or the northern Pacific Coast.

Habitat: Prefers deciduous forests and woodlots below 3,500 feet; they also frequent wooded urban areas. As secondary-cavity nesters, they nest in natural cavities, abandoned woodpecker holes, and sometimes in nesting boxes (4 x 4 x 8 inches with a 1¼-inch hole cut 2 inches below the top) mounted 10–20 feet above the ground in wooded areas. They line their nests with mosses, rootlets, bark shreds, grasses, fur, and feathers.

Eggs: Females lay 3–10 white eggs peppered with spots or dots of reddish-brown, gray, and purple; 1 brood per breeding season. Both parents incubate the eggs; incubation takes about 12 days. Fledglings leave the nest about 14 days after hatching.

Food: In spring and summer they feed primarily on insects. Fall and winter fare includes seeds, nuts, and berries. They will come to feeders for sunflower seeds, cracked nuts, peanuts, and suet.

Habits: They take one seed at a time and either store it or wedge it into a crack so they can hack it open. In winter they join mixed-species foraging flocks. They "threaten" other birds by partially spreading their wings and tails and making half-turns, with their necks and heads extended. Pairs mate for life, and both parents "bill sweep" in or near their nest, swinging their upper bodies back and forth while holding insects in their beaks for their young.

Carolina Wren
Thryothorus ludovicianus

Ron Austing

Carolina Wrens, the largest wrens in eastern North America, are familiar energetic backyard songsters. These active wrens often carry their tails at jaunty angles over their backs. They are creatures of thickets, where they explore the tangles' dark crevices, holes, and tunnels for insects. Troglodytidae, the scientific name for the wren family, means "cave dweller" and refers to the dark places where wrens forage as well as to the cavities or domed nests they build.

You can attract Carolina Wrens to your backyard by planting dense shrubbery, providing birdbaths and other sources of water, and by filling feeders with suet or peanut butter-suet mixes.

Identification Flashes and Distinguishing Features:

Their relatively large size, buffy underparts, white lines over their eyes, and jauntily held tails readily distinguish Carolina Wrens from other birds.

Size: 5.5 inches (14 centimeters)

Color: Both males and females have reddish-brown upperparts with white throats and eye stripes; their underparts are buffy. They have slender, down-curved bills.

Voice: They make loud, ringing *teakettle, teakettle, teakettle* or shorter *sweetheart, sweetheart, sweetheart* songs and long, drawn-out *chirrrrrrrrrrrrr* calls.

Range: Permanent residents from southern New Hampshire to the Gulf Coast; westward to central Kansas; south to Mexico. Sometimes will winter slightly north and west of this range; suffer heavy population drops in severe winters.

Habitat: Frequents woodlots, thickets, hammocks, swamps, and residential areas. They build nests in almost any available cavity, including old woodpecker holes and holes in fence posts, stonewalls, tree stumps, and buildings as well as nesting boxes, pails, pockets of hanging cloths, and mailboxes. Both parents build a domed nest of leaves, grasses, twigs, mosses, weed stalks, feathers, debris, and occasionally snake skins. They line their nest with finer materials.

Eggs: Lays 4–8 white to pale-pink eggs that may be heavily dotted or blotched with dark brown; 2–3 broods per breeding season. The female incubates the eggs for 12–14 days. Fledgings leave the nest 12–14 days after hatching.

Food: Primarily insects (spiders, beetles, moths, caterpillars, roaches, grasshoppers, sow bugs, millipedes, and snails). They also eat small lizards. They will come to feeders for suet and suet mixes.

Habits: They sing at all times of day throughout the year. They are the most commonly seen wrens in the Southeast.

Bewick's Wren

Thryomanes bewickii

Bewick's Wren is native to the U.S. west of the Appalachians. This tame species lives near farms, homes, and small towns. Populations have mysteriously declined east of the Mississippi River since the 1960s.

Nesting in natural cavities, they have been known to nest in anything providing shelter, from mailboxes, to baskets, to cow skulls. They will build in nest boxes.

Ron Austing

Identification Flashes and Distinguishing Features:

Look for the distinguishing white eye stripe, long, slightly decurved, bill, and the long rounded tail with white spots on the feather tips.

Size: 5.25 inches (14 centimeters)

Color: The color varies geographically from, mousy gray-brown in the West to rusty brown in the East. There is a white eye stripe and barring on the wings. The underparts are whitish to grayish. The long rounded tail has dark brown or black barring and white spots on the tips of the feathers.

Voice: The male makes a *chip, chip, chip, de-da-ah, tee-dee*; like a Song Sparrow; except high, thin, buzzing, and variable. It often ends in a thin trill. The call is a flat *jipp*.

Range: Residents of the western U.S. eastward to the Appalachians.

Habitat: Frequents shrub and scrub bushes including thorn scrub, thickets with scattered trees, semi-open areas including agricultural land, and around human habitation. Both sexes build the nest in the cavity of almost anything—tree, man-made structures, hollow log, post, etc. Nest is built of twigs, moss, bits of snakeskin, and grass; it is lined with feathers.

Eggs: Lays 4–11 white eggs with flecks of purple, brown, and gray; 1 brood per year, possibly 2 in the South. Female incubates eggs for 12–14 days and broods the young. Fledglings leave the nest 14 days after hatching. Both parents feed the young.

Food: Mostly insects and sometimes spiders. They feed on the ground or in trees.

Habits: Noisy, tame, and bold. They hop while holding their tail high above, flicking it from side to side. When they sing, the tail points downward with the head held back. The male builds several "dummy" nests in his territory for the female to choose from and then helps to finish construction.

House Wren

Troglodytes aedon

Persistent singers and noisy scolders, male House Wrens busy themselves building "dummy" nests in every available suitable cavity before the females arrive in the spring. The females make the final choice of the one nesting site for the pair. House Wrens are so territorial that they may destroy nests and kill the eggs and young of other birds, including other House Wrens.

Ron Austing

You can attract House Wrens to your backyard by providing suitable nesting boxes (see Habitat, below) and offering suet or peanut butter-suet mixes.

Identification Flashes and Distinguishing Features:

Their lack of distinguishing features makes House Wrens easy to identify.

Size: 4.75 inches (12 centimeters)

Color: The plainest members of the wren family, both sexes have brownish-gray upperparts, grayish-buff underparts, and indistinct pale stripes over their eyes. Their tails, wings, and flanks have black bars.

Voice: They produce a bubbling, energetic *tsi-tsi-tsi-tsi-oodle-oodle-oodle* song.

Range: Permanent residents of mid-Atlantic Coast, central California coast south to Mexico, and southeastward through western Arizona to Mexico. Summer residents from the mid-Atlantic Coast to the mid-Pacific Coast northward. They winter south of these ranges excluding a swath from western Tennessee to northern Texas.

Habitat: Prefers deciduous low woody vegetation, thickets, tangles, brush piles, and areas around human habitation. They nest in natural cavities in trees, stubs, fence posts, old woodpecker holes, and nesting boxes (4 x 4 x 6 inches with a 1-inch hole cut 2 inches from the top) mounted on posts or suspended from limbs 5–10 feet above the ground in wooded areas or gardens. The male builds the nest from sticks and twigs, and the female lines it with grasses, feathers, paper, leaves, plant fibers, and hair.

Eggs: Lays 5–9 white eggs speckled with reddish or brown dots; 2-3 broods per breeding season. The female incubates the eggs; incubation takes 13–15 days. Fledglings leave the nest 12–18 days after hatching.

Food: Primarily insects (wasps, ants, beetles, moths, crickets, grasshoppers, flies, ticks, spiders, and millipedes). They also eat snails. Sometimes will come to feeders for suet or peanut butter-suet mixes.

Habits: They are known for their persistent vocalizations and for the wide variety of places they choose as nesting sites.

Eastern Bluebird

Sialia sialis

Ron Austing

Eastern Bluebirds rank among the best-known and best-loved North American birds. Bright-blue upperparts and red-brown breasts and throats make the males hard to miss.

You can attract them by providing nesting boxes; House Sparrows and European Starlings will compete fiercely with them, but you can eliminate some of the competition by making bluebird-size boxes (see Habitat, below). They will come for water and to feeders for mealworms and commercial "bluebird mixes."

Identification Flashes and Distinguishing Features:

You will readily identify male Eastern Bluebirds by their bright-blue upperparts and reddish-brown breasts and throats.

Size: 7–7.75 inches (18–19 centimeters)

Color: Males have blue upperparts, reddish-brown breast and throat, and white belly and undertail coverts. Females are paler and duller with pale blue-gray heads. Immature birds have grayish upperparts, gray-and-white spotted underparts, bluish tails.

Voice: They make soft, melodious *purity* or *tur-a-lly* calls and *cheer-up cheerful charlie* songs.

Range: Permanent residents from southern Indiana to the Gulf Coast (excluding southern tip of Florida), and from Atlantic Coast to central Texas. Summer residents north of this range into Canada. They winter into western Texas, eastern New Mexico, and extreme southern Louisiana.

Habitat: Frequents open country, orchards, gardens, and parks. Builds their nest in natural cavities in trees, fence posts, old woodpecker holes, and nesting boxes (5 x 5 x 8 inches with a 1½ hole cut 2 inches from the top) mounted 5–10 feet above the ground on posts spaced 100 yards apart in open areas. Females build nests from grasses, weeds, and pine needles and line them with finer grasses, hair, and feathers.

Eggs: Lays 3–7 (1 less egg for second brood) pale-blue, blue-white, or white unmarked eggs; 2-3 broods per season. The female incubates the eggs; incubation takes 12–14 days. Fledglings leave the nest 15–20 days after hatching.

Food: Mostly insects taken from a low perch (grasshoppers, crickets, beetles, millipedes, katydids, and spiders). Also eats small reptiles, amphibians, fruit, and berries. Will come to feeders for mealworms, peanut butter-suet mixes, cornmeal mixtures, and commercial "bluebird mixes."

Habits: Thousands of bluebirds nest in boxes placed along roadsides and other sites. Most bluebirds remain on nesting grounds south of southern Indiana during winter months and use the boxes for night roosts. Sometimes they huddle with other bluebirds for warmth.

Western Bluebird

Sialia mexicana

Unlike the Eastern Bluebird, the Western Bluebird displays a brilliant blue throat. Its chestnut breast and sides distinguish it from the Mountain Bluebird.

Because it nests in holes of trees, the populations have been adversely affected by the dwindling numbers of large old trees.

Tom Vezo

Identification Flashes and Distinguishing Features:

Look for the bright blue throat and chestnut on upper back and shoulders to distinguish it from other bluebirds.

Size: 7–7.75 inches (18–20 centimeters)

Color: The male has a bright blue head, upperparts, and throat; breast, sides, and flanks are chestnut-red; also a touch of chestnut on upper back and shoulders. The belly and crissum are grayish white. Female has brownish gray upperparts and a pale gray throat. Breast, sides, and flanks show slight chestnut color; they also have a white eye ring. The juvenile is brownish gray with white-spotted upperparts and underparts and bluish wings and tail.

Voice: The song resembles *f-few, f-few, fawee*; the call is a *pa-wee* or *mew*.

Range: Residents of the West from mid-Oregon south through western California; southern Utah south to Mexico, and central New Mexico west through Arizona. Summers from southern British Columbia south through western Montana west and south through central California, and into Colorado. Winters in the extreme southern tip of Nevada and western Arizona, and southern New Mexico south to Mexico.

Habitat: Frequents open woodlands, grasslands with scattered trees, and farmlands. The nest is built by both sexes 2–50 above ground in a tree cavity or bird box; it is constructed of grass, weeds, stems, pine needles, twigs, and sometimes hair and feathers.

Eggs: Lays 3–8 pale blue to bluish white eggs; 2 broods per year. The female incubates the eggs; incubation takes 13–14 days. The fledglings are brooded by the female and leave the nest in 15–22 days. Both parents feed the young.

Food: Diet consists of insects, worms, spiders, and snails. They forage on the ground and hunt in the air. In winter they eat berries. They will eat from feeders with mealworms, peanut butter and suet mixture, cornmeal mixes, and bluebird mixes, currants, and raisins.

Habits: They live in pairs or in small colonies. Will roost communally in winter, sharing the same cavity for a night to keep warm.

Mountain Bluebird

Sialia currucoides

The solid brilliant blue hue of the male Mountain Bluebird distinguishes it from other bluebirds. It is found in most abundance about a mile and a half above sea level in the tree-covered mountains and open landscapes of the West. The population of this species is at risk due to the decline of its habitat. The Mountain Bluebird will nest in nest boxes.

Tom Vezo

Identification Flashes and Distinguishing Features:

Look for the overall brilliant blue coloring of the male.

Size: 7–7.25 inches (18–19 centimeters)

Color: The male is a bright blue overall with pale blue underparts; belly and undertail coverts are white. The female is a dull brownish gray overall; blue wing coverts, tertials, and secondaries are white-edged. There is a white eye ring, and the undertail coverts and belly are white. The juvenile is similar to the female but with pale whitish streaking and spotting on the sides and breast.

Voice: Makes a low warbling *tru-lee*, but are mostly silent. Their call is a *phew*.

Range: Permanently reside in the central western states from southern Colorado and northern New Mexico westward to central and northeastern California and into southern Oregon. They summer to the north of this region into Canada and on up into Alaska. They winter south of this range from central New Mexico westward to southern California.

Habitat: Prefers tree-covered mountain ranges and open landscapes, but winters in lower desert and semidesert areas. Both sexes build the nest in a natural tree cavity, protected areas on buildings, or in a nest box. They construct the nest of grass, weed stems, pine needles, twigs, and hair or feathers.

Eggs: Lays 4–8 pale blue to bluish white eggs, very rarely white; 2 broods a year. The female incubates the eggs; incubation takes 13–14 days. The female broods the young for the first 6 days. The fledglings stay in the nest 22–23 days after hatching. Both parents feed the young.

Food: Eats insects, caterpillars, some fruits, and some berries. In the summer, they mostly eat insects. They catch insects mid-air and on the ground, hovering from above then dropping on their prey.

Habits: Lives as solitary individuals, in pairs, or small family groups.

Wood Thrush

Hylocichla mustelina

Wood Thrushes, the best-known eastern spotted thrushes, frequent moist woodlots in summer. These noted songsters often visit wooded lawns and gardens.

You can attract Wood Thrushes to your backyard by including berry-producing shrubs in your naturescape and providing water.

Fred J. Alsop III

Identification Flashes and Distinguishing Features:

Their rufous-red upperparts and black-spotted underparts distinguish Wood Thrushes from other birds.

Size: 7.75–8 inches (19–20 centimeters)

Color: Both males and females have rich rufous-red crowns, napes, and backs, olive brown rumps and tails, and white underparts that are heavily spotted with large, round black markings. They have pink legs.

Voice: They make musical flute-like to bell-like songs of phrases of *ee-oh-lee, ee-oh-lay* notes that rise and fall in pitch; given in both early morning and at dusk. Call is rapid *pit-pit-pit* notes.

Range: Summer residents of the East, from Maine to northern Florida, west to central Minnesota, and south to northeastern Texas.

Habitat: Prefers cool, humid deciduous forests, parks, gardens, and wooded urban areas. Females build robinlike nesting cups on crotches of branches using leaves, mosses, grasses, mud, and sometimes paper. They line their nests with rootlets (robins use grasses).

Eggs: They lay 2–5 pale-blue to blue-green eggs; 1–2 broods per breeding season. The female incubates the eggs, and the male guards the nest whenever the female leaves; incubation takes 13–14 days. Fledglings leave the nest 12 days after hatching.

Food: Primarily insects and other small invertebrates that they forage on the ground or glean from foliage (earthworms, ants, beetles, crickets, spiders, moths, and caterpillars). They also eat fruit and berries, especially in fall.

Habits: Like other thrushes, they sing beautiful songs; you will hear their best songs at dusk. They have become more accepting of people and often build nests close to homes in residential, wooded neighborhoods. When alarmed, they raise their head feathers into a crest.

American Robin

Turdus migratorius

American Robins are the largest North American thrushes and among the best-known birds on the North American continent. Even young children recognize "Robin Redbreast." These large songbirds frequent our lawns and have even become urban dwellers.

Fred J. Alsop III

You can attract American Robins by including lawn areas and berry-producing plants in your yard, nesting shelves or ledges (see Habitat, below), and providing water. They especially enjoy birdbaths, pools, and running water.

Identification Flashes and Distinguishing Features:

Their large size and orange-red breasts make American Robins easy to identify.

Size: 10 inches (25 centimeters)

Color: Males have gray-brown upperparts with black heads, tails, and wings and white rings around their eyes. They have chestnut to brick-red breasts and bellies, white lower bellies and undertail coverts, white tail corners, and yellow bills; their throats are streaked white and black. Females are paler versions of the males, and juveniles are similar to their parents but with underparts heavily spotted with black.

Voice: They sing a back-and-forth *cheer-up, cheer, cheer, cheerily cheer-up*. They also make loud *hip, hip, hip* or *hup, hup, hup* calls.

Range: Permanent residents throughout most of the U.S. In summer, breeds north to coast of Arctic Ocean.

Habitat: Frequents open woods, farmlands, and parks and gardens in urban areas. Females build bulky nesting cups in the forks or on horizontal branches of deciduous trees or conifers and sometimes on ledges or "nesting shelves" placed on the side of a building. They work grasses, string, cloth, paper, and weeds into the mud interlinings of their nests and then line the finished nests with fine grasses.

Eggs: They lay 3–7 unmarked "robin's-egg blue" eggs; 2–3 broods per year in the South, fewer in the North. The female incubates the eggs; incubation takes 12–14 days. Fledglings leave the nest 14–16 days after hatching.

Food: Primarily earthworms found by sight on lawns, golf courses, and fields; also eat grasshoppers, crickets, moths, cicadas, beetles, caterpillars, butterflies, weevils, cutworms, termites, and ants. They occasionally eat fruit and berries (dogwood, bayberries, pokeberries, and chinaberries) and will come to feeders for mealworms or bread.

Habits: The males are very territorial and often fight each other or their own reflections in windows, mirrors, or the chrome on cars.

Gray Catbird
Dumetella carolinensis

These tame little birds live in shrubbery, and their genus name, *Dumetella*, refers to a "thicket dweller." Although they are members of the Mockingbird family, they aren't as good at mimicry as their cousins.

You can attract Gray Catbirds to your backyard by including shrubbery in your naturescape, providing water, and offering raisins, cheese, nuts, and cereals.

Fred J. Alsop III

Identification Flashes and Distinguishing Features:

Look for the black crowns and tails on their gray bodies.

Size: 8.5–9 inches (22–23 centimeters)

Color: Dark slate-gray bodies, black caps, long black tails, and reddish undertail coverts.

Voice: They make mockingbird-like phrases, but with no repetition of phrases. They mix catlike *meow* or down-slurred *mew* sounds into their songs. Sometimes they mimic frogs and other birds.

Range: Permanent residents in a swath along the Atlantic and Gulf Coast from New England to Texas; summer residents north of their permanent range to Canada, west to Idaho and western Washington.

Habitat: Prefers woodland undergrowth, hedgerows, thickets, gardens, and ornamental plantings. The female, with the help of her mate, builds a deep nesting cup with a bulky foundation of vines, twigs, weeds, grasses, and bark strips and lined with rootlets, hair, fine grasses, and pine needles.

Eggs: Lays 2–6 deep bluish-green unmarked eggs; 2 broods per year. The female incubates the eggs; incubation takes 12–13 days. Fledglings leave the nest 10–11 days after hatching.

Food: About half of their diet consists of insects (caterpillars, moths, crickets, beetles, beetles, cicadas, dragonflies, centipedes, and spiders). Also fruit and berries (dogwood, grapes, blackberries, and blueberries). Will come to feeders for cheese, raisins, peanuts, boiled potatoes, and cereals.

Habits: These often fearless birds allow close approach, sometimes becoming tame to the continued presence of people in their territory. If you make "squeaking" or "pishing" sounds with your hands, they will quickly come to investigate.

Northern Mockingbird

Mimus polyglottos

They are noted for their mimicry of other birds' songs and calls as well as for their ability to incorporate these and other sounds (roosters' crows, dogs' barking, piano notes, machines, frogs, police whistles, etc.) into their songs. They sing day and night during the breeding season.

Ron Austing

You can attract Northern Mockingbirds to your backyard by including berry-producing plants in your naturescape, providing water, and filling feeders with suet, suet mixes, fruit, or bread.

Identification Flashes and Distinguishing Features:

Look for the white flash spots and the white edge on the long tails of these basically grayish birds.

Size: 10 inches (25 centimeters)

Color: Both males and females have medium-gray upperparts, pale-gray to whitish underparts, darker gray to blackish wings and tails, large white patches on their wings, and white outer tail feathers. Juveniles have heavily spotted underparts.

Voice: They make loud, abrupt *check* calls as well as rich, varied songs composed of phrases, including mimicry of other birds and sounds, repeated 3–5 times in a row. Displaying birds often "leap" into the air from a high perch and sing both on the way up and on the way back down. Females sing in fall to establish their winter territory.

Range: Permanent residents south and east of a line from New Hampshire to southern California, and up the Pacific coast. They summer slightly north of this range, occasionally as far north as Canada.

Habitat: Frequents trees, shrubs, and desert scrub. Well adapted to areas of human habitation. Both parents build their nesting cup low to the ground using twigs for the outer layer and leaves, vines, wool, string, paper, fine grasses, rootlets, and hair for the lining.

Eggs: Lays 2–6 blue-and-green eggs that are heavily marked with brown spots and blotches; 2–3 broods per breeding season. The female incubates the eggs; incubation takes 12–13 days. Fledglings leave the nest 11–13 days after hatching.

Food: Almost 60 percent of their diet consists of animal foods (insects, worms, spiders, snails, frogs, lizards, and small snakes). Also eats fruit and berries and will come to feeders for suet, raisins, cut apples, or bread.

Habits: In spring males sing most of the day and sometimes well into the night. They aggressively defend their young and dive at intruders, including people, cats, and dogs. They also defend winter territory to protect food supplies. When foraging on the ground, they spread their wings with a jerk above their backs to startle insects into moving, making them easy prey.

Brown Thrasher

Toxostoma rufum

Ron Austing

Although Brown Thrashers are not the mimics that Gray Catbirds or Northern Mockingbirds are, they are excellent songsters and occasionally mimic parts of the songs of other birds. They frequently sing from high, exposed perches. These large reddish-brown birds often forage on the ground, sometimes dashing across the road like miniature roadrunners.

You can attract Brown Thrashers to your backyard by including thick shrubbery in your naturescape and providing water.

Identification Flashes and Distinguishing Features:

Their large size, rufous-red upperparts, streaked underparts, and long tails distinguish Brown Thrashers from other birds.

Size: 11.5 inches (29 centimeters)

Color: Both males and females have rich rufous-red upperparts, white to buff underparts that are heavily streaked with dark brown to black, long, dark decurved bills, yellow eyes (adults), long rounded tails, and white wing bars.

Voice: They make mockingbird-like phrases, repeating each phrase 2–3 times. They also make loud *smack* notes.

Range: Permanent residents from New York south to the Gulf of Mexico, west to eastern Texas and Oklahoma. They spend the summer breeding season north and gradually northwest of this range to western Montana and into Canada. They winter slightly west of their permanent range into central and southern Texas.

Habitat: Frequents the edges of woodlots, old brushy fields, farmlands, roadsides, brier patches, and gardens. Both parents build nesting cups close to the ground in dense thickets, low tangles, shrubs, and low trees. Their nests often have 4 levels: a base of larger twigs topped with layers of leaves, smaller twigs, and coarse grasses.

Eggs: Females lay 2–6 pale-blue to white eggs covered with small reddish-brown spots; 2–3 broods per year. Both parents incubate the eggs; incubation takes 11–14 days. Fledglings leave the nest 9–13 days after hatching.

Food: They usually forage on the ground, using their bills to dig in the soil and turn over leaves to expose food. About 70 percent of their diet consists of insects and other invertebrates. They also take small salamanders, frogs, snakes, and lizards. They occasionally feed on fruit, berries, acorns, and waste corn.

Habits: Often loud and musical. They aggressively defend their young, sometimes flying at the head of an intruder. They tolerate people and frequent yards and gardens.

Curve-billed Thrasher

Toxostoma curvirostre

The Curve-billed Thrasher is a nonmigratory resident of the southwestern U.S. south to Mexico. They are often found near water sources, including birdbaths and dripping faucets, all of which are scarce in the desert and brushlands it occupies.

In addition to water, this thrasher is attracted to feeders with fruit.

Ron Austing

Identification Flashes and Distinguishing Features:

Look for the curved black bill, spotted underparts, buffy undertail coverts, and bright orange eyes. The juveniles have straighter bills and yellow eyes. Notice indistinct spotting in the westernmost race.

Size: 11 inches (28 centimeters)

Color: They have gray-brown upperparts and buff-gray underparts. The breast is faintly spotted. The tail is white to gray-buff tipped. The eyes are orange to orange-yellow. Juveniles' eyes are yellow.

Voice: Call is *whit-wheet* which can include up to 3 notes, and often a repetitive melodic song, intricate with low trills and warbles.

Range: They reside in the southwestern U.S. and Mexico, from southern Colorado to Mexico, southern Texas to southwestern Arizona. Sometimes seen in southeast California, as well as slightly north and south of this range.

Habitat: Frequents tropical lowlands, semi-desert, and desert regions. The nest is built by both sexes 2–8 feet above ground in a shrub, cactus, or tree. The nest is softened with twigs and grass. Couples often reuse the nest through the year.

Eggs: They lay 1–5 pale blue-green eggs with pale brown spots; 2 broods per year. The female primarily incubates, swapping with the male during the day; incubation lasts from 12–15 days. The female broods the fledglings shading them from the sun. The young leave the nest 11–18 days after hatching. Both parents feed the young.

Food: Using their bills, they dig in the ground for insects and also eat spiders, small reptiles, snails, fruits, seeds, and berries.

Habits: Couples stay paired throughout the year. They sometimes build a roosting platform in the winter that becomes the nest in the spring.

European Starling
Sturnus vulgaris

Ron Austing

These Eurasian songbirds were introduced into New York City in the late nineteenth century, and in the past hundred years they've become established in many parts of North America. These aggressive generalists seem perfectly adapted to settle a new world and have been most effective in doing so. They greatly benefit farmers by eating destructive insects in large numbers.

You can attract European Starlings by providing water and filling feeders with suet, suet mixes, or table scraps. They will aggressively seek and defend nesting sites and will accept nesting boxes with holes at least one and one-half inches in diameter.

Identification Flashes and Distinguishing Features:

Their short tails and squatty appearance make it easy to distinguish European Starlings from other black birds. Also, they walk instead of hopping.

Size: 8.5 inches (22 centimeters)

Color: During breeding season both males and females have shiny oily greenish-purple plumage and yellow bills. The rest of the year they have dark bills and blacker plumage with white spots and crescent-shaped markings. Juveniles have dark bills and ashy gray-brown plumage with white throats.

Voice: They sing cascades of squeaky chatter, twitters, chirps, and *pheeweWWe* ("wolf whistle") sounds. They imitate the calls and songs of pewees, bobwhites, killdeers, and phoebes.

Range: Permanent residents of the entire U.S., southern Canada, and in the coastal area around Anchorage, Alaska.

Habitat: These secondary-cavity nesters look for natural cavities, woodpecker holes (which they aggressively commandeer), holes in buildings, pipes, and nesting boxes with entrance holes at least 1½ inches in diameter. They build loosely constructed nesting cups from grass, straw, paper, leaves, weeds, debris, and cloth. They line their nests with finer grasses, hair, and feathers.

Eggs: Females lay 4–8 pale-blue or greenish-white eggs that are usually unmarked; 2–3 broods per breeding season. Both parents incubate the eggs; incubation takes 12–14 days. Fledglings leave the nest about 21 days after hatching.

Food: They forage on the ground for a variety of insects and other invertebrates (clover weevil, cutworms, Japanese beetles, grasshoppers, snails, spiders, and earthworms). They also eat fruit and berries as well as weed seeds and grain. They occasionally forage in garbage and will come to feeders for small grains, suet, suet mixes, and bread.

Habits: Often flutter their wings rapidly during singing displays. They aggressively compete for nesting sites. Mixed-species flocks of starlings, blackbirds, and robins may number into the hundreds of thousands or even millions.

Cedar Waxwing

Bombycilla cedrorum

Ron Austing

Flocks of these sleek brown-crested birds with their black masks appear to fill fall dogwoods, early spring holly trees, or spring blossoming apple trees. In a few hours or days, they may be gone just as quickly as they arrived, following their erratic path to the next bounty of fruit. They are named for the drop-shaped red tip that forms on the secondary wing feathers (and sometimes tails) of adults; this tip resembles the red wax that was once used to seal letters.

You can attract Cedar Waxwings by including plants that bear small fruit or berries in your naturescape. You can also attract them by providing water.

Identification Flashes and Distinguishing Features:

Look for the distinctive yellow-tipped tails on these crested grayish birds.

Size: 7 inches (18 centimeters)

Color: The colors on these birds blend into one another like wet watercolor. Both sexes have brown crests; pale-brownish upper breasts, heads, and backs; pale yellow lower breasts and bellies; and blue-grayish wings, rumps, and upper tails. They have white undertail coverts; the outer halves of their tails are dark with a bright yellow terminal band. Most adults have red tips on their secondary wing feathers. They have black masks that extend from their foreheads through their lores to behind their eyes.

Voice: They emit high-pitched trilled *hziss, hzisss, hzisss* whistles.

Range: Permanent residents of the northern U.S. from the northern Atlantic Coast west to the northern Pacific Coast of Oregon and Washington. They summer north into Canada and winter in the southern U.S.

Habitat: They nest in open stands of scattered trees or in shrubs and place their nesting cups in forks or on horizontal limbs. Both parents carry grasses, twigs, weeds, mosses, string, lichens, and plant fibers to the nesting site, where the female weaves them into a cup and lines it with rootlets, fine grasses, and hair.

Eggs: They lay 2–6 pale-gray to bluish-gray eggs lightly coated with small black dots; 1–2 broods per breeding season. The female incubates the eggs; incubation takes 12–16 days. Fledglings leave the nest 14–18 days after hatching.

Food: In the summer they eat primarily insects taken on the wing flycatcher-fashion. They also eat fruit, berries, sap, and petals. In late summer they may get drunk on fermented fruit.

Habits: Nomadic wandering flocks search for new food sources, and they occasionally nest in loosely formed colonies. During courting they pass flower petals back and forth, and when feeding, several birds may perch side by side and pass a berry or cherry back and forth until one of them eats it.

Yellow Warbler

Dendroica petechia

The Yellow Warbler has the widest range of any other North American warbler; establishing summer residency from Canada to Mexico, and from the Atlantic to the Pacific Coast. It has an interesting response to brood parasitism by Brown-headed Cowbirds. When a cowbird lays eggs in this warbler's nest, the female covers all of the eggs up, including her own. Then she will often lay new eggs on top. Several layers have been found in a single nest.

Ron Austing

Identification Flashes and Distinguishing Features:

Look for the plump yellow body and the bright red streakings on the male's underparts which distinguish it from the female and other warblers.

Size: 5 inches (13 centimeters)

Color: The male is bright yellow overall with reddish streakings on the underparts. The eyes are dark. The female has a yellowish olive back, wings, and tail; there are yellow wing bars and edging.

Voice: Makes a fast warbling *sweet-sweet, I'm so sweet* or *tseet-tseet-tseet-titi-deet*.

Range: They spend the summer breeding season throughout the northern two-thirds of the U.S. and into Canada southward along the New Mexico/Arizona border into Mexico. They winter in Mexico.

Habitat: Frequents the forest edge, thickets, and grasslands with scattered trees. The nest is built primarily by the female in the fork of a tree or bush 6–14 feet, and up to 60 feet, high. It is firmly constructed of plant material, moss, and animal hair; surrounded with spider's silk and cocoon material; and softened with delicate materials.

Eggs: Lays 3–6 grayish, green, or bluish white eggs marked with grays, olives, and browns, circled at the large end; 1–2 broods per year. The female incubates; incubation takes 11–12 days. The young are brooded by the female. The fledglings leave the nest 9–12 days after hatching. Both parents feed the young.

Food: Forages in bushes, shrubs, or trees for insects, larvae, and some fruit.

Habits: These birds are active and travel solitary or in pairs. They are vulnerable to habitat loss, mostly in areas near water.

Yellow-rumped (Myrtle/Audubon's) Warbler

Dendroica coronata

These conspicuous birds draw attention to themselves with loud *check* calls and their habit of darting out of branches to hawk passing insects. Their bright-yellow rump patches (they are often called "butter butts") will help you identify them. Their wing tips often conceal their rump patches when the birds are perched, but the yellow flashes will be highly visible in flight. You can attract them by including berry-producing plants in your naturescape, providing water, and offering suet.

Myrtle

Ron Austing

Identification Flashes and Distinguishing Features:

Their small size, streaked underparts, and bright-yellow rump patches help distinguish Yellow-rumped Warblers.

Size: 5.5 inches (14 centimeters)

Color: Plumage varies geographically; breeding males have gray-black upperparts and face, black chest, white streaks on their sides and flanks, white chin and throat (Myrtle), or yellow chin and throat (Audubon's); white wing bars, broken eye ring, narrow eye stripe (Myrtle), and yellow patches on the sides of their chest, crown, and rump. Breeding females look like washed-out males. In winter both sexes have brown upperparts with yellow rump patches and streaked-brown underparts.

Voice: Most often makes loud *check!* sounds. Their spring migration song is a musical trill that is weaker in the middle and often sung in 2 parts, with the second part at a higher pitch.

Range: Permanent residents of eastern Arizona, southwestern New Mexico, and southeastern Utah; and the northern Pacific Coast. Winters in a line from Maryland west and gradually south to southern California southward into Mexico. Summers in Maine across to northern Minnesota; and in the West throughout most of Canada to Nevada, western South Dakota to the Pacific Coast.

Habitat: A variety of temperate vegetation and habitats. They nest in conifer trees at high elevations and build nesting cups on horizontal branches, often near the trunk, using twigs, bark strips, plant down, and fibers. They line nests with finer grasses and hair and cover the eggs with lots of feathers when the female leaves the nest.

Eggs: Lays 3–5 white or creamy-white eggs spotted and blotched with browns at the large end, often in a wreath design; 2 broods per season. The female incubates the eggs for 12–13 days. Fledglings leave the nest 10–12 days after hatching.

Food: In summer they eat small insects and spiders gleaned from trees, by flycatching, and by foraging on the ground. In winter they eat primarily berries and small seeds. They will come to feeders for suet, peanut butter-suet mixes, and doughnuts.

Habits: They are the most common wintering warblers over most of the southern U.S. and are often seen in conspicuous flocks.

Prothonotary Warbler

Protonotaria citrea

The Prothonotary Warbler spends the summer breeding season in the wetland regions of the East, earning its previous name of Golden Swamp Warbler. Like Lucy's Warbler in the West, this warbler builds its home in the hollows of trees. These birds are curious and will approach birders who squeak and pish.

The Prothonotary Warbler will nest in nest boxes.

Ron Austing

Identification Flashes and Distinguishing Features:

Look for the golden yellow head, neck, and underparts; large dark eyes; blue-gray wings; and long black bill.

Size: 5.25 inches (13 centimeters)

Color: The male's head, neck, and underparts are golden yellow. The back is olive-green and wings are blue-gray. The tail is blue-gray with large white patches, and the undertail coverts are white. The female has a bright yellow throat, face, and breast. The crown and nape are greenish yellow, and the back is greenish. The wings, rump, uppertail coverts, and tail are gray. There are white spots on the inner web of tail feathers, and the belly and undertail coverts are white.

Voice: Makes a loud, ringing, recurring *zweet*, somewhat up-slurred as *sweet, sweet, sweet, sweet*. The call is a noisy *chip-chip*.

Range: Spends summer breeding season in the East from southern Wisconsin and Michigan south to the Gulf Coast, the East Coast westward to central Oklahoma.

Habitat: Prefers wetland areas—swamps, marshes, and woodland areas near streams and wetlands. The male builds several nests and the female picks one and completes it. The nest is built 5–10 feet above ground, near water, in a hollow or cavity of a tree, a post, or a nest box. The nest is built with grass, moss, leaves, and sticks; it is softened with feathers and rootlets.

Eggs: They lay 4–6 pinkish or cream eggs with brown and gray spots; 2 broods per year in the South. The female incubates the eggs; incubation takes 12–14 days. The female broods the young. Both parents feed the young. The fledglings leave the nest after 11 days.

Food: Eats insects, spiders, larvae, seeds, crustaceans, and snails.

Habits: Lives as solitary individuals or in pairs. Uses bill when foraging for food, digging into crevices, and picking food from floating logs and from the water.

Spotted Towhee

Pipilo maculatus

Once categorized as a western race of the Rufous-sided Towhee, the Spotted Towhee has varying amounts of white spotting among its different geographic populations. It is fairly common in chaparral, brushy thickets, and along forest edges.

You can attract this towhee to your feeder with a mixture of oats, suet, and flax seeds.

Ron Austing

Identification Flashes and Distinguishing Features:

Look for the white spotting on the upperparts, wings, and tail, which is distinguished geographically. The undersides of the tail flash white when in flight.

Size: 7–7.5 inches (18–19 centimeters)

Color: The head and chest of the male is blackish and the upperparts are blackish olive. The belly and median underparts are white. The sides, flanks, and undertail coverts are cinnamon-rufous. The wings have two white wing bars and white spots. The tail is black with white tips on the underside of the outer tail feathers. The eyes are red. The female has a dark brown head, neck, breast, and upperparts. There are white spots on the back. The wings are dark brown with two white wing bars and white spots. The tail is dark brown with white tips on the underside.

Voice: Birds from interior populations sing a song similar to Bewick's Wren with 2 *chip* notes followed by a trill. Coastal birds produce a fast or slow trilling. Their call is a mewing *guee*.

Range: Permanent residents of the West from Washington south and across to the western tip of Texas. They spend summer from Idaho east to the mid-Dakotas and southward. They winter from southwestern Iowa south through eastern Texas.

Habitat: Prefers shrubs, brushy thickets, and the edges of forest land. The female builds the nest on sheltered ground or in a low tree or shrub. The nest is built of twigs, leaves, rootlets, grass, and bark; it is softened with grasses.

Eggs: They lay 2–6 gray-brown or creamy white eggs; 2 broods per year. The female incubates; incubation takes 12–14 days. The young are brooded by the female. The fledglings leave the nest after 9–11 days. They are fed by both parents.

Food: Insects and larvae, spiders, seeds, and fruit; occasionally small lizards or snakes. They will eat from a feeder with a mixture of suet and small seeds.

Habits: Travels solitary or in pairs and stays in small family groups after nesting season. If the female is surprised on the nest, she will scurry away like a rodent as a distraction.

Eastern (Rufous-sided) Towhee

Pipilo erythrophthalmus

They are often called Ground Robins because of their robin-like appearance, or Cheewinks because of their call notes. They frequent thickets and forage on the ground, making lots of noise as they rake over dried leaves with a "double-scratch" (kicking backward with both feet at the same time).

You can attract Eastern Towhees to your backyard by providing water and offering small seeds either on the ground or on platform feeders low to the ground.

Fred J. Alsop III

Identification Flashes and Distinguishing Features:

Look for the black upperparts and rufous sides of male Eastern Towhees and the brown upperparts and rufous sides of the females.

Size: 7–7.5 inches (18-19 centimeters)

Color: Males have black upperparts with large white corner tail patches; rufous sides, flanks, and undertail coverts; and white bellies. Females have brown instead of black plumage. Except for Florida races, both males and females have red eyes.

Voice: They make sharp, loud *cheewink* or *towhee* sounds. Male song resembles *drink-your-tea-ee-ee-ee-ee* with much variation and often omitting first or last notes.

Range: Permanent residents from Ohio to Gulf Coast, Atlantic Coast to southeastern Kansas, and northeastern Oklahoma. Summers north of this range to Canada; winters southwest of permanent range from central Oklahoma to south central Texas coast.

Habitat: Frequents barrens, open brushy fields, thickets, roadside edges, parks, residential areas with ornamental plantings, hedgerows, and young clearcuts. Females build bulky nesting cups on or near the ground. They make their nests from bark, grasses, weeds, twigs, leaves, and string, and line them with finer grasses, hair, pine needles, and rootlets.

Eggs: Lays 2–6 creamy-white to pale-gray eggs with reddish-brown dots or spots; 2–3 broods per breeding season. The female incubates the eggs; incubation takes 12–13 days. Fledglings leave the nest 10–12 days after hatching.

Food: Forages on the ground and eats spiders, millipedes, snails, earthworms, lizards, salamanders, and small snakes. They also eat fruit, berries, and seeds of weeds and grasses. They will come to feeders for black oil sunflower seeds or millet.

Habits: Cowbirds frequently parasitize towhees by laying eggs in their nests so the towhees will raise the cowbird young. During breeding season males often sing from high, exposed perches. They live alone, either singly or in pairs.

Canyon Towhee

Pipilo fuscus

The Canyon Towhee was once paired with the California Towhee as one species named the Brown Towhee. Now considered separate, the Canyon Towhee is more pale with a reddish crown that resembles a cap, and a dark spot on the center of its chest. This towhee is not as aggressive as the California Towhee. They are attracted to feeders with seeds.

Tom Vezo

Identification Flashes and Distinguishing Features:

Look for the overall gray appearance with the reddish cap and dark central chest spot.

Size: 8 inches (20 centimeters)

Color: Sexes are similar: gray overall with a reddish cap, buff throat and upper breast, and a necklace of light dusky streaks. They have a whitish patch on the belly and cinnamon undertail coverts. There is a dark central chest spot. Juveniles have streaked underparts, two cinnamon wing bars, and darker streaked upperparts.

Voice: Produces 1–2 introductory chips, then quickened chips, *chwee, chwee, chilly, chilly, chilly*. The call is a garbled *chedep*, or *chee-yep*, and a light *ssip*.

Range: They are found from southwestern Texas across New Mexico, Colorado, Arizona, and south into Mexico.

Habitat: Frequents canyon slopes with brush, juniper, or piñon. The nest is built primarily by the female, usually 3–12 feet above the ground. It is built in the thick part of the tree with stems, grass, and sticks; it is softened with leaves, bark chips, and animal hair.

Eggs: Females lay 2–6 light green or blue eggs with flecks and splotches of brown and black; 2–3 broods per year. The female incubates the eggs; incubation takes 11 days. The female broods the young. The fledglings leave the nest 8–9 days after hatching. Both parents feed the young.

Food: Eats grains, insects, and seeds foraged on the ground. They double scratch in soil and leaf litter.

Habits: A pair mates for life. They are often in small groups after breeding season. They hop rather than walk on the ground.

California Towhee

Pipilo crissalis

The California Towhee and the Canyon Towhee together were previously called the Brown Towhee. The California Towhee is darker brown and lacks the dark central breast spot; they hop instead of walking. As the name implies, they are native to California south to Baja California. They will visit feeders with seeds.

Tom Vezo

Identification Flashes and Distinguishing Features:

Look for the chestnut brown crown, cinnamon undertail coverts, and brownish gray body.

Size: 9 inches (23 centimeters)

Color: They are brownish gray overall with a chestnut brown crown, buff lores, a buff throat with conspicuous border of dark spots, and cinnamon undertail coverts.

Voice: The call is a sharp metallic *chink* or a thin high-pitched *ssee*. They produce a rising series of metallic *chink* notes, slurring towards the end.

Range: Residents of the California coast north to southwestern Oregon and south to Baja California; in some locations they have moved out of coastal areas due to urban development.

Habitat: Prefers dry areas of shrubs, thickets, and scrub vegetation. The nest, built mostly by the female, is found 4–12 feet above ground. Built in thick foliage with bark pieces, sticks, weeds, and grass; it is lined with animal hair, bark chips, and leaves.

Eggs: Female lays 2–6 light blue or greenish eggs with brown and black markings; 2–3 broods per year. The female incubates; incubation takes 11 days. The female broods the young; fledglings leave the nest after 8 days, but are tended for several weeks after by both parents.

Food: East grains, seeds, and insects, and will come to a feeder for seeds. They will forage in the open, but prefer to forage near cover, on the ground under foliage, outdoor buildings, and fences.

Habits: Defending their territory, they will actively pursue intruders. They mate for life. The male will watch over the female while she eats. A mated pair will forage separately and then repeatedly performs a display of sideways posturing and bowing. If the mate does not respond properly to the ritual, it is attacked as if a territorial intruder.

American Tree Sparrow

Spizella arborea

The American Tree Sparrow spends winter primarily in the U.S. after nesting farther north in the tundra region from Newfoundland to Alaska. They are common

throughout the northern two-thirds of the U.S. from eastern Washington State to the northern tip of Texas to Pennsylvania and up the northeastern coast. They travel in flocks as large as thirty-five to forty birds.

A birdfeeder with a wild birdseed mixture should attract these birds to your backyard.

Ron Austing

Identification Flashes and Distinguishing Features:

Look for the rufous crown, gray head and nape, rufous stripe behind the eye, and single, dark, central breast spot.

Size: 6.25 inches (16 centimeters)

Color: Both male and female have black and rufous streaking on the scapulars and back with a gray chin, throat, breast, and underparts. There is a dark central spot on the breast. The tail is notched. The head and nape are gray and the crown is rufous. There are rufous patches on the breast, sides, and flanks. The bill is two-toned: black above and yellow below. The juvenile has more streaking on the head, breast, and sides; the upperparts are pale.

Voice: Males sing during breeding season and to establish territory. The call is *tweedle-eet, tweedle-eet.* The song is composed of several clear notes followed by a trilled melody with many variations.

Range: Winters throughout a large portion of the northern two-thirds of the U.S., and nests in the northern tundra region from Newfoundland to Alaska. The males will typically winter farther north than females and juveniles.

Habitat: Frequents small coniferous and conifer-deciduous groves, open brush and weedy field areas, and marshes. They nest 1–5 feet above ground on clumps of grass, occasionally in shrubbery or trees. The nest is built by the female with sticks, bark, grass, and moss; the nest is lined with feathers, hair, and fur.

Eggs: Females lay 3–7 light blue or greenish white eggs with brown markings; 1 brood per breeding season. Incubation takes 12–13 days; the female incubates. Fledglings leave the nest after 8–10 days.

Food: Mostly seeds, but feeds on insects, caterpillars, berries, and catkins of willow in the summer. They forage by scratching on the ground, in shrubbery or trees, and in the snow.

Habits: Lives in pairs during breeding season and in flocks during the winter.

Chipping Sparrow
Spizella passerina

Chipping Sparrows rank among the smallest and most common backyard sparrows. They require short, sparse grass for foraging.

You can attract Chipping Sparrows to your backyard by including lawn areas as well as dense shrubbery in your naturescape, providing water, and filling feeders with millet and other small seeds.

Ron Austing

Identification Flashes and Distinguishing Features:

Look for their chestnut crowns, unmarked underparts, white stripes over their eyes, and black lines "through" their eyes.

Size: 5.5 inches (14 centimeters)

Color: Adults have streaked brown upperparts, white throats, white stripes over their eyes, black lines "through" their eyes, gray faces, grayish unstreaked underparts, dark bills, and whitish wing bars. During breeding season, adults have chestnut caps. Juveniles have streaked crowns and underparts.

Voice: They make one of the easiest songs to learn: a series of *chip-chip-chip-chip-chip-chip-chip* notes all on the same pitch, like a small machine gun.

Range: Permanent residents from Maryland to southeast Mississippi, and a region encompassing the borders of Arkansas, Louisiana, Texas, and Oklahoma. They winter from the South Carolina coast south into Florida, from eastern Mississippi into southern Louisiana west through Texas, extreme southern New Mexico, southwest Arizona, and the southwestern tip of California. They summer throughout the northern three-quarters of the U.S., most of Canada, and eastern Alaska.

Habitat: Frequents open grassy woodlands, pine woodlands, parks, orchards, gardens, farmlands, suburbs, and Christmas tree farms. Males help the females build nests in conifer and other trees, shrubs, and vines. Makes well-woven nesting cups from dead grasses, rootlets, and weed stems and lines them with finer grasses and hairs from horses, dogs, cattle, and people.

Eggs: Lays 2–5 pale-blue eggs with dark brown, black, gray, and blue splotches circling the larger end; 2 broods per breeding season. The female incubates the eggs, and the male feeds her while she is on the nest; incubation takes 11–14 days. Fledglings leave nest 8–12 days after hatching.

Food: Small insects and small seeds; they will come to feeders for millet and other small grains.

Habits: They are tame and approachable and will learn to accept food from your hand. After the nesting season, pairs and young birds join flocks of other chippys or mixed species flocks.

Field Sparrow
Spizella pusilla

Ron Austing

These small, slender, long-tailed birds are often seen in old fields and thickets. Their song can be heard in rural areas during the day and on moonlit summer nights. Their populations seem to be decreasing over much of their range, perhaps due to changes in their habitat, particularly the turning under of weedy fields in the winter and the clearing of brushy fencerows.

You can attract Field Sparrows to your backyard by providing water and filling feeders with millet and other small seeds.

Identification Flashes and Distinguishing Features:

Look for unmarked underparts, white eye rings, pink bills.

Size: 5.75 inches (15 centimeters)

Color: Brownish, dark-streaked upperparts; unstreaked grayish-buff underparts; gray faces with brown stripes behind their eyes; white eye rings and wing bars; and pink bills.

Voice: They sing a series of clear, plaintive whistles that starts slow and evenly spaced but accelerates until it fades, like a ball bouncing faster and faster until it stops.

Range: Permanent residents from Ohio to the Gulf Coast (excluding Florida peninsula) and from Atlantic Coast to north central Texas. Summers north of this range from southern Maine through central Minnesota to northeastern Montana southward. Winters in Florida, southern Louisiana into central and southern Texas.

Habitat: Frequents old fields and thickets, brier patches, young pine plantations, old clearcuts, clearings, and brushy pastures. Sometimes nest on or near the ground; other times they build elevated nests in blackberry tangles, small conifers, bushes, weed patches, and saplings. Males help females make open nesting cups from dead grasses, weed stems, and leaves; they line their nests with finer grasses, rootlets, and hair, especially horsehair.

Eggs: Lays 2–6 creamy-white, bluish-white, or greenish-white eggs with brown, gray, and purple blotches around the larger end; 2–3 broods per breeding season. The female incubates the eggs; incubation takes 10–17 days. Fledgings leave the nest 7–8 days after hatching.

Food: In summer they eat insects, usually taken from ground. In fall and winter they eat small seeds (grass and weed seeds). They will come to feeders for millet and other small seeds.

Habits: They are persistent singers during the breeding season, and they sing from weed tops, short trees, or other low perches. They do not frequent residential areas.

Lark Bunting
Calamospiza melanocorys

The state bird of Colorado, groups of a hundred plus of these birds gather in the spring and fly in circular formations that appear as a rolling wheel of birds. When traveling across the prairie, the rear birds fly over the front birds and settle into vegetation. The Lark Bunting will occasionally eat from feeders with small grains and seeds.

Brian E. Small

Identification Flashes and Distinguishing Features:

Look for the black or slate-gray body with the large white wing patches and the bluish gray bill.

Size: 7 inches (18 centimeters)

Color: The male is black or slate-gray overall with large white wing patches and a bluish gray bill; tail is short with white tips on all but the central tail feathers. The female has streaked gray-brown upperparts, an un-streaked belly, bluish gray bill and white wing patches with a bit of buff; underparts are white with dusky streaking. The male and female have similar plumage in winter, with the males showing more black primaries.

Voice: Produces a flutelike warbling of whistles and trills. The call is *hoo-ee*. They sing in groups.

Range: Summers in the West within a narrow strip from southern Saskatchewan south to the northern tip of Texas, central Kansas to central Colorado. They sometimes summer slightly outside this range to the east and west. They winter farther south into central, south and western Texas west through southern New Mexico and Arizona; south into Mexico.

Habitat: Prefers open areas—grasslands, scrublands, and grasslands with scattered trees. The female builds the nest in a grassy depression with grass and rootlets. The nest is softened with hair and plant down.

Eggs: They lay 3–7 pale blue or greenish blue eggs, sometimes spotted reddish brown; 2 broods per year. The female incubates, though the male sometimes helps; incubation takes 11–12 days. The female broods the young. The fledglings leave the nest 8–9 days after hatching. Both parents feed the young.

Food: Eats insects, caterpillars, and seeds. They will eat from feeders with small grains and seeds.

Habits: Travels in pairs or in flocks. Establishing territory, the male will fly 20–30 feet up, flashing the white wing patches, sing, then descend with jerks to the ground. Several males will often participate in display fights.

Fox Sparrow
Passerella iliaca

Fred J. Alsop III

These large sparrows get their name from their rusty upperparts and "foxy-red" tails. They frequent woodlands and thickets, especially near water. They forage on the ground and usually visit feeders only when snow covers the ground. Many people think they are the best singers in the sparrow family.

You can attract Fox Sparrows to your backyard by providing water and offering black oil sunflower seeds, bread crumbs, or millet and other small grains either on the ground or on platform feeders close to the ground.

Identification Flashes and Distinguishing Features:

Look for large sparrows with gray heads, heavily streaked underparts, and rufous-red tails.

Size: 6.75–7.5 inches (17–19 centimeters)

Color: Grayish head and back, rufous-red upperparts and tail; whitish to pale-gray underparts with rich rufous streaking that often forms a central stickpin. They show great geographical variation in both color and size.

Voice: They make clear, flutelike notes that rise and fall in pitch.

Range: Winter residents from southern Illinois to the Gulf Coast, the Atlantic Coast through central Texas, and through southern sections of New Mexico and Arizona. Also winters on the Pacific Coast. Summers west of Pacific Coast to central Wyoming, central Colorado north through Canada and into Alaska.

Habitat: Frequents dense woodland thickets and forests. Males help the females build open-cup nests either on the ground or close to the ground in small bushes, conifers, or willows. They make their nests from small twigs, bark strips, grasses, and weed stems and line them with fine grasses, rootlets, feathers, and hair (cattle, horse, moose, and caribou).

Eggs: They lay 2–5 pale-green or blue eggs that may have brown spots; 2 broods per year. The female incubates the eggs for 12–14 days. Fledglings leave nest 9–11 days after hatching.

Food: Primarily seeds, berries, and fruit. Takes insects and other invertebrates on the ground and occasionally forages on the ground under feeders filled with black oil sunflower seeds, bread crumbs, or millet or other small grains.

Habits: When foraging on the ground, they dig through leaves, humus, and snow with a strong towhee-style "double-scratch" (pushing both feet backward at same time). They often forage in shadows cast by trees, which camouflages them. They sing in spring in their southern wintering range prior to migrating northward. They are somewhat shy and travel in flocks.

Song Sparrow
Melospiza melodia

Ron Austing

These familiar sparrows nest in hedges and shrubs and forage on the ground beneath feeders. Sometimes called "little brown birds," they are among the least mysterious bird species in North America, thanks to the classic studies of housewife and ornithologist Margaret Morse Nice, who followed the lives of hundreds of individual Song Sparrows around her Ohio home.

You can attract them by including shrubbery in your naturescape, providing water, and offering millet and other small grains on the ground or on platform feeders.

Identification Flashes and Distinguishing Features:

Look for sparrows with heavily streaked underparts and a large central breast spot.

Size: 5.75–7.5 inches (14–19 centimeters)

Color: Brown upperparts, heavily spotted, streaked whitish underparts, white throat and belly, gray face with thin dark lines "through" eyes, brown malar marks, dark central spot on breast, thin central crown stripes, and long rounded tail. Shows geographical variation in both color and size.

Voice: They make quizzical *what?* calls. Their song typically begins with 2-3 clear whistled notes followed by a buzzy trill that sounds like *maids, maids, maids put on your tea kettle-kettle-kettle,* with much variation.

Range: Permanent residents from New Hampshire to Virginia westward; range narrows through Nebraska and southern South Dakota, then widens through central Montana to Washington, and south through Colorado, eastern Arizona and southern California. Winters throughout southern U.S. south of this range excluding southern tips of Florida and Texas. Summers north of this range into Canada.

Habitat: Frequents woodland edges, swamps, roadsides, brushy overgrown fields, cities, and suburbs. Female usually builds nest on ground, well-hidden in vegetation or close to ground in low shrubs, thickets, or cattails. Makes nest with grasses, leaves, and bark; lines it with finer grasses, rootlets, and hair.

Eggs: They lay 2–6 pale greenish-white eggs that are almost completely covered with brown, reddish-brown, and gray spots, dots, and blotches; 2–3 broods per breeding season. The female incubates the eggs; incubation takes 12–14 days. Fledglings leave the nest 9–16 days after hatching.

Food: Primarily seeds, especially weed seeds, but more than half of summer diet is insects and other invertebrates (caterpillars, spiders, beetles, wasps, army ants, and grasshoppers). Also eats grasses, small fruit, and berries. Forages on ground under feeders for millet and other small grains.

Habits: Often pump their tails up and down in flight. They sing from elevated perches year-round.

White-throated Sparrow
Zonotrichia albicollis

These plain-breasted, white-throated sparrows have a yellow spot between their eyes and bills. The similar White-crowned Sparrow lacks yellow lores and dark bill.

You can attract White-throated Sparrows by including shrubbery and brush piles in your backyard, providing water, and offering millet and other small grains either on the ground or on platform feeders close to the ground.

Ron Austing

Identification Flashes and Distinguishing Features:

Look for their dark-and-light striped crowns, yellow lores, and unstreaked breasts.

Size: 6.25–7.5 inches (16–19 centimeters)

Color: Brown upperparts with bold dark to blackish streaking, gray face and breast, paler gray to white belly and undertail coverts, white throat, white wing bars, and yellow lores. They can have either black heads with white stripes or dark-brown heads with tan to gray stripes.

Voice: They make sharp chink or high-pitched *seeet* notes. They make a thin 2-note whistle followed by 3 sets of triple notes that sounds like *Poor Sam Peabody, Peabody, Peabody.*

Range: Permanent residents in New Hampshire west through New York into northern Pennsylvania. Winters in southern U.S. south of this range from Atlantic Coast to eastern Kansas gradually southwest crossing northern Texas into southern New Mexico and Arizona. Summers in northern section of states bordering Canada in the East, from Maine to Minnesota, and most of Canada.

Habitat: Frequents woodland edges, brushy fields, brush piles, and shrubby areas. Females build nesting cups on the ground or in low dense shrubs; nests are concealed by vegetation, roots of stump, or rootwad. Makes nest from grass stems, weeds, conifer needles, mosses, bark fibers, and twigs, and lines with rootlets, fine grasses, and hair.

Eggs: Lays 3–6 creamy-white, bluish, or greenish eggs heavily marked with spots, dots, and blotches of browns, grays, and sometimes black; 1–2 broods per year. Female incubates eggs 11–14 days. Fledglings leave nest 7–12 days after hatching.

Food: Eats primarily small seeds, buds, and a variety of fruit and berries. In spring may feed on new buds high in trees. Also feeds on insects and other invertebrates (crickets, spiders, and beetles). They will come to feeders for black oil sunflower seeds and small grains.

Habits: Flocks live in thickets during the winter. If you make "squeaking" and "pishing" noises on the back of your hand, they (along with chickadees and titmice) will come quickly to investigate.

White-crowned Sparrow

Zonotrichia leucophrys

They look very similar to White-throated Sparrows but have puffy black-and-white striped crowns and pink bills. They are often found near abandoned farmsteads, feedlots, and hoglots on their wintering grounds. You can attract White-crowned Sparrows to your backyard by including shrubbery and brush piles in your naturescape, providing water, and offering black oil sunflower seeds, cracked corn, and small grains either on the ground or on platform feeders near the ground.

Ron Austing

Identification Flashes and Distinguishing Features:

Look for sparrows with unmarked breasts, black-and-white striped crowns, and pink bills.

Size: 6.5–7.5 inches (17–19 centimeters)

Color: Brownish upperparts with dark streaking; gray face, neck, and breast that blends to buffy wash on sides and flanks; white throat, belly, undertail coverts, and wing bars; pink bill; bold black-and-white striped crown; black lines "through" their eyes; and white lines over their eyes. Juveniles have streaked underparts; immatures look like adults but have tan-and-brown striped heads.

Voice: They sing clear, plaintive *more wet wetter chee zee* whistles.

Range: Permanent residents along Pacific Coast from central California northward; and throughout Utah into north and northeastern Nevada, and western Colorado. Winters in most of southern U.S. excluding southern Atlantic Coast and Florida peninsula. Summers in the Northwest, and most of western and northern Canada and Alaska.

Habitat: Frequents open country, and abandoned farmsteads. Females build bulky nesting cups on the ground or close to the ground in shrubs or small trees. Makes nest from grasses, mosses, and bark; lines with finer grasses, rootlets, feathers, and hair.

Eggs: Lays 2–6 pale-blue to green eggs heavily spotted with brown, purple, and black; 2–4 broods per breeding season. The female incubates the eggs; incubation takes 11–14 days. Fledglings leave the nest about 7–12 days after hatching.

Food: Primarily weed seeds, grass seeds, willow catkins, and moss capsules. In summer they feed on insects (ants, mosquitoes, beetles, caterpillars, and spiders). Will come to feeders for black oil sunflower seeds, small grains, and cracked corn.

Habits: When foraging on the ground, they dig through leaves, humus, and snow with a strong towhee-style "double-scratch" (pushing both feet backward at same time). Winters in flocks, often in thickets and brushy areas. Sings in early spring and during migration. Make "squeaking" and "pishing" noises on the back of your hand, and they (along with chickadees and titmice) will come quickly to investigate.

Slate-colored

Dark-eyed Junco

Junco hyemalis

The Dark-eyed Junco is a geographically variable species with five races: Slate-colored, Gray-headed, Pink-sided, White-winged, and Oregon. The five differ in color but display comparable habits. You can attract Dark-eyed Juncos to your backyard by including shrubbery and brush piles in your naturescape, providing water, and offering black oil sunflower seeds, millet, and other small seeds either on the ground or on platform feeders near the ground.

Gray-headed

Pink-sided   White-winged

Tom Vezo (left)   *Tom Vezo* (right)

Identification Flashes and Distinguishing Features:

Although variable, most races have gray or brown head and breast that sharply contrasts with a white belly; white outer tail feathers show in flight.

Size: 5.75–6.5 inches (14–17 centimeters)

Color: Slate-colored: dark gray hood, gray upperparts sometimes with brown at center of back; white belly and undertail coverts; light pinkish bill; female is paler gray, sometimes with brownish wash. Oregon: blackish hood, rufous-brown to buffy brown back and sides; females are similar but less brightly colored. Pink-sided: blue-gray hood, black lores, bright pinkish cinnamon sides. White-winged: pale gray above, often with two, thin white wing bars, more white on tail. Gray-headed: pale gray hood and underparts with rufous back. All juveniles are more streaked on their upperparts and underparts.

Voice: They make smacking, sucking *tack, tack, tack* notes and sing one-pitch, jingling, bell-like trills.

Range: Slate-colored: winters in eastern North America, not often seen in the West. Oregon: winters in the West, rare in the East. Pink-sided: breeds in the Rockies. White-winged: breeds in Black Hills area. Gray-headed: resident in southern Rockies.

Habitat: Frequents old brushy-weedy fields, thickets, cedar stands, woodland edges, roadsides, hedges, parks, gardens, and lawns with shrubbery. Females build nesting cups on the ground, often on slopes, banks, edges of trails or roads, and rocky ledges; nests are concealed by vegetation, rootwads, and fallen logs. Sometimes they build nests in low conifer branches, bushes, or shrubs. They build compact nests from grasses, weed stems, pine needles, mosses, and bark shreds and line them with rootlets, fine grasses, and hair.

Eggs: Lays 3–6 pale bluish-white to gray eggs with heavy spotting and blotches of browns, purples, and grays often concentrated at the larger end; 1–3 broods per breeding season. The female incubates the eggs for 11–13 days. Fledglings leave the nest 9–13 days after hatching.

Food: Primarily seeds (grass, weed, and hemlock), fruit, berries, and small grains. Half of summer diet is insects and other invertebrates. They will come to feeders for black oil sunflower and thistle seeds and wild bird mix.

Habits: They winter in mixed-species flocks. Aggressive males often spread their tails at rivals, displaying their white outer feathers.

Northern Cardinal

Cardinalis cardinalis

Named for the red-robed Roman Catholic dignitaries, Northern Cardinals have been selected as the official bird of seven states. Among the most recognized and popular birds of the eastern United States, they live in a great variety of habitats.

You can attract Northern Cardinals to your backyard by including shrubbery in your naturescape and providing water. They will become regular visitors at feeders filled with sunflower seeds.

Ron Austing

Identification Flashes and Distinguishing Features:

Male cardinals are the only bright-red birds with crests. Female cardinals are the only red-billed birds with crests.

Size: 7.5–9.25 inches (19–24 centimeters)

Color: Males have brilliant red plumage, thick reddish beaks, crests, and black faces. Females have olive-gray upperparts, bronzy golden-buff underparts, and reddish bills, wings, crests, and tails. Juveniles look like "browner" females with dark bills.

Voice: They make sharp *chip* notes and widely varied songs of rich, whistled notes in three common patterns: *whoit, cheer, cheer, cheer; cheer, whoit, whoit, whoit, whoit;* and *cheer, pret-ty, pret-ty, pret-ty.* They sing year-round; the males' song is stronger, but females sing, too.

Range: Permanent residents of the eastern half of the U.S. and Mexico west along the Rio Grande into southwestern New Mexico and southeastern Arizona.

Habitat: Lives in a variety of habitats: shrubbery, open woodlands, thickets, brushy areas, forest edges, parks, forests, and suburban gardens. Females build deep nesting cups in thick shrubs or low in small trees. Makes nest from twigs, vines, leaves, weeds, coarse grasses, bark, paper, and string and lines it with finer grasses, rootlets, and hair.

Eggs: Females lay 3–4 grayish, greenish, or bluish-white eggs heavily blotched and spotted with grays, browns, and purples; 2–4 broods per season; male often takes care of 1 brood while female incubates subsequent clutches of eggs for 12–13 days. Fledglings leave the nest 9–11 days after hatching.

Food: More than 50 kinds of medium to large insects and more than 30 kinds of seeds, fruit, and berries. Also eats waste corn, tree buds, blossoms, and grains. Will come to feeders for sunflower seeds and cracked corn.

Habits: Forage on or near the ground. Males are territorial; when winter flocks break up, they attack their reflections, which they mistake for rival males, in windows, mirrors, and chrome car parts. They are attracted to birdbaths. Lowers red crest at will.

Pyrrhuloxia

Cardinalis sinuatus

The Pyrrhuloxia resides in the Southwest, from the southwestern border of Texas through southern New Mexico and Arizona and on into Mexico. They are highly territorial with both sexes defending their territory until established, after which the male is responsible. The Pyrrhuloxia resembles a gray cardinal.

They will visit feeders and birdbaths.

Ron Austing

Identification Flashes and Distinguishing Features:

Look for the overall gray appearance with red edgings and the red-tipped gray crest. The yellow bill resembles a parrot's bill.

Size: 8.75 inches (22 centimeters)

Color: The male is gray with a red-tipped crest, red face, red mottling from the throat to the belly, and red edging on the wings. The female is similar with less red and a browner gray appearance. Her crest is red-tipped and there is a red ring around the eye. In winter the yellow bill on both sexes will turn grayish yellow.

Voice: Similar to the Northern Cardinal, they make a progression of loud whistles, *chewee, chewee, chewee; wheet, wheet, wheet.* The call is *plik* or *chink.*

Range: They reside from southwestern Texas through southern New Mexico and Arizona southward.

Habitat: Frequents areas of scrub vegetation, semidesert, desert, thickets, and the edge of forests. The female builds the nest 5–15 feet above the ground in a shrub or thicket. The nest is constructed of thorny twigs, weeds, grass, and bark pieces; softened with fine roots and hairs.

Eggs: They lay 3–4 grayish white or greenish white eggs with flecks of brown; 1 brood per year. The female incubates the eggs; incubation takes 14 days. The young are brooded by the female. The fledglings leave the nest 10–11 days after hatching. They are fed by both parents.

Food: They eat flower spikes, fruits, berries, seeds, insects, and larvae. They forage for food in trees, bushes, but more often, hopping on the ground.

Habits: Lives solitary or in pairs during breeding season, but will form flocks and join mixed species flocks in the winter. The male will sing from an exposed perch.

Rose-breasted Grosbeak

Pheucticus ludovicianus

The males of these showy cardinal-size finches sing incessantly, producing a sweet song. Rose-breasted Grosbeaks frequent gardens in northern areas of their range and have earned the nickname "potato-bug birds."

You can attract Rose-breasted Grosbeaks to your backyard by providing water and filling feeders with sunflower seeds.

Ron Austing

Identification Flashes and Distinguishing Features:

Look for the rosy red breast on the black-and-white males and large conical bills and the wing bars on the buffy-tan females.

Size: 7–8.5 inches (18–22 centimeters)

Color: Males have black heads and upperparts; white rumps, corner tail feathers, wing patches, and underparts; red breasts (brownish on 1–2 year-olds) and wing linings; large, thick, light colored bills. Females and juveniles have brownish-black upperparts, white throats, white lines "through" eyes extending back to necks, buffy-white underparts heavily streaked with black, and yellow wing linings.

Voice: Makes sharp *peek* notes and beautiful, clear, sweet robinlike singsong patterns. Males often sing from the nest; females sing softer.

Range: Spends summer breeding season in the Northeast across Canada and from Minnesota to central Missouri, and the northern Atlantic Coast to eastern Nebraska. They also summer south into the Blue Ridge Mountains. They migrate across the Southeast to winter in Mexico.

Habitat: Frequents thickets, moist deciduous woodlands, swamps, orchards, and suburban areas in summer. During migration they can be found anywhere there are broad-leafed trees. Both parents build a poorly constructed nesting cup in shrubs or forks of small trees. Makes nest from weed stems, small twigs, and straw; lines with finer grasses, rootlets, and hair.

Eggs: Lays 3–5 bluish, grayish, or greenish eggs with spots and blotches of brownish red. Both parents incubate the eggs for 13–14 days. Female may begin a second nesting while male cares for the brood. Fledgings leave the nest 9–12 days after hatching.

Food: They eat the seeds and blossoms of elm, hickory, and beech trees as well as insects (potato beetles, locusts, cankerworms, grasshoppers, and moths). They will come to feeders for sunflower seeds.

Habits: Males appear affectionate; courting pairs often touch bills. They frequent feeders in May during spring migration.

Black-headed Grosbeak

Pheucticus melanocephalus

The Black-headed Grosbeak is a summer visitor to the West. The male and female are known to aggressively defend their territory from other grosbeaks. They are recognizable by their lemon-lined wings which flash in flight.

They will visit feeders offering various seeds. They are so tame that they will sometimes take food from your hand.

Ron Austing

Identification Flashes and Distinguishing Features:

Look for the large dark conical bill, the lemon-lined wings, black head, and cinnamon-orange hind collar.

Size: 7–8.5 inches (18–22 centimeters)

Color: The male's head is black and the underparts are cinnamon. There are two white wing bars, black upperparts with brown edging to the feathers, a cinnamon-orange hind collar and postocular stripe, and a cinnamon rump. There are lemon linings on the wings. The female has a brown head and upperparts with dark streaking. The crown has a white median stripe. The throat and underparts are pale cinnamon. There is a lemon wash on the belly, fine brown streaks on the sides and flanks. There are two white wing bars.

Voice: Their song is like a robin's with back-and-forth warbled phrases. It is lower pitched than the Rose-breasted Grosbeak. They make a high squeaky *plik*.

Range: They are summer residents of the West from extreme southwestern Canada to Mexico, and mid-Nebraska westward.

Habitat: Prefers open woodlands, riparian woodlands, and the edge of forests. The female builds the nest 4–25 feet above the ground in the thick part of a tree or shrub. They often nest near water. The nest is made of sticks, weeds, roots, and pine needles; the nest is lined with finer materials.

Eggs: They lay 3–4 light greenish or bluish eggs spotted reddish brown; 1 brood per year. Both sexes incubate; incubation takes 12–14 days. The female broods the young with some help from the male. The fledglings leave the nest after 11–12 days. The young are fed by both parents.

Food: They eat seeds, insects and larvae, berries, and fruits. They will eat from a feeder.

Habits: Travels alone or in pairs during breeding season. They may form flocks during the winter. While incubating and brooding, both parents may "whisper" songs.

181

Lazuli Bunting

Passerina amoena

The western counterpart to the Indigo Bunting in the East, the Lazuli Bunting is found in open forests, thickets, and dry canyon regions during the summer breeding season. To attract females, the male spreads and flutters his wings to show off his color; he sings to establish his territory, which he aggressively defends.

Ron Austing

The Lazuli Bunting visits feeders with small seeds and grains.

Identification Flashes and Distinguishing Features:

Look for the male's bright turquoise head, white wing bars, and cinnamon upper breast. The female has a grayish brown head and upperparts.

Size: 5.25 –5.75 inches (14–15 centimeters)

Color: The male has a bright turquoise throat, head, and upperparts; 2 broad white wing bars; cinnamon upper breast; white underparts with a cinnamon wash on the flanks; blackish wing and tail with blue-edged flight feathers. The juvenile is cinnamon with white underparts. The female has a grayish brown head and upperparts, a buff wash on the throat and breast, white underparts, 2 pale buffy wing bars, grayish blue uppertail coverts and rump, and blackish wings and tail with blue-edged flight feathers.

Voice: The call is a "wet" *plik*. Sings various phrases, some are paired and somewhat buzzy, *see-see-sweet, sweet-zee-see-zeer*.

Range: Spends summer breeding season from southwestern Canada to northwestern New Mexico, western South Dakota to California. Winters in southeastern Arizona and western Mexico.

Habitat: Prefers open forests, thickets, scrub areas, and dry canyons, often near streams. The female builds the nest 2–4 feet above ground, sometimes up to 10 feet above ground. The nest is built in a fork of a bush or a small tree and constructed of grass, weeds, and leaves; softened with finer grass and mammal hair.

Eggs: They lay 3–5 plain pale bluish white eggs; 2–3 broods per year. The female incubates; incubation lasts 12 days. The fledglings leave the nest after 10–12 days. Though both parents feed the young, the female is the primary provider.

Food: Foraging on the ground and low in trees and bushes, they eat primarily seeds, and in the summer, insects and caterpillars. They will eat small seeds and grain from feeders.

Habits: During breeding season, they travel alone or in pairs. At the end of breeding season, they join flocks and mixed species foraging flocks with other buntings and sparrows and move to higher elevations

Indigo Bunting

Passerina cyanea

Ron Austing

These sparrow-size birds frequently perch on utility wires, fly up from highways into roadside thickets, and visit feeders during winter months and migrations. In strong light males appear to be a brilliant, iridescent indigo blue; in poor light or when backlighted, they may look black.

You can attract Indigo Buntings by including hedges and thickets in your naturescape, providing water, and filling feeders with sunflower and millet seeds.

Identification Flashes and Distinguishing Features:

The male's brilliant indigo-blue plumage and sparrow size makes them easy to identify.

Size: 5.5–5.75 inches (13–14 centimeters)

Color: Males at least 2 years old have bright indigo-blue bodies with blue to purplish heads and rusty wingbars; bellies of younger males have patches of brown and sometimes white. Females and juveniles are rich brown without obvious streaking; female heads may have slight crested appearance.

Voice: They sing varied high-pitched phrases, with the beginning phrases paired and often followed by a short trilled *sweet-sweet, sweeter-sweeter, here-here*. They also make wet *tsick* sounds, as if they're trying to spit out feathers.

Range: Spends summer breeding season in eastern two-thirds of the U.S. They winter in southern Florida and southern Texas.

Habitat: Frequents brushy weedy areas, agricultural areas, woodland edges, roadside thickets, hedges, and clearings for utility wires. Females build nests close to the ground in the crotches of saplings, thickets, brier patches, weed stems, and canebreaks. Makes well-woven nesting cup of grasses, weed stems, bark fibers, Spanish moss, and paper on a base of leaves or sometimes snake skin. Lines nest with finer grasses, hair, feathers, plant down, and rootlets.

Eggs: Lays 3–4 unmarked white eggs, occasionally marked with purple or brown spots ; 2 broods per breeding season. The female incubates the eggs; incubation takes 12–14 days. Fledglings leave the nest 9–12 days after hatching.

Food: Insects (grasshoppers, caterpillars, cicadas, beetles, weevils, flies, cankerworms, mosquitoes, spiders), plant foods (seeds of grasses, goldenrod, dandelion, thistle, small grains), and small fruit and berries (elderberries, blackberries, privet berries). Will come to feeders for black oil sunflower seeds, millet, and safflower seeds.

Habits: Persistent singers; often sing from shaded perches through the heat of summer days. Males often sing while displaying in a slow flight with rapidly beating wings.

Painted Bunting

Passerina ciris

Once sold on streets as a cage bird, Painted Buntings were called "nonpareil"—the incomparable. The males are among the most colorful of North American songbirds.

You can attract Painted Buntings to your backyard by providing water and filling feeders with millet and other small grains.

Ron Austing

Identification Flashes and Distinguishing Features:

The males are unmistakable—no other buntings or other birds have such colorful plumage.

Size: 5–5.5 inches (13–14 centimeters)

Color: Males at least 2 years old have blue heads, yellow-green backs, purplish-red rumps, red underparts and eye rings, and green-washed wings and tails; 1-year-old males are mostly green with blue head patches. Females have green upperparts and yellow-green underparts. Juveniles are drab brown with greenish washes.

Voice: They sing sweet, high-pitched, thin-spaced *you-eta, you-eta, I eaty you too* notes.

Range: Summer residents of the Atlantic Coast from North Carolina to northern Florida, and the middle southern U.S. from southern Missouri to Mexico, and from Mississippi across through Texas. They winter in southern Florida.

Habitat: Frequents open country, brushy weed-grown fields, gardens, railroad clearings, roadside thickets, woodland edges, and riparian thickets. They build their nests close to the ground in trees, thick brush, or vines. They make well-woven cups of leaves topped with dried grasses, bark, and weed stalks and lined with finer grasses, rootlets, and hair.

Eggs: Females lay 3–5 pale bluish-white eggs with brown spots; 2–3 broods per breeding season. The female incubates the eggs; incubation takes 11–12 days. Fledglings leave the nest 12–14 days after hatching.

Food: They eat primarily small seeds of grasses but also take some insects (boll weevils, grasshoppers, wasps, caterpillars, crickets, and spiders). They will come to feeders for millet and other small grains and wild bird mixes.

Habits: Sings from exposed perches atop low shrubs, small trees, or utility wires. They are often shy and retiring. Males are polygamous and often fiercely combat rival males to the point of injury—most unusual behavior for birds.

Red-winged Blackbird

Agelaius phoeniceus

Red-winged Blackbirds can be found along highways, in the willows and cattails bordering fishing holes, and in cultivated fields. They travel and forage with other blackbirds, robins, and starlings, and winter flocks may number into the millions. They migrate northward in early spring, making them the true "harbingers of spring."

Fred J. Alsop III

You can attract Red-winged Blackbirds to your backyard by providing water and offering millet and other small grains either on the ground or on platform feeders close to the ground.

Identification Flashes and Distinguishing Features:

Look for the yellow-bordered red shoulder patches on male Red-winged Blackbirds. Females look like large, heavily streaked sparrows and have light lines above their eyes.

Size: 7.5–9.5 inches (19–24 centimeters) Males are larger than females.

Color: Males have glossy black bodies with red shoulder patches (epaulets) bordered by yellow. Females have brown upper-parts, grayish-white underparts heavily streaked with brown, and light lines above their eyes; they may have a red wash on their shoulders, chins, and cheeks.

Voice: Males sing loud, reedy *konk-ah-reee* songs.

Range: Permanent residents throughout most of the U.S. excluding states bordering Canada, where they spend the summer breeding season. They winter in Mexico.

Habitat: Frequents freshwater and saltwater marshes, brush and willows bordering water, dry upland fields, wet meadows, and farmlands with tall grasses. Females build loose nesting cups attached by plant fibers to plant stalks or branches. They make their nests from rushes, cattail strips, grasses, rootlets, and mosses and line them with mud and inner linings of finer grasses, hairs, plant down, and rushes.

Eggs: They lay 3–5 pale-blue to green eggs with black, brown, and purple spots, blotches, and scrawls on the larger end; 2–3 broods per breeding season. The female incubates the eggs; incubation takes 11–12 days. Fledglings leave the nest about 10 days after hatching.

Food: More than 73 percent of their diet is seeds, grains, fruit, and berries. Also eats insects and other invertebrates (beetles, caterpillars, grasshoppers, spiders, snails), especially in summer. They will come to feeders for small mixed seeds, wild bird mixes, and bread.

Habits: Often live in loose colonies; males become polygamous if there are surplus females. Males actively defend their territories, driving away predators, other male blackbirds, and cowbirds. Dominant males display red shoulder patches; subordinate males hide them.

Common Grackle

Quiscalus quiscula

They behave gregariously year-round and winter with other blackbirds, starlings, and robins. Mixed-species flocks can number in the millions.

You can attract Common Grackles to your backyard by providing water and offering millet and other small grains either on the ground or on platform feeders low to the ground.

Ron Austing

Identification Flashes and Distinguishing Features:

You can identify males in flight by their long tails folded into a distinctive keeled-"V" shape.

Size: 11–13.5 inches (28–34 centimeters)
Males are larger than females.

Color: Males have iridescent greenish bodies and heads with a glossy black-purplish sheen; females are duller but blacker. They have long black bills and yellow eyes.

Voice: They make squeaking sounds that sound like a squeaky gate hinge.

Range; Permanent residents in most of the eastern half of the U.S. They summer north and west of this range in most of Canada east of British Columbia, and from Maine across to Montana, south to northeastern New Mexico. They winter in southwestern Texas.

Habitat: Frequents various urban and suburban habitats and nests either singly or in small colonies in shrubs, bushes, or deciduous or evergreen trees. Females build loose, bulky nests from weed stalks, grasses, debris, and twigs, sometimes on a mud foundation cup. They line their finished nests with finer grasses, hair, and feathers.

Eggs: Lays 4–7 pale-greenish to yellow-brown eggs sometimes with brown, black, and lavender spots, blotches, and scrawls concentrated at the larger end; 1–2 broods per breeding season. The female incubates eggs; incubation takes 13–14 days. Fledglings leave the nest 16–20 days after hatching.

Food: A variety of animal fare (boll weevils, Japanese beetles, wasps, army ants, spiders, earthworms, snails, mice, lizards, frogs, fish, crayfish, eggs, baby birds, and salamanders). They also eat grains, weed seeds, corn, acorns, fruit, and berries.

Habits: Their gregarious behavior makes them conspicuous along roadways during breeding season. They are often seen in large mixed-species flocks, which invade cities and towns to feed on lawns.

Boat-tailed Grackle

Quiscalus major

These large blackbirds, with their seven-inch (eighteen centimeter) keeled tails, stay close to coastal marshes and lowlands. The low-lying terrain of Florida provides the ideal habitat, and they are common backyard birds across the state. They sing and display noisily from buildings, signs, and utility lines and poles in coastal areas as well as on beaches and dunes.

Fred J. Alsop III

You can attract them to your backyard by providing water and offering grains either on the ground or on platform feeders low to the ground.

Identification Flashes and Distinguishing Features:

Look for the large keeled tails on the iridescent blue-purple-black males and bronze-colored females.

Size: Males are 16–17 inches (41–43 centimeters); females are 12–14 inches (30–36 centimeters)

Color: Males have iridescent blue-black bodies with glossy purple upperparts. Females are tawny, buffy brown with darker brown wings and tails, and dark eyes.

Voice: They sing a noisy jumble of "electric" whistles, rattles, and loud *jeebs*.

Range: Permanent residents throughout Florida and in tidal and coastal marshes along the entire Gulf Coast, and from Florida through the Carolinas to Long Island on the Atlantic Coast; they are seldom found more than 20 miles inland.

Habitat: Frequents coastal areas, marshes, islands, and land around marinas. Females build nests in bushes and trees near water. They make bulky nesting cups from twigs, reeds, cattails, coarse grasses, paper, string, Spanish moss, rags, cattle dung, or mud and line them with finer grasses, hair, and feathers.

Eggs: Lays 3–5 bluish-gray to pale-blue eggs with brown, black, and lavender dots, blotches, and scrawls; 2–3 broods per breeding season. The female incubates the eggs; incubation takes 13–15 days. Fledglings leave the nest 12–15 days after hatching.

Food: Primarily eat insects and other invertebrates (grasshoppers, beetles, grubs, snails, mussels, fish, nestlings, eggs, crayfish, shrimps, crabs, frogs, small snakes, and lizards) taken on the ground. Also eat some grains.

Habits: Travels in small flocks except during breeding season, and they nest in loose colonies. They are large, noisy, and conspicuous. Courtship displays of the males include puffing up their plumage, bobbing and bowing to females, and spreading their wings and tails while constantly and loudly vocalizing.

Great-tailed Grackle

Quiscalus mexicanus

Ron Austing

This bird nests closely with the Boat-tailed Grackle in coastal eastern Texas and western Louisiana and was once considered one in the same species; however, they do not breed with each other.

The Great-tailed Grackle often walks on the ground with its large tail straight up in the air.

Identification Flashes and Distinguishing Features:

Look for the black body with iridescent purple head and neck on the male. The female is smaller and has a dark brown head and upperparts with a cinnamon-buff breast and throat. There is a faint iridescent purple on the plumage.

Size: 10.5–18.5 inches (27–48 centimeters)

Color: The male has a black body with an iridescent purple head, neck, and underparts. The eyes are golden yellow. The tail is long and keel-shaped. The female has a dark brown head and upperparts, buff-cinnamon supercilium and border to auriculars, and a cinnamon-buff breast and throat. The eyes are yellowish white; brown-eyed females occur in the East where their range overlaps with Boat-tailed Grackles.

Voice: Makes loud chatters, squeaks, gurgles, shrieks, and piercing ascending whistles. There is a high-pitched squeal of *may-reee, may-reee*. The call in flight is *chak*.

Range: They reside primarily in the southern U.S. west of the Mississippi River. They migrate to the northern edge of this region during breeding season, as far north as Nebraska and sometimes into South Dakota, west to the Pacific Coast.

Habitat: Prefers to be near water in open areas with some trees, marshes, thickets, parks, agricultural, and urban areas. The nest is built by the female. In trees, they build 5–15 feet above ground with Spanish moss, mud, cow dung, feathers, and debris. In marsh vegetation, they build bulky nests less than 2 feet above water with cattails, grasses, and dried rushes. Females will steal nesting material from one another.

Eggs: They lay 3–4 light gray to light blue eggs with reddish purple markings; 1–2 broods per year. The female incubates; incubation takes 13–14 days. The female broods the young. Fledglings leave the nest 20–23 days after hatching. The female feeds the young.

Food: Eats insects, snails, small fish, frogs, shrimp, small birds, eggs and nestlings, fruits, berries, seeds, and grains. They often steal food from other birds. They forage on the ground and when wading in water.

Habits: Noisy, they travel in groups and small flocks. They are polygamous to promiscuous. The male will claim territory within a colony and will display and sing in front of a group of females. The female chooses the male.

Brown-headed Cowbird

Molothrus ater

Cowbirds have earned notoriety as brood parasites—they lay their eggs in other birds' nests, leaving the foster parents to raise young cowbirds, often at the expense of their own young. Cowbirds may be a factor in the recent population declines of many songbirds. Fragmentation of forests and development of open farmlands have benefited this species.

If you want to attract cowbirds, despite their parasitic breeding behavior, place millet and other small grains either on the ground or on platform feeders low to the ground.

Fred J. Alsop III

Identification Flashes and Distinguishing Features:

Look for brown-headed birds with a moderately heavy bill.

Size: 7–8.25 inches (18–21 centimeters)

Color: Males have metallic greenish-black bodies and coffee-brown heads with conical black bills. Females have unmarked ashy brownish-gray coloring. Juveniles are paler than females and have heavily streaked underparts.

Voice: They sing bubbly *glug-glug-glee* notes. The flight note of males is a high-pitched, slurred *cowbird*. Females make dry rattling sounds.

Range: Permanent residents from New Hampshire to central Florida westward to central Iowa then gradually southwestward to southern Arizona and New Mexico; north up the Pacific Coast to Washington. Summers north of this entire range into Canada. Winters in southern Florida, southern tip of Texas, and southwestern Arizona.

Habitat: They frequent farmlands, pastures, woodland edges, openings in deciduous and coniferous woodlands, shade trees, and gardens. They do not build nests; they lay their eggs in the nests of at least 214 North American host species.

Eggs: Females usually lay 1 egg each morning and may lay more than 30 eggs per season in host nest(s); some hosts remove cowbird eggs, others build new nests over old ones to cover cowbird eggs, and others abandon their nests. Eggs are white to grayish white with brown speckles concentrated at larger end; incubation takes 10–13 days.

Food: Primarily grass seeds, weed seeds, grains, corn, and dandelions. They also eat insects and other invertebrates (grasshoppers, ants, wasps, beetles, spiders, and caterpillars) and some fruit. They will come to feeders for small grains.

Habits: They lift up their tails when they walk. Their genus name, *Molothrus*, means "vagabond." The wandering habits of ancestral cowbirds that followed roaming buffalo herds on the plains may account for their parasitic breeding behavior.

Baltimore (Northern) Oriole

Icterus galbula

These showy, musical birds place their distinctive deep-pouch nests so high and so well screened that they're usually not discovered until the leaves fall in autumn, after the birds have already migrated south. They were reclassified in 1973 as Northern Orioles, but new information in 1996 has restored both their name and species status.

You can attract them by providing water, slices of citrus fruit, and feeders filled with suet or commercially available Oriole nectar.

Ron Austing

Identification Flashes and Distinguishing Features:

Look for their orange backs, shoulders, and underparts and black heads, tails, and wings.

Size: 7–8.25 inches (18–21 centimeters)

Color: Males have black bodies with bright orange backs, shoulders, underparts, and corner tail patches; females look like washed-out males and have greenish-yellow to yellow-orange bodies and tails, dark heads and wings with white wing bars.

Voice: They make clear *hew-it* calls and loud, clear, flutelike songs composed of low-pitched, 2-note phrases broken by softer single notes. They incorporate "chatter" calls into their songs.

Range: Summer residents from Maine to Virginia gradually southwest to northern Louisiana, northwest through much of Kansas and Nebraska north through the central Dakotas to Canada. Winters in Florida, along the southern Atlantic Coast, and in Mexico.

Habitat: Frequents tall trees in residential areas, streamside borders, roadsides, orchards, and woodland edges. Females weave 5 to 6-inch-deep, grayish pouches suspended by the rim between tree forks or drooping branches. Makes nest from grasses, milkweed fibers, hairs, string (including short strands of yarn), monofilament fishing line, and grapevine bark and lines it with finer grasses, hairs, plant fibers, and cottony materials.

Eggs: Lays 4 grayish to bluish white eggs with brown and black spots, streaks, and scrawls concentrated at the larger end; 1 brood per breeding season. The female incubates the eggs; incubation takes 12–14 days. Fledglings leave the nest 12–14 days after hatching.

Food: Especially fond of caterpillars but also eats other insects as well as fruit, berries, and flower nectar. Will come to hummingbird or oriole nectar feeders as well as feeders filled with cut oranges and other citrus fruit, suet, and peanut butter-suet mixes.

Habits: Often nest in yards and sometimes come to feeders. They sing from treetop perches throughout the summer.

Bullock's Oriole

Icterus bullockii

Although Bullock's Oriole breeds with the Baltimore Oriole in a hybrid zone in the Great Plains, it is considered a separate species. The face pattern and the white wing patches differentiate the bright orange male from other orioles.

Bullock's Oriole will visit feeders providing suet, sliced orange, and nectar water.

Fred J. Alsop III

Identification Flashes and Distinguishing Features:

In the male, look for the orange face; black cap, nape, bib, and eye stripe; black back; black wings with large white patch; and orange underparts and rump. The female is olive-brown with a yellow face, throat, and breast.

Size: 7–8.25 inches (18–21 centimeters)

Color: The male has an orange face, underparts, and rump; a black cap, nape, bib, and eye stripe; a black back; and black wings with a large white patch. The tail is black with orange outer tail feathers. The female is olive-brown with a yellow face, throat, and breast. The belly and rump are buffy gray, sometimes washed yellow-orange. The tail is olive.

Voice: Makes precise, clear whistled single and double notes. Some notes are gruff or scratchy. The call is a rough nasal *cheah*, sometimes repeated. They also make a loud rattle.

Range: They spend the summer breeding season in the West, from southern Canada to Mexico, western Kansas to the West Coast. They winter in Mexico.

Habitat: At home in open shaded areas, grasslands, forest edges, and foothill oak forests. The female builds the nest with some help from the male. The nest is built 6–15 feet above the ground, hanging from the end of a branch, often in cottonwood or willow, or in a clump of mistletoe. The nest is constructed of plant fiber, horse hair, string, and bark; it is softened with moss, plant down, wool, and hair.

Eggs: They lay 4–5 light blue or pale gray eggs with dots of brown, gray, or black, 1 brood per year. The female incubates the eggs; incubation lasts 12–14 days. The fledglings are brooded by the female and leave the nest after 12–14 days. Both parents feed the young.

Food: Foraging in trees and bushes, they eat insects and larvae, berries, fruit, and also drink nectar.

Habits: During breeding season travel is solitary or in pairs. After nesting they travel in small groups. Couples spend a lot of time together; both members of the pair will attack predators.

Purple Finch

Carpodacus purpureus

Superficially similar to the increasingly common House Finches, Purple Finches rely on backyard feeders whenever their food supply is weakened. They have expanded their breeding range because of the fragmentation of northern coniferous forests, the establishment of Christmas tree farms, and increased plantings of ornamental evergreens and shrubs.

You can easily attract Purple Finches to your backyard by providing water and filling feeders with black oil sunflower seeds.

Ron Austing

Identification Flashes and Distinguishing Features:

Male Purple Finches look like sparrows that have been dipped in raspberry juice. Look for the broad white stripes above the eyes of the brown females.

Size: 5.5–6.25 inches (14–16 centimeters)

Color: Males have bright raspberry red heads, backs, rumps, and most of their underparts; whitish lower bellies and undertail coverts; dark lines "through" their eyes; dark wings; and deep forked tails. Females and juveniles have brownish upperparts, gray-brown underparts with heavy brown streaking, wide brown ear patches, and white lines over their eyes.

Voice: They make *chur-lee* calls and rich, rapid, somewhat high-pitched warbles.

Range: Permanent residents in the extreme Northeast and along the Pacific Coast. Winters in eastern half of the U.S. Summers throughout Canada.

Habitat: Frequents open woodlands and suburbs. Females build shallow nesting cups on horizontal branches, usually in conifer trees. They make their nests from twigs, grasses, weed stems, mosses, and rootlets and line them with finer grasses, hair, and wool.

Eggs: Lays 3–5 pale greenish-blue eggs speckled with brown and black; 1–2 broods per breeding season. The female incubates the eggs; incubation takes 13 days. Fledglings leave the nest about 14 days after hatching.

Food: Weeds, grasses, tree seeds, and tree buds. They especially enjoy fruit and berries (blackberry and raspberry). In late spring and summer, they feed on insects, particularly caterpillars and beetles. They will come to feeders for black oil sunflower seeds, millet, and small grains.

Habits: Often gives distinctive sharp musical chipping sounds while in flight.

House Finch

Carpodacus mexicanus

In 1940 California cagebird dealers illegally trapped House Finches, a western species, in the wild and shipped them to pet store dealers in New York City for sale as Hollywood Finches or Linnets. The U.S. Fish and Wildlife Service stopped the trafficking, and the New York dealers released their birds into the city. The birds established themselves in the parks and residential areas of the "Big Apple" and have slowly increased their range.

You can attract House Finches by providing water and filling feeders with black oil sunflower and thistle seeds, wild bird mixes, and small grains.

Identification Flashes and Distinguishing Features:

Look for sparrow-size red-and-brown males and streaked brown females.

Size: 6 inches (15 centimeters)

Color: Males have brown upperparts, caps, and ear patches; red rumps, foreheads, eye stripes, chins, throats, and breasts; whitish underparts with brown streaks on their sides and flanks; and whitish wing bars. The amount and intensity of their red coloring varies; some males are orange. Females and juveniles have brown, streaked plumage.

Voice: They make nasal *wheer* calls and high-pitched, warbled 3-note phrases that often end in ascending quizzical notes.

Range: Permanent residents throughout much of the U.S. excluding Florida, much of the Gulf Coast area, the northern border of Michigan and northeastern Minnesota, and extreme north central Montana.

Habitat: Found in cities, parks, farms, open woods, and suburbs. Females build nests in trees, nesting boxes, ledges, trees, shrubs, ornamental bushes, or vines. They make their nests from grasses, twigs, debris, string, leaves, hair, rootlets, and plant stems and line them with finer materials.

Eggs: Lays 2–6 bluish-white to pale-green eggs speckled with black dots; 1–3 broods per breeding season. The female incubates the eggs; incubation takes 12–14 days. Fledglings leave the nest 11–19 days after hatching.

Food: More than 85 percent of their diet is seeds (grasses, thistle, and dandelion). They also eat some insects. They will come to feeders for thistle and black oil sunflower seeds and small grains.

Habits: They seem to have a commensal relationship with people. Some populations have been stricken with a form of conjunctivitus that produces swollen, crusty eyes and may indirectly cause death in birds that depend on good eyesight for survival. Cleaning feeders regularly and raking away seed hulls and droppings beneath feeders helps control the spread of the disease.

Pine Siskin

Carduelis pinus

These small brownish, heavily streaked northern finches often travel in flocks with many thousand birds. When their boreal forest evergreen seed supply is sparse, irruptive flocks may turn up in conifers or at feeders throughout the U.S.

Fred J. Alsop III

You can attract Pine Siskins to your backyard by providing water and filling feeders with thistle or black oil sunflower seeds.

Identification Flashes and Distinguishing Features:

Look for brown, heavily streaked sparrow-size birds that have small bills and yellow streaks in their wings and tails.

Size: 4.5–5.25 inches (11–13 centimeters)

Color: Gray-brown upperparts and buffy-white underparts with heavy streaking above and below; buffy-white wing bars; broad yellow stripes that show as yellow patches on folded wings; and dark, short notched tails with some yellow plumage.

Voice: They make notes that resemble a miniature chain saw and American Goldfinch-like songs with buzzy *shreeeeeee* notes.

Range: Permanent residents in the North including all of Maine and west along the U.S./Canadian border; also in the West from western Montana to the Pacific Coast and south to the central New Mexico/Arizona border. Winters throughout the U.S., except for central and southern Florida and the southern tip of Texas. Summers in Canada and southeastern Alaska.

Habitat: Frequents coniferous forests as well as evergreens in parks, cemeteries, suburbs, and gardens. Females build nests on horizontal conifer branches, well-concealed by needles. Makes shallow nesting cup from twigs, needles, grasses, bark, and mosses, and lines it with finer grasses, mosses, rootlets, fur, and feathers.

Eggs: Lays 3–5 pale bluish to greenish eggs with black, brown, and lavender dots and spots concentrated at the larger end, often forming a wreath; 2 broods per breeding season. The female incubates the eggs, and the male feeds her while she is on the nest; incubation takes 13 days. Fledglings leave the nest about 15 days after hatching.

Food: Seeds of conifer and deciduous trees as well as weed and grass seeds and thistle. In late spring and summer they take insects (aphids, beetles, and caterpillars) and also drink sap from sapsucker drill wells. They are fond of calcium salts and during winter often flock to mortar joints or sides of roads that have been salted for ice removal.

Habits: Extremely tame and approachable, they sometimes will eat from your hand. They enjoy bathing and drinking at birdbaths.

Lesser Goldfinch

Carduelis psaltria

The Lesser Goldfinch inhabits the Southwest and is appreciated for the large amount of weed seed it eats. As the name implies, it is smaller than the American Goldfinch. The color of the male's plumage varies based on its range.

They will visit birdbaths and feeders with thistle, mixed seeds, and sunflower seeds.

Ron Austing

Identification Flashes and Distinguishing Features:

Look for the bright yellow-green underparts and the black cap. The wings are black with white edging and white wing bars. The color of the back of the male varies—black in the East and greenish olive in the West.

Size: 4.5 inches (11 centimeters)

Color: The male has a black cap, bright yellow-green underparts, and black wings with white edging. There is a white wing patch at the base of the primaries. The female is greenish olive above and yellowish green below with two white wing bars.

Voice: Makes an intricate warbling, twittering, excited series of *swee* notes. The call is a mewing *tee-yee* and a drawn *zweeir*.

Range: Permanent residents of the West and Southwest from Texas westward and along the coast of California into Oregon, south into Mexico. In the summer they are seen on the northern edge of their range into Colorado, Utah, and Nevada.

Habitat: Prefers open areas such as grasslands, grasslands with scattered trees, and the edge of forests. The nest is built by the female 2–30 feet above the ground across the limb of a tree or bush, or set in tall weeds. The nest is constructed of plant fibers, grasses, and bark; it is softened with feathers, and plant down.

Eggs: They lay 3–6 light blue eggs; 1–2 broods per year. They are late nesters. The female incubates the eggs; incubation takes 12 days. The male feeds the female during incubation. The young are brooded by the female. The fledglings leave the nest 11–15 days after hatching. Both parents feed regurgitated milky seed pulp to the young.

Food: Forages in brush, shrubs, and weedy fields for weed seeds, other seeds, and insects.

Habits: Travels in pairs or in small flocks, and forages in flocks. Pairs stay together in winter and possibly mate for life. The male courts the female with a song in flight; the male also feeds the female during courtship.

American Goldfinch

Carduelis tristis

Fred J. Alsop III

Sometimes called "Wild Canaries," the goldfinch's genus name *Carduelis* refers to a fondness for thistle. The species name tristis means "sad" and points to their often heard plaintive *dear-me! (babeee)* notes.

You can attract American Goldfinches to your backyard by including late summer and early fall wildflowers in your naturescape, providing water, and filling feeders with black oil sunflower seeds or thistle.

Identification Flashes and Distinguishing Features:

In spring look for the unmistakable bright "canary" yellow and black cap, wings, and tails of male American Goldfinches.

Size: 5 inches (13 centimeters)

Color: In spring males have bright yellow bodies, white rumps and undertail coverts, black caps, notched tails, and wings with white bars. Females are duller yellow overall with olive-green backs and no black caps. During winter both males and females are browner and greener overall; males do not have black caps and may show more yellow wash than females.

Voice: Makes distinctive *per-CHICK-o-ree* calls when in flight. They also sing canary-like series of twitters, chips, and trills with *swee* or *babeee* notes incorporated into songs.

Range: Permanent residents across the U.S. from Maine south to the central Southeast; westward range narrows to a small area in northeastern Colorado, then widens in a circular shape to the Washington coast; also down the Pacific Coast to Mexico. Winters south of this range throughout the U.S., and summers north to Canada.

Habitat: Frequents areas abundant in thistle, including overgrown fields, vacant lots, towns, suburbs, and other areas with scattered trees. Females build well-woven nesting cups in weed patches, brier patches, shrubs, vines, and trees. They make their nests from plant fibers and line them with milkweed, thistle, or cattail down.

Eggs: Lays 4–6 unmarked pale bluish-white eggs; 1–2 broods per breeding season. The female incubates the eggs, and the male feeds her when she is on the nest; incubation takes 10–12 days. Fledglings leave the nest 11–17 days after hatching.

Food: Prefers thistle seeds but also eats weed, grass, and tree seeds and catkins, tree buds, and flower heads. They also take insects, some fruit, and berries. They will come to feeders for thistle, small grains, and black oil sunflower seeds.

Habits: They nest in late summer when small seeds from wildflowers and weeds are readily available; adults feed regurgitated seeds to their young. They remain in flocks until July, when they pair for breeding.

Evening Grosbeak
Coccothraustes vespertinus

At first glance you might mistake these finches for large goldfinches until you notice the massive white bills and dark heads of the males. These birds are something special. Evening Grosbeaks live in western mountains and northern coniferous forests, but every third or fourth winter when their populations are large or the supply of tree seeds is small, they invade the South, sometimes in huge numbers.

Ron Austing

You can attract Evening Grosbeaks to your backyard by providing water and filling feeders with black oil sunflower seeds.

Identification Flashes and Distinguishing Features:

Look for large yellow, black, and white males and gray and white females with big bills. Listen for their loud, strident calls.

Size: 7.75–8.5 inches (19–21 centimeters)

Color: Males have burnt to bright-yellow bodies; black wings with large white patches; black notched tails; blackish heads, throats, and breasts; yellow foreheads, lores, and stripes over eyes; and massive white (pale greenish in the spring) bills. Females and juveniles have silver-gray upperparts, buffy underparts, black wings and tails with white patches, white throats, yellowish collars, and large white bills.

Voice: Makes loud, far-carrying House Sparrow-like *peet peet kreeck* calls and Purple Finch-like songs.

Range: Permanent residents from Maine along the edge of the Canadian border to eastern Minnesota; and from central Montana to the Pacific Coast south to northern California, and from southeastern Idaho southeastward to central New Mexico across to eastern Arizona and south to Mexico. Winters in the northeastern half of the U.S. sometimes as far south as Texas and through the southeast.

Habitat: Frequents coniferous forests. Females weave shallow nests on conifer branches hidden by needles and sometimes in deciduous trees or shrubs. Their nesting cups are interwoven twigs, mosses, and lichen, lined with rootlets.

Eggs: Lays 3–5 bluish-green eggs with brown, gray, purple, and black spots and specklings; 1–2 broods per breeding season. Females incubate eggs; incubation takes 11–14 days. Fledglings leave the nest 13–14 days after hatching.

Food: Primarily tree seeds and buds. In summer they take insects (cankerworms, spruce budworms, and beetles). They also eat fruit and berries (dogwood, cherries, and choke-cherries). They will come to feeders for sunflower seeds.

Habits: Travels in flocks most of the year. They are fond of calcium salts and during winter will flock to mortar joints or sides of roads that have been salted for ice removal; unfortunately many are killed by vehicles. They drink water from birdbaths.

House Sparrow
Passer domesticus

Ron Austing

The species name *domesticus* means "about the house," which describes this bird's surroundings—they live where people live. Introduced into New York City in the nineteenth century, this European species has spread across North America.

You can attract House Sparrows by providing water and nesting boxes with holes at least one and one-half inches in diameter. Placing a dowel perch beneath the hole will encourage them to nest in the box. You can also attract them by offering millet, wild bird mixes, and other small seeds.

Identification Flashes and Distinguishing Features:

Look for the gray crowns and black bibs and chins on males. Look for the yellowish bills and tan eye stripes on females.

Size: 5.5–6.5 inches (14–17 centimeters)

Color: Males have rich brown upperparts streaked with black; ashy-buff underparts; gray crowns, cheeks, and rumps; white wing bars and face patches; black lores, chins, and bibs; and blackish conical beaks. Females have brown upperparts with blackish streaks, ashy-buff underparts with indistinct streaking, buffy lines over their eyes, and yellowish bills.

Voice: They make loud, repeated *cheap, cheap, cheap* sounds.

Range: Permanent residents throughout the U.S. excluding Alaska, and most of southern Canada.

Habitat: Found in cities, suburbs, parks, farms, and along highways. Both parents build a nest in natural cavities, nesting boxes, holes in buildings, behind shutters, on rafters, under eaves, and behind highway signs. They make their nests from grasses, debris, string, paper, weeds, and straw and line them with feathers. A bulky dome conceals the finished nest.

Eggs: They lay 3–7 whitish, blue-white, or green-white eggs with tan, brown, and gray spots and blotches; 2–3 broods per breeding season. The female incubates the eggs; incubation takes 10–14 days. Fledglings leave the nest 14–17 days after hatching.

Food: In spring and summer they feed on insects and other invertebrates (ants, worms, crickets, grasshoppers, beetles, wasps, moths, flies, caterpillars, and spiders). They also take fruit, seeds, and waste grains (corn, oats, and wheat). They will come to feeders for millet, wheat, and other small grains.

Habits: Usually seen in noisy flocks. They sleep in communal roosts, except during breeding season, in shrubs, conifers, or ivy vines on buildings. House Sparrows had commensal relationships with horses, picking undigested grain seeds from their droppings. When horse populations declined due to the coming of the automobile, House Sparrow populations declined as well.

Helpful Resource Materials

Books

Adler, Bill Jr. *Outwitting Squirrels: 101 Cunning Stratagems to Reduce Dramatically the Egregious Misappropriation of Seed from Your Birdfeeder by Squirrels.* Chicago: Chicago Review Press, 1996.

Alsop III, Fred J. *Smithsonian Birds of North America.* New York: DK Publishing Inc., 2001.

Brown, Robert M., Sheila Buff, Tim Gallagher and Kristi Streiffert. *National Wildlife Federation Where the Birds Are.* New York: DK Publishing Inc., 2001.

Burton, Robert. *The National Audubon Society North American Birdfeeder Handbook.* New York: Dorling Kindersley Publishing Inc., 1995.

Jones, Jon Oliver. *Where the Birds Are: A Guide to All 50 States and Canada.* New York: William Morrow and Co. Inc., 1990.

Kress, Stephen W. *The National Audubon Society Bird Garden.* New York: Dorling Kindersley Publishing, 1995.

National Geographic Society. *Field Guide to the Birds of North America*, 4th ed. Washington, D.C.: National Geographic Society, 2002.

National Wildlife Federation. *Gardening With Wildlife Kit.* Washington, D.C.: National Wildlife Federation, 1990.

Sibley, David Allen. *National Audubon Society, The Sibley Guide to Birds.* New York: Alfred A. Knopf, 2000.

Stokes, Donald. *The Bird Feeder Book.* Canada: Little, Brown & Company, 1987.

Stokes, Donald and Lillian Stokes. *The Hummingbird Book.* Boston: Little, Brown & Company, 1989.

Terres, John K. *Songbirds in Your Garden.* Algonquin Books of Chapel Hill, 1994.

Videotapes

Attracting Birds to Your Backyard with Roger Tory Peterson, produced by Nature Science Network.

Birds of the Backyard: Winter into Spring with George Harrison, produced by Company for Home Entertainment.

How to Start Birdwatching with Diane Porter, 1994.

Hummingbirds Up Close, produced by Nature Science Network, 1988.

Audiotapes

Backyard Bird Songs, produced by Houghton Mifflin as part of the Peterson Field Guide Series, 1991.

Index and Checklist

About the Author

Fred J. Alsop III holds a Ph.D. degree in zoology from the University of Tennessee at Knoxville and teaches biological sciences at East Tennessee State University. A Kentucky native, Fred is an avid birder and field biologist who has identified more than 3,300 species of birds in nineteen countries and has led natural history tours to many parts of the world. He has photographed birds for more than thirty years, and his photographs have appeared in numerous publications.

Fred has published more than 125 articles on birds in regional, national, and international journals. He is the author of several books including *Birds of the Smokies*, a national award-winning book; *Smithsonian Birds of North America*; *Smithsonian Handbooks, Birds of North America Eastern Region*; *Smithsonian Handbooks, Birds of North America Western Region*; and *Backyard Birds*.

He served two terms as a national lecturer for the Research Society of Sigma Xi and has taught numerous workshops for state and federal wildlife officers and biologists on field identification of birds as part of the international Partners in Flight program. He is recognized as an authority on the avifauna of Tennessee.

Fred is a public speaker, scuba diver, private pilot, and tennis player. He and his wife, Cathi, live in Johnson City, Tennessee.

About his Friends

Ron Austing has been one of the premier photographers of birds in North America for more than fifty years. His outstanding color shots have graced the pages of every major nature magazine published in the U.S. as well as many other countries, and his bird pictures are a major part of almost every bird book that has used photos for illustrations, including this one. His unmatched videography, frequently seen on national television, is hallmarked by tight images of his wild subjects and serves to illustrate his vast ornithological knowledge. Ron makes his home in Dillsboro, Indiana.

Ray Harm is a renowned wildlife artist who pioneered the limited edition print business in the 1960s. This adopted Kentuckian and West Virginia native is internationally known and highly honored for his beautiful and accurate paintings of wildlife and Ray has become famous as a painter of birds. Unlike almost all of today's commercial wildlife artists, Ray renders his true-to-life paintings only from his own original field sketches backed up by his knowledge of natural history—a history he has learned by spending countless hours in the field observing and sketching his subjects. Dr. Harm is a World War II veteran, a former rodeo cowboy, a ranch cowboy, a musician, a pilot, author, and lecturer. He and his wife, Cathy, live on their ranch near Sonoita, Arizona.

It has been my honor and privilege to have been their friend for more than thirty years.